W9-ACE-265

DISCARDED

Shelton State Libraries
Shelton State Community College

Moses and the Monster and Miss Anne

DISCARDED

HQ
1438
.E23
M67
2009

Moses and the Monster and Miss Anne

CAROLE C. MARKS

UNIVERSITY OF ILLINOIS PRESS
Urbana and Chicago

© 2009 by Carole C. Marks
All rights reserved
Manufactured in the United States of America
C 5 4 3 2 1
∞ This book is printed on acid-free paper

Library of Congress Cataloging-in-Publication Data
Marks, Carole.
Moses and the monster and Miss Anne /
Carole C. Marks.
p. cm.
Includes bibliographical references and index.
ISBN 978-0-252-03394-0 (cloth : alk. paper)
1. Women—Eastern Shore (Md. and Va.)—History.
2. Eastern Shore (Md. and Va.)—Social conditions.
3. Women—Eastern Shore (Md. and Va.)—Biography.
4. Tubman, Harriet, 1820?–1913.
5. Cannon, Lucretia P., d. 1829.
6. Carroll, Anna Ella, 1815–1894.
7. African American abolitionists—Eastern Shore
   (Md. and Va.)—Biography.
8. Criminals—Eastern Shore (Md. and Va.)—Biography.
9. Slaveholders—Eastern Shore (Md. and Va.)—Biography.
10. Slavery—Eastern Shore (Md. and Va.)—History.
I. Title.
HQ1438.E23M67   2009
973.7'115—dc22   2008034991

To René
Still here, after all these years

Contents

Acknowledgments

There are a number of people I wish to thank: Joan Catapano and the editors of the University of Illinois Press, who never gave up on this project despite many setbacks, and anonymous readers for the press who gave wise counsel.

Historian Anne Boylan, who interrupted her busy schedule to read and comment on every chapter, providing invaluable historical insight. John Creighton, whose studies on Harriet Tubman go back nearly thirty years and whose guidance and wisdom were invaluable. Carole and Bill Walsh and René Marks, who cheerfully traveled to every historical site from Cambridge to Gettysburg. Junius Banks, my wonderful Uncle Duke, who clipped and sent relevant newspaper items right up to his death. I also wish to thank members of the Harriet Tubman Historical Reading group, including Pat Lewis, Kate Larson, Mrs. Evelyn Townsend, Vernetta Pinder, Kay McEly, Jay Meredith, David Honig, and Royce Sampson.

Matthew Countryman, Rachel Countryman, Elizabeth Higginbotham, Peter Kolchin, Darlene Clark Hine, Florence Bonner, Lynn Weber, Jean Bohner, Walter Allen, Bob Newby, James Jones, Amalia Amaki, and Paul Jones, colleagues who are always willing to listen and debate. Chris Densmore, Swarthmore College Library, and Chris Becker, Maryland Historical Society. Archival and editoral assistance from my friends at the Schomburg Center, and special thanks to Howard Dodson and Sylviane Diouf; University of Delaware graduate students Chris Steinbrecher and Guenevere Mead; Vince de Forest and Sheri Jackson from the National Forest

Service; and Constance Manoli-Skocay, Concord Free Library, Delaware Historical Society, Special Collections at the University of Delaware.

The next generation: Emilie, Emma, Mason, Elisha, and Miguel, who are full of hope and wisdom beyond their years. And most of all, to Harriet Tubman, whose faith and spirit guided each step of this journey.

Introduction

There ain't no sin and there ain't no virtue.
There's just stuff people do.
   —*John Steinbeck*, The Grapes of Wrath

A few miles of land between the Chesapeake Bay and the
Delaware River are all that really attaches the Eastern Shore of Maryland
to the mainland of the United States. One of the earliest settled regions
of colonial America, its inhabitants prided themselves on their independence, perseverance, and lavish hospitality. Yet positioned as it was
east of most main roads of travel, strangers did not go there by accident.
Called a "land where time stood still," it may seem incredibly arrogant
or merely boastful to write of this area as the first staging ground on the
road to freedom and to focus on three women, "dangerous women," as
major catalysts of that journey. But the Eastern Shore was no ordinary
place and these women played important, though contradictory, roles in
that passage. Their homemade, homegrown tools, with unanticipated
accuracy, chipped away at the very foundation of American slavery. Historian Barbara Fields astutely observed about Maryland's long and complicated antebellum history that "the simultaneous growth of a free black
population hopelessly entangled with the slaves lodged a conspicuous
anomaly in the heart of the slave order." "Slavery," she said, "in some
sense defined freedom."[1]
   Harriet Tubman, slave rescuer, outlaw, and the most famous of the
three, was called "the Moses of her people" and had a $10,000, (some
said $40,000) price on her head.[2] Patty Cannon, kidnapper of free blacks,
was a member (some said head) of a ruthless gang and was called "the
most celebrated woman allied with crime in the history of Maryland and

Delaware." Anna Ella Carroll, slaveholder, "a military genius" by her own account and the "unrecognized member of the Lincoln cabinet" by others, conspired with Governor Thomas Holliday Hicks to keep Maryland in the Union, when many, perhaps most, state legislators clamored to join the Confederacy.[3]

Behind the myths, masks, and exaggerations that sometimes they and others fashioned about them (one historian claimed that much of the material of the underground railroad belongs in the realm of folklore rather than history)[4] lie somewhat ordinary, obscure individuals who "labored in a private way without the applause of the crowd," as Frederick Douglass once said of Tubman. Poet John Greenleaf Whittier, himself a worker in the cause of abolition, wrote that society was, on occasion, borne along by "*comparatively obscure individuals*, scarcely understood by contemporaries, and perhaps even by themselves, who begin a great reform which lifts the world" (emphasis mine).[5] This was the calling and the contribution of the three and is the subject of this work.[6]

Moses and the Monster and Miss Anne attempts to color in the space between the myth and the reality of these women. It is filled not simply with historical evidence, which in any case is sparse at best, but also with the sociological imagination and inventiveness of an age. All three women were products and creators of their times. As Anne Firor Scott once wrote of another trio, "In this age of statistical sophistication, it is a bold historian who builds any case upon three examples, yet in these we see exemplified cultural values which were those of many of their contemporaries." They were "experimenting in idiosyncratic and opportunistic ways, like so many others of this time, with the expanding economy, political change and the emergence of organizations and institutions to deal with the social consequences of that growth."[7]

The three women grew up in a social and political maelstrom, a historical present that constituted the major context of their lives. Like their neighbors, they too struggled with matters of work and law and the intended and unintended consequences of economic transformation and redundancy. But they are best understood as three "dangerous" women whom society deemed misfits, women on opposing sides of a moral divide who, for differing reasons, challenged the structure and content of a fragile American social system newly separated from its colonial roots and struggling to invent itself.[8]

A more mismatched trio hardly seems possible. Harriet Tubman devoted her life to delivering her people from bondage. Anna Ella Carroll devoted hers to saving the Union while attempting to preserve in some form the right to own slaves. Patty Cannon, alleged thief and murderer, was devoted to kidnapping and snatching free people into servitude. Extraordinarily different—and yet these Eastern Shore women shared roots in a common land. Between 1815 when Carroll was born, 1820 (or 1822) when Tubman is thought to have been born, and 1829 when Cannon died, they lived within twenty-five miles of each other: Carroll first near Pocomoke City and later in Dorchester County; Tubman in Bucktown, near Cambridge; and Cannon at Johnson's Crossing, now called Reliance, Delaware, on the Delaware-Maryland border. In 1837 Carroll and her family moved to Dorchester County—even closer to Harriet Tubman.

There is no evidence that the three ever met. I like to think that at some point they came together by accident in some public place—in a country store in Cambridge, or in front of the courthouse, or perhaps on the docks of the Choptank. They would not of course greet each other. Anna Ella Carroll would not deign to speak to a tavern-keeper, and neither Carroll nor Cannon would acknowledge a slave—except of course to give an order. But as historian Catherine Clinton has concluded, "Tubman came of age at the heart of a crossroad, where abolitionists, kidnappers, slavecatchers, and fugitives hid out from one another."[9]

At times, the lives of these three women were mirror images of each other, inseparable opposites drawn in sharp relief of black and white, good and evil. At times their struggles merged into a tapestry of independence and defiance. Had they met in jail (a fate some Maryland lawmakers, at various times, had in mind for all three), the women would have instantly recognized their shared roots.

And they were not of different worlds. Casual and incidental contact between the races regardless of class, though infrequent in the lower South, was not unusual on the Eastern Shore because of its many small farms and large populations of free and freed blacks and slaves. Those who ran large estates knew by name many of their slaves because of constant interaction over long periods of time. Poorer whites, in a pattern of laboring that could be even harsher than plantation slavery, hired black labor, slave and free. Whites and blacks sometimes labored side by side. Blacks were even rumored to be members of slave-trading gangs.

But more particularly their worlds collided with a cast of characters in common: abolitionists, slave owners, wealthy lawyers, politicians, and also-rans who floated in and out of all their lives. Heading the list was Thomas Holliday Hicks, sheriff of Dorchester who claimed to have issued the arrest warrant for Patty Cannon in 1829 and took her to the jail in Georgetown where she later died. Hicks was also a lawyer in Dorchester County and persuaded Edward Brodess, owner of Harriet Tubman, to settle a dispute with his guardian in an orphan's court, prolonging a legal entanglement that figured prominently in Tubman's need to escape.[10] And later, with Anna Ella Carroll's acknowledged help, then-Governor

Hicks kept the state of Maryland, rich with Confederate sympathizers, in the Union in 1861.

Josiah Bayly, Cambridge attorney and later state attorney general, was Patty Cannon's lawyer and possibly the Cambridge lawyer who provided information to Harriet Tubman about her mother's status from the will of Athow Pattison, her owner.[11] John Clayton, lawyer and later senator from Delaware, early in his career took on the task (with a religious vengeance inherited from his Quaker family) of pursuing Patty Cannon and her son-in-law Joseph Johnson. In 1829 Clayton was instrumental in having the entire gang indicted (mostly in absentia). Clayton was also one of the few politicians to respond to Anna Ella Carroll's constant appeals on behalf of her out-of-work father and arranged a job for him during the brief administration of Zachary Taylor.[12] And it is possible, though we do not know for certain, that the Cannon-Johnson gang, prominent slave dealers of the area, may have handled both the sales of slaves from Kingston Hall, the Carroll home, and the sale of Harriet Tubman's older sisters. These were only the prominent Maryland connections.

On the national level, Tubman and Carroll had mutual friends in William Seward, Gerrit Smith, Franklin Sanborn, Lucretia Mott, and Elizabeth Cady Stanton, a who's who of the anti-slavery movement. Seward arranged for Tubman to buy one of his houses in Auburn, New York, while she was still a fugitive. Seward was also a member of Abraham Lincoln's cabinet and had frequent contact (though perhaps less frequent agreement) with fellow Republican Anna Ella Carroll. Gerrit Smith, a wealthy abolitionist from New York, on occasion entertained Harriet Tubman in his home and may have introduced her to John Brown. Smith was also an acquaintance of Anna Ella Carroll and gave her money so that she could "buy" her remaining slaves in order to set them free. Elizabeth Cady Stanton, Smith's cousin and sister-in-law, drew Tubman into the woman suffrage movement and in later years took up the cause of Carroll as she sought compensation from the government for her unacknowledged war activities.

Protestant, particularly Quaker, connections between Philadelphia and the Eastern Shore accounted for many of these prominent contacts and explained the unusual acquaintance of black and white. But the story was more complicated than the moral outrage of small religious sects.

Cannon, Tubman, and Carroll were products of Maryland's Eastern Shore, a land and culture ancient and distinct. "An old and rich country—Maryland—fit for kings, and slaves," it was said.[13] Natives shared a curious combination of traits: ambition, thrift, rebellion—and isolation. "I am an Eastern Shoreman with all that name implies," Frederick Douglass told an audience in 1877. "Eastern Shore corn and Eastern Shore pork gave me my muscle. I love Maryland and the Eastern Shore." It was a curious admission from a highly vocal and disgruntled escaped slave ("decay and ruin are everywhere visible") and yet not without precedent.[14]

The Eastern Shore, bearing the aspect of a shoal rising from the sea, appears more like an island than a peninsula, surrounded by water, with Chesapeake Bay on one side and the Atlantic Ocean on the other.[15] The Chesapeake, said to be the largest estuary in the United States, is the center of the region and, to a significant extent, another lead player in this drama. Traversing the peninsula near its center and flowing into the bay is the Choptank, the longest and best known of the Eastern Shore rivers. Local historian Hulbert Footner observed that a spiritual line existed between the people who lived to the north of the Choptank and those who lived to the south. The south, it was said, had a greater spirit of nonconformity, increased independence, and greater lawlessness.[16] "Civilization ends at the Choptank," H. L. Mencken once observed.[17] While resisting the implied claim that the Choptank was a boundary of refinement and cultivation, I will point out that the southern half was the early home of the three women of this work.

The women were raised in a region filled with religious dissenters and nonconformists, people who lived by their own design. Inhabitants "nourished and ripened and handed down their own notions undisturbed."[18] Less patriarchal and more secular than New England and their neighbors to the south, Eastern Shoremen and women developed a culture sui generis. Many believed slavery evil, influenced by the presence of both Quakers and Methodists whose strong teachings against the institution were well known. By 1700, Quakers were the largest religious group in the area. But slaveholders were also plentiful as were Catholics on the western shore, who by charter from the King retained a tight pecuniary control of much of the land, east and west. No single religious group dominated and, though the Church tried to legislate against it, intolerance of all against all was ever present.

The Eastern Shore was also part of the early formation and consolidation of American slavery. Tobacco was the first staple of Maryland slavery and planters grew rich from its harvests. Though relying first on the labor of a combination of European indentured servants and African laborers, with the restoration of the monarchy planters were forced to turn to the more expensive but dependable labor of the slave trade. By 1720 the transformation was complete and slaves for life worked the land.

As late as 1749 tobacco represented 90 percent of the aggregate agricultural production of Maryland, but its dominance was not to last. The demise began with soil depletion and the cultivation of a heartier tobacco crop south and west that resulted in a migratory shift. As historian Walter

Johnson explained, "By the end of the eighteenth century slave coffles were a common sight on the roads connecting the declining Chesapeake—its soil exhausted by a century of tobacco planting—to the expanding regions of post-Revolutionary slavery, the Carolinas to the south and Kentucky and Tennessee to the west." Substitutes were found in wheat and soy but unlike tobacco they did not require a yearlong, fixed labor supply.[19] Eastern Shore slaves—loved, feared, or considered merely chattel—were increasingly redundant. With greatly reduced incomes and resources slaveholders struggled to recover not only their wealth but their lifestyle. It was a conundrum whether or not to sell their only liquid asset (in human form)—a question that slaveholders struggled with for several generations.

Each of our subject women openly participated (though women rarely did) in attempts to resolve the dilemma. Patty Cannon labored in the burgeoning industry of domestic slave dealing, a quasi-legal business combining legal slave trading and illegal kidnapping in which money was earned by selling off redundant segments of the Eastern Shore black population. Harriet Tubman, slave for life, became part of an elaborate rescue network that attempted to prevent others from being wrenched from their families, sold, and sent to harsh climates by traders like Cannon. Anna Ella Carroll, a slaveholder who recognized the evils of slavery and eventually bought the freedom of those she owned, promoted schemes of colonization and compensation to end the evil practice without bringing financial ruin to her kind and undermining the Constitution, that sacred document she believed gave license to the institution of slavery in the first place.

Moses (Tubman), the Monster (Cannon), and Miss Anne (Carroll) were not, of course, the only Shore natives involved in such activities. Slave trading and, more particularly, free black kidnapping was a booming industry on the Eastern Shore. The Underground Railroad also flourished there, with blacks and whites risking their lives and fortunes to help fugitives escape. Early in the nineteenth century, colonization societies sprang up as well—societies with illustrious memberships. (Women, careful to remain in their sphere, formed "auxiliaries" to these societies.) But most of these activities were run by men in public, while the Chesapeake women accomplished much of what they did in private.

When Tubman, Cannon, and Carroll lived there, Maryland "was a society divided against itself," effectively separated into three parts.[20] Northern Maryland embraced six counties and included the port city of Baltimore on the western side of the Chesapeake. Southern Maryland also embraced six counties and was an agricultural region devoted to slavery, tobacco production, and later wheat. The Eastern Shore, an area on the opposite side of the bay, embraced seven counties "neither as slave and black as Southern Maryland nor as free and white as Northern Maryland."[21] Separated from the rest by the Chesapeake, this area developed a way of life little influenced by strangers. Tourists stopped but briefly there; European immigrants settled in the more commercialized north.

About one-third of Maryland's 1790 population of 320,000 lived on the Eastern Shore, with the other two-thirds divided equally between north and south. The racial and labor composition of the three sections, however, did not mirror the population split. Overall, the state's population included 209,000 whites, just over 8,000 free blacks, and just over 103,000 slaves. Northern Maryland (including Baltimore) had about 87,000 whites (42 percent of the total white population), nearly 2,000 free blacks (25 percent of Maryland's free blacks), and nearly 16,000 slaves (about 15 percent of the slave population). In composition it was similar to the nonslaveholding North. By contrast, Southern Maryland was most like the slaveholding South, with the exception of its "sizeable" free black population. It had nearly 56,000 whites (27 percent), just over 2,000 free blacks (26 percent), and almost 49,000 slaves (47 percent). The Eastern Shore fell in between. It had 65,141 whites (31 percent of the population), almost 4,000 free blacks (nearly 49 percent), and almost 39,000 slaves (over 37 percent).[22] The great worry for whites on the Eastern Shore was the large and growing free black population—nearly half of those in the state—and its intermingling with the slave population.

Cleavages between the sections were ever apparent. Residents of the Eastern Shore identified themselves as such and less often as Marylanders, a situation that sometimes made united effort difficult. In 1850 then-Dorchester County representative Thomas Holliday Hicks drew up a bill of secession from Maryland. It was not the first. Like the others, it did not pass.

Waterways served as a major source of transport because distance from neighbor to neighbor was substantial. The Nanticoke River, which flowed through Seaford and then southward into the bay, was four miles from Cannon's home in Delaware. "Down the Nanticoke they sailed to the Chesapeake Bay and the concentration of points of Norfolk and Washington; or the slavers coasted straight to Mobile or New Orleans."[23] Black captives were thrown into the hold of a slave dealer's ship and never seen again. Fugitive escapes also involved watercraft—as when a stolen vessel, hidden in the marshes, carried Harriet Tubman's niece down the Choptank River to the Chesapeake to Baltimore and Harriet and freedom. Carroll's second home was on the Choptank, another river that emptied into the bay. She claimed that her familiarity with waterways, honed from her early years on the Eastern Shore, informed the battle plan that took the Union army down the Tennessee River rather than the Mississippi and saved the Union.[24]

Cannon's, Tubman's, and Carroll's shared roots in Maryland were accompanied by marginalization in a changing economy, a second common trait. Slavery was at the heart of this marginalization. The first African laborers were hardly distinguishable from the European indentured servants brought to labor in the same fields. As historian Philip Morgan wrote, "Not only did many blacks and whites work alongside one another, but they ate, caroused, smoked, ran away, stole, and made love together." Life was harsh, mortality high, and prosperity often unobtainable, even for those who had enough wealth to own others. Still there was opportunity in this early slave society. "Some slaves were allowed to earn money; some even bought, sold, and raised cattle; still others used the proceeds to purchase their freedom" and that of their family members.[25] When the monarchy was restored in England, the supply of white indentured servants bound for the colonies declined sharply. Landowners were forced to turn to the expensive African slave trade for a more reliable source of labor. Over time, as this system consolidated, "colonists [under Maryland law] were permitted to buy and hold enslaved Africans for a lifetime, and to 'own' the lifetime rights to their children, and children's children, as well."[26] Slaves for life became slaves even into the next generation.

"Men and women of the South, and honest ones, too," W. E. B. DuBois wrote, "have striven feverishly to paint Negro slavery in bright alluring colors. They have told of childlike devotion, faithful service and lighthearted irresponsibility, in the fine old aristocracy of the plantation. Much they have said is true. But when all is said and granted, the awful fact remains congealed in law and indisputable record that American slavery was the foulest and filthiest blot on nineteenth century civilization."[27] The misery of "one doomed to live without knowledge, without the capacity to make anything on his own and to toil that another may reap the fruits," as Frederick Douglass described the enslaved, permeated the region and its people and stunted its growth.[28]

The slave society that had defined the region for nearly one hundred years was severely shaken in the second half of the eighteenth century. Soil depletion ended the reliance on tobacco, the major source of wealth. Diversification was key to survival and often meant a dramatic reduction in the need for slaves as shifts into wheat, rye, and barley production required fewer laborers or more temporary ones. Paralleling the fall of tobacco was the increased use of cash as opposed to barter to pay for goods and services. This change forced the offspring of subsistence farmers, who had once lived simply off the fat of the land, into the cash economy. Still, as historian Catherine Clinton observed, "By the time of the American Revolution, slavery was as much a part of Maryland as the tobacco planted in its soil and the oysters harvested from its muddy shores. Although they were shifting into grain agriculture by 1800, slaveholders on the Eastern Shore owned, on average, eleven slaves apiece."[29]

Obviously the economic dilemmas of the three Eastern Shore women were of different scales. Anna Ella Carroll inherited the tobacco wealth of her grandfather, centered in land and slaves, which sustained her for many years but evaporated over time. Patty Cannon, who lived on rented land, went into the business of slave dealing, one of the few cash-yielding employments available to yeoman farmers in the region. Harriet Tubman, slave for life, became "redundant" when soil depletion and tobacco collapse reduced the need for so many slaves and the "extras"— defined by a variety of individual circumstances from good (potential breeders) to bad (troublemakers)—were sold away. Families were broken up and children, in particular, sent to more lucrative slave markets in the South. Tubman, having freed herself, returned many times to save the vulnerable members of her family. Slavery, then, gave these separate struggles a common thread.

Though the Chesapeake slave holdings were small compared to those farther south, the dominance of the system over the entire region and its inherent economic irrationality were apparent. "It is generally supposed," Frederick Douglass wrote in his 1855 autobiography, that "slavery, in the state of Maryland, exists in its mildest form . . . divested of those harsh and terrible peculiarities which mark it in the southern states." Douglass was referring to Maryland's less severe climate, the less grueling nature of its tobacco and wheat harvest as compared to rice and cotton, and to the fact that many slaves in the state were better clothed and fed. But, he also claimed, "Slave-rearing there is looked upon as a legitimate trade; the law sanctions it, public opinion upholds it, the church does not condemn it."[30] Historian Barbara Fields was even stronger in her criticism suggesting that the region "imparted an extra measure of bitterness to enslavement" because it "set close boundaries on the liberty of the ostensibly free and played havoc with bonds of love, friendship, and family among slaves and between them and free black people."[31]

Still, over time, blacks of the Chesapeake, because of their relative longevity, were represented by a variety of circumstances from slave for life to slave for a specified period to freed to born free. Even the simple act of distinguishing slave or free became difficult as their numbers grew. In the 1760s, "deeds of manumission" (papers describing the individual and specifying the terms and constraints of freedom) were issued to aid in identification. The presence of so many free blacks was feared both because of the ambiguity of their status (Did they have rights? Were they citizens?) and their potential to influence and corrupt the slave society. And the mingling of the two groups, a practice used to keep slaves from running away and to increase their stock, blurred the once-reliable visual cues. As historian Peter Kolchin noted, "Before the Revolution, skin color demarcated most freed people from slaves." But the free black population "darkened" in the 1780s and 1790s.[32]

Slaves with false papers and free men with no papers made the job of verification even more difficult. Between 1790 and 1810, the number of free African Americans in Maryland increased from 8,093 to almost 34,000. By 1820, over one-third of the population was free. Many whites hoped freed blacks, given the precariousness of their situation, would choose to leave rural areas for nearby cities, but they were disappointed. Others sought, by law, to forcibly remove the newly freed. That too failed. For the most part, Chesapeake free blacks "remained in their old neighborhoods" near to family, near to friends, near to a familiar way of life. It was not because of opportunity that the freed blacks stayed. Their jobs were grueling, dirty, and the pay was low. Historian Ira Berlin called free blacks slaves without masters.[33] In Maryland, nonslaveholding whites, a majority of whites in most counties, held many of the petit bourgeois occupations. They were the artisans, the shopkeepers, and the commercial farmers. "Consequently," as Fields observed, "free blacks did not occupy a unique or legitimate place within Maryland society, but instead formed an anomalous [and problematic] adjunct to the slave population."[34] Loggers like John Tubman, Harriet's first husband, and Ben Ross, her father, represented something of an elite segment of the free population because of their skills. Most free workers were unskilled and remained in unstable and dire circumstances.

Slaves formerly harvesting tobacco were sometimes hired out, that is, used as a cheap alternative to free labor. Paid for their work, their earnings were shared with owners in a system fraught with inequities and abuse. But the introduction of the cotton gin in 1793, which quickened the process of harvesting, gave new life to the dying institution of slavery—a new venue in the South and West and a new outlet, for those who wished to sell, for the underused slaves of the East. It created a "spectacular long term increase in the value of slaves, growing demand and limited supply."[35] As prices rose, slave owners in the East found that outright sale was more profitable than hiring out. Prominent owners were also able to use slaves as collateral for bank loans, that is, to borrow against their potential sale price thereby maintaining, at least temporarily, accustomed affluence. Bankers loaned "rich" slaveholders money readily, knowing that if they fell behind, slaves could be sold. Slave populations grew. A "natural increase" of slaves began in the eighteenth century (attributed to diet, climate, and better treatment) but grew greater in the nineteenth as new markets increased sales, particularly of the young.[36]

Among slave families, this informal "breeding" and involuntary migration was horrific. Children, too young to know or remember their birth families, were lost forever. "About one million slaves moved west between 1790 and 1860, most of them departures from Maryland, Virginia and the Carolinas," Peter Kolchin found.[37] This was perhaps the first of the great internal migrations. Of course, some owners left the area and took their slaves. They were, as William Faulkner once noted, "younger sons sent out from some old quiet country like Virginia or Carolina with the surplus negroes to take up new land."[38] But many more sold off their holdings to pay their debts—sold them with reluctance and some regret but sold them nonetheless. "Slaveholders," Walter Johnson wrote, "populated the new states of the emerging Southwest—Alabama, Mississippi, and Louisiana—with slaves brought from the East: 155,000 in the 1820s; 288,000 in the 1830s; 189,000 in the 1840s; 250,000 in the 1850s."[39] Ironically, the lifework of our three women—slaveholder, slave trader, and slave rescuer—were tied in opposing ways to the same forces and contradictions of regional change that transformed their lives.

A third area of convergence related to rules, laws, and the rule of law. Many citizens in the early republic valued above all, citizenship, rights, and individual authority. They retained a lingering "revolutionary ethos," combining support for religious freedom with liberty and the pursuit of happiness. They were suspicious of kings, nobility, and oligarchies. "He who governs best, governs least," they intoned.

Like many of their fellow Shoremen, the three women opposed (for very different reasons) forms of state authority. By her actions it may be inferred that Patty Cannon believed that the state should not interfere with the rights of citizens to earn a living, be it smuggling or owning slaves. Harriet Tubman believed in the right to be free, a privilege that trumped all other considerations. Anna Ella Carroll believed that the rights of property were sacred and guaranteed by the Constitution, a document that also gave, in Daniel Webster's words, "solemn guarantees to slavery."[40] All three believed themselves justified in challenging the state on these issues.

Establishment of the rule of law and the formation of legal statutes of slavery codified as state policy was of paramount importance in a fledging society like that of the United States in the 1800s. Making laws and getting people to obey them were difficult tasks that consumed every level of government, particularly in a country founded on the notion that laws could be unjust and citizens had a right to protest them. A degree of individual participation and oversight unprecedented in other societies developed here. Familiarity with local issues was high, even in the absence of newspapers and other printed media. One of the greatest features of this new society was, as Charles Francis Adams described it, "politics as a form of mass entertainment, a spectacle with rallies, parades and colorful personalities."[41] Participation in political issues was at times pronounced.

At the same time, because of the vastness of the land and isolation of much of the population, engagement and enforcement varied widely. Law in remote areas was, like beauty, in the eye of the beholder. It was often easier to revert back to a system granting absolute power to those thought to be in charge, thus bringing to the powerless security and protection. But part of the power of the new society was that it often chose not to revert back to old systems.

From the colonial period, both the law and understanding of society had regional variations. Northerners favored natural rights and individual freedom and had a taste for civil disobedience. New Englanders were always more litigious than Southerners.[42] Southern slaveholders recognized three distinct levels of law: constitutional law (which they championed as strict constructionists); biblical law (which they interpreted literally, particularly as in its Old Testament support of slavery); and state law (which more than anything, they created for those they controlled). The last refers to the common and statutory law toward which they had the most lenient view. For that reason, particularly in the rural areas, the rule of law was tenuous at best. Local authorities had neither the means nor access to routinely identify, capture, and convict miscreants. Moreover, historian Charles Sydnor found, Southern life in particular was defined and made exciting by its veneer of lawlessness, "a high proportion of street fights, duels, harsh treatment of slaves, quickness to resent insults, and a common practice of carrying pistols and other weapons."[43] Regulating such behavior was almost impossible. Explained Sydnor, "It is generally accepted that the countryman is something of an individualist who shapes his actions according to local custom and his own notions of how he should behave rather than according to the dictates of law books."[44]

Still, Sydnor rejected the claim that in the rural South local law was held in disrespect, preferring instead the suggestion that the slaveholder "on his own estate was lawgiver, executive, and judge."[45] He held power normally exercised by the state over such acts as burglary, assault, and larceny. Planters routinely settled some controversies without going to court. And the attitude that formal law should be reserved for the most egregious cases did not reside with the gentry alone. Community sentiment supporting extralegal activity was widespread. Andrew Jackson's mother advised her son, "Never tell a lie, nor take what is not your own, nor sue anybody for slander or assault and battery. Always settle them cases yourself."[46]

White Maryland feared free blacks—feared their potential competition and their influence over slaves. Many whites wanted them gone. This backdrop led to contradictory attitudes on the part of most whites toward quasi-legal activities like "slave dealing." Capturing a runaway slave and returning him to his owner was legal and generally accepted. Stealing a slave belonging to someone else was illegal and carried a severe penalty. Such activity was to be avoided. Capturing a free or freed black and selling them into slavery was improper, but for many not egregious, behavior.

Kidnappers of free blacks were helped by the fact that blacks could not testify in court— proof that they were in fact not slaves had to be given by a reputable white person. That this was an almost impossible burden did not worry enough people to change the practice. What was believed instead was that free blacks had redress. Many judges did attempt to investigate claims of improper actions. Also, freed slaves could be taken back into slavery for the debts of their owners and for bad acts of their own. So, for many whites, the kidnapping and selling of "so-called" free blacks into slavery was unfortunate but not really offensive. Evidence of this is found in the fact that efforts to pass laws to protect free blacks from kidnapping failed in most states, including Maryland.[47] It was also the case that slave traders and kidnappers were protected by powerful slave owners who hinted that traders, though disgusting and ill-bred, performed deeds of public good, that is, reduced the free black population in the region.

For those who did not own slaves, slave trading was a way to participate materially in the complex new industry that involved capturing fugitive slaves and returning them to their owners for a fee, brokering the sale of redundant slaves for local owners, and kidnapping and selling free blacks. Slave trading was a business that could lead to wealth. "As soon as the African trade was closed, the interstate traffic began to assume the aspect of a regular business. The heyday of the trade fell in the piping times of peace and migration from 1815 to 1860."[48] Slave trading flourished from Delaware to Kentucky and throughout the upper South. It was not work for the faint-hearted though. Free blacks in particular fought back when they could, armed themselves when they could, and were aided at times by sympathetic whites. Children were the most vulnerable in these circumstances and the most frequently snatched. Seasoned kidnappers quickly became rich. The line between illegal kidnapping and legal trading became very murky. "The large trading firms," Walter Johnson observed, "were often family businesses, passed from one generation to another, and their principals were men of means: they lived in large houses, attended fine dinner parties, and held public offices."[49] Patty Cannon, her son-in-law, and their gang controlled the Eastern Shore peninsula.

Several pieces of national legislation further complicated public attitudes toward the interstate slave traffic. Framers of the Constitution, wishing to create a compromise between the anti-slavery North and the pro-slavery South, particularly South Carolina, created a provision to end the slave trade twenty years hence. "It ought to be considered as a great point gained in favor of humanity," James Madison wrote in the Federalist Papers, "that a period of twenty years may terminate forever, within these States, a traffic which has so long and so loudly upbraided the barbarism of modern policy; that within that period it will receive a considerable discouragement from the federal government, and may be totally abolished, by a concurrence of the few States which continue the unnatural traffic in the prohibitory example which has been given by so great a majority of the Union."[50] The general feeling was that this compromise was vital to keeping the thirteen colonies together. And perhaps more important, the "side" opposing slavery, the prohibitory example, represented a hodgepodge of viewpoints from "a mistake to be corrected in time" to "a sin against God" and many points in between, making a "do nothing" solution the most expedient.

In addition to banning the international slave trade, the framers added an important clause in the Constitution saying that "persons held to service or labor in one state . . . escaping into another will not be discharged from such service" and "shall be delivered up on the claim of the party, to whom such service or labor may be due."[51] The general interpretation of this clause was that fugitive slaves escaping into free states, regardless of free state laws, could be claimed by and returned to slaveholders. Southerners took succor in the constitutional acceptance of their "property rights" but soon realized that their ability to reclaim fugitives hinged on the support and cooperation of the local community to which the slaves had fled.

The Fugitive Slave Law of 1793 was not mainly about fugitive slaves but fugitives from justice and failed to satisfy many slaveholders on the borders. This law reiterated the right of a slave owner to recover his lost property in any place where it was found. It added that the slave owner could apply to a district or circuit judge of the United States for a certificate to enable him to recover his slave. For slave dealers such as Patty Cannon, a quasi-legal, community-sanctioned industry was born.

Congress enacted a second fugitive slave law as part of the 1850 Compromise, a deal struck with North and South to save the Union. This law outlined the rights of slave owners to pursue their property with the aid and support of local authorities. For fugitives like Harriet Tubman, escape to neighboring free states no longer ensured safety.

A fourth area of convergence was the "intense conflict over gender relations," as historian Anne Boylan described it, which marked the period between the 1790s and the 1830s. It was, she said, "a crucial era of nation building filled with political change and religious upheaval."[52] Each of our three women struggled to make a living in a changing public sphere hostile to women's work and to their participation in the political realm. Writer Bayard Taylor observed, "The development of the Eastern Shore, like that of Virginia, and I suspect the entire South, depends on the young men, of course, yet it is virtually in the hands of women." Their views of gentility, he said, are more like "those which the early settlers brought with them than those of even aristocratic Europe at the present day."[53] Tubman and Cannon represented familiar ambiguous gender roles soon to be obsolete.[54] They were agrarian figures who chopped wood, ploughed fields, drove cattle, and shot guns. Once typical, over time the very fact of their labor acquired the stigma of "debased status" and "an aura of vague disreputability." Both were said to have strength equal to men, again crossing the line of what women ought to do. "The idea of a lady doing such a thing was repugnant," one Southern diarist noted.[55] Tubman and Carroll were also said to escape pursuers by adopting male disguises. Cross-dressing, even Jefferson Davis discovered, was believed to threaten the very foundation of Southern society. The traits of the sexes, Brenda Stevenson explained, "were God-ordained and distinctive."[56]

Carroll, though unmarried, attempted to retain her status as a Southern lady by adopting opposing genteel disguises, at one time that of "a republican mother," and at another as the faithful servant of her widowed father. But Carroll also knew well "that in 19th century America, politics was regarded as the privilege and responsibility of men."[57] She knew it and literally schemed to operate, at times flagrantly, outside these rules. With her first major publication, she observed, "For the first time, I appear before the public. As a woman, I shrink with timidity and distrust."[58]

Beginning in the late eighteenth century, the label "strong-minded" was attached to women who were educated, independent, politically active, and outside the norm. Louisa May Alcott's little women were said to be strong-minded, especially Jo. Sojourner Truth, who dared to speak her mind in public, proclaiming on one occasion, "All the gold of California, all the wealth of this nation, could not restore to me that which the white people have wrested from me," was also called strong-minded. Strong-mindedness became a badge of honor for suffragists of the nineteenth century and a pejorative one to those who "had no wish to extend her influence or position."[59] Please don't call Miss Anna Ella Carroll strong-minded, her family told biographers. Yet Carroll, who had "no political, religious, or personal animosities to resent," was a paid lobbyist and apologist for slavery, anti-Catholicism and colonization. What could the weak-minded have stood for?

Tubman and Cannon shared in this insularity of mind as strong individualists with great physical strength, wit, humor, and a claim to supernatural powers. Patty Cannon was said to be "a handsome, fascinating woman and also a Gypsy, a very strong and masculine woman."[60] One tale was that she could "take hold of a Negro man, however young and strong, trip and throw him upon his face, and tie him before he could recover himself."[61] Harriet Tubman, Sarah Bradford wrote, "worked only as a field-hand for many years, following the oxen, loading and unloading wood, carrying heavy burdens, by which her naturally remarkable power of muscle was so developed that her feats of strength often called forth the wonder of strong laboring men."[62] Each rejected a notion of a woman's place, preferring as Carroll once said, "to stand in their own shoes."[63]

Carroll too was a strong individualist having wit, humor, and great intelligence. While there were no claims regarding her physical prowess, a stubborn will made her appear to some as overly aggressive. Indeed, family members found it necessary to insist that she was feminine, sociable, and charming. Yet it was also said that she had not a trace "of refined female delicacy," defined instead as "a healthy country girl with a strong vital body."[64] All three women occupied peripheral places out of step with a society that boasted a new, restrictive set of domestic values, behaviors, and expectations. Carroll, the only literate one of the three, continually felt compelled to write in dismissive terms of knowledge and learning. Women's magazines in particular emphasized the ideal of sensitivity, grace, compliance, and dependence. The home was depicted as an idealized space presided over by women who should be pious, humble, and submissive. By contrast, Cannon's home was a tavern and Tubman spent much of her time in the woods. Carroll, the only one to never marry, lived most of the time in hotels.

Women like Cannon were shunned more for their unladylike behavior than for their ill deeds. It was generally agreed that in her normal conversation Cannon was witty, and that she loved to demonstrate her wrestling ability, employing a famous "side hold." In an 1841 narrative, she was accused, among other things, of poisoning her husband and of murdering her own infant to show her cruelty and power. Though there was sparse evidence of any of her crimes and none of this one, the authors did not permit lack of evidence to influence their work. Their outrage is expressed in the comment, "She, who should have made her faithful arm a pillow for the head of her husband conspired to raise it against his domestic peace, his life, that the bosom that should have been filled with fidelity and affection treacherously contrived a plan of fatal destruction."[65] Tubman was not accused of unladylike behavior, nor would such labels be typical for a slave. "While middle-class white women were placed on a moral pedestal and depicted as pure, physically fragile symbols of 'good' womanhood," historian Shirley Yee observed, "black and poor white women shared the stigma of 'bad' womanhood."[66] Tubman's mostly female biographers, though very sympathetic, seemed to take pains to underscore the differences between her behavior and theirs. They questioned her closely about her actions. Knowing she carried a gun, they asked if she would use it. "If any man gave out, he must be shot," Tubman explained of her expeditions. A prominent abolitionist used "shocking terms" to describe Tubman's treatment, "stripped and whipped and handled with insolent hands and sold to the highest bidder."[67] Such terms at once elicited outrage and distance. White women would never be publicly stripped and whipped. Civil War diarist Mary Chestnut once commented on another set of boundaries, different but strangely similar. Chestnut described herself as "sickened" at the sale of mulatto women in silk dresses. "I tried to reason," she wrote, "this is not worse than the willing sale most women make of themselves in marriage—nor can the consequences be worse. The Bible authorizes marriage and slavery—poor women! Poor slaves!"[68]

Tubman's abilities found an important outlet in the Civil War and she was publicly credited with involvement in a number of scouting raids and campaigns. Abolitionist hero John Brown called her General Tubman. She was greatly admired in her time, though never granted veteran's benefits for her war activities despite waging a thirty-five-year battle with the federal government. Carroll, a woman with no military experience, developed (according to her records) a brilliant battle plan to save the nation that had to be hidden because, said one cabinet member, the society would never stand for this. She too never received recognition from the government although Congressional committees, over a period of twenty years, validated her claims with letters of support from key people involved. "Generally historians," C. Kay Larson has observed, "dismiss her claim to the Tennessee River Campaign as self-promotion."[69]

Still these women of the Eastern Shore were not invisible to society. Myths and exaggerations about their exploits emerged in their lifetime and after their death. Patty Cannon, the monster, was variously depicted as a sadistic desperado, gang leader, baby killer, and wife who poisoned her husband. Harriet Tubman, who tried and succeeded in rescuing most of her family, was transformed from "an ordinary specimen of humanity" into a combination of Moses and modern day Joan of Arc. Anna Ella Carroll became an unnamed and unheralded member of Lincoln's cabinet.

It is usual to write of their heroic deeds and misdeeds—actions central to this work as well—but less usual to think about their rise and fall in the world through their own efforts and decisions: to marry or not, to bear children or not, to lead or follow—what historian Anne Firor Scott called, "the high cost of self-making."[70]

1 | The Monster's Handsome Face

O thou monster ignorance, how deformed dost thou look!
—*Love's Labor's Lost*

On July 4, 1826, Thomas Jefferson and John Adams died within hours of each other. Their deaths symbolized the end of the infancy of the nation, the withering away of the last vestiges of the "founding father mantle" and the beginning of urban-industrial economic expansion. Though opposed on many points of policy, neither man had thought the nation would come so far so fast and neither wanted it to. Jefferson, who feared the premature embracing of manufacture because of the inevitable corruption of morals, said on one occasion, "It is the manners and spirit of a people which preserve a republic in vigour, degeneracy in these is a canker which soon eats to the heart of its laws and constitution."[1]

By 1826, the new republic was still struggling to invent the content and fabric of its government. In that year, Anna Ella Carroll began her schooling under the careful tutelage of her father; Harriet Tubman, age six, started her first job; and after almost thirty years of kidnapping defenseless blacks, Patty Cannon went into retirement.

Slave dealing, like smuggling in general, was a lucrative occupation ignored by the public, condemned by a few religiously driven moralists, pursued by those on society's margins, and invented to keep the gentry rich. As historian Walter Johnson explained, "Slaveholders who had arranged the sale in the first place, tried to maintain an artificial and ideological separation of slavery from the market, separating themselves as much as possible from the evil they had initiated—a sale of humans . . . and the evildoers—the traders."[2]

Consider for example Bushrod Washington, a justice of the U.S. Supreme Court and nephew of the nation's first president. In 1816 Washington was appointed president of the American Colonization Society, a organization that promoted the return of slaves to Africa, viewing repatriation as the most humane solution to the terrible legacy. Washington called slavery "the only stain of our political institutions."[3] However, he also owned slaves, and living on the inherited estate of Mount Vernon, found like many others in that area that his land was exhausted and his financial situation in disarray. So, in August 1821, while still president of the society, he sold fifty-four of his ninety slaves to two planters on the Red River in Louisiana for $10,000, or about $185 each. Washington thought or at least hoped, because of his position, that the sale would remain private. Many Virginia planters, including his friends, had conducted similar sales without public comment. Washington, however, was not as lucky and a local newspaper, with a hint of surprise, reported on the transaction in some detail. An outcry against Washington developed, with questions raised about his true anti-slavery loyalties. Washington was furious, expressing outrage at the failure of his associates—anti-slavery activists—to understand his sacrifice. He had, he explained, at his own expense taken pains to ensure that husbands and wives would not be separated.[4] He felt his actions were above reproach. Slave trading was, after all, legal.

Unlike its opposite, a reverse Underground Railroad (as it was sometimes called) sent once-free blacks deep into slavery. Without adequate or consistent record keeping, we are as ignorant of how many blacks were sold south as escaped north. In many cases, black families could only pray that missing family members were actually in the "promised land." Slave dealing was not the calling of only a few unscrupulous racketeers, but the main livelihood of many in the area who reaped profits through the high prices paid for slaves in the Cotton Belt.[5] The growing population of free blacks, a group both feared and disliked, increased the temptation to fatten profits by dipping into that reserve. In Maryland, the crime of stealing slaves was dealt with harshly, while the kidnapping of free blacks was only winked at. In Delaware, slave stealing was a capital offense and a penalty of thirty-nine lashes and the ears nailed to a board could be exacted for the kidnapping of free blacks. But prosecutions for the latter were uncommon, particularly when jurisdiction was an issue. It was no accident that Patty Cannon lived on the border between the states.

Patty Cannon's name was well known on the Eastern Shore. "She was," author Hal Roth once wrote, "the most celebrated woman criminal in the history of Maryland and Delaware." Some called her "the wickedest woman ever to walk on American soil."[6] Unfortunately, tales of her exploits far exceed the documentary evidence of her life. Said to be in the business of slave dealing for over thirty years, few records exist of her crimes and indictments and even fewer of the more mundane events of her life such as births, marriages, deaths, and tax bills. Accounts at that time were at best haphazard, and those who wished to remain outside the boundary of public scrutiny could do so with ease.

Despite her notoriety, Patty Cannon was never found guilty of the crime of kidnapping, nor for selling free black people into servitude. She was indicted in 1821 along with husband Jesse Cannon, son-in-law Joe Johnson, daughter Mary Johnson, son Jesse Jr., and John Stevenson, an accomplice, for kidnapping a free Negro, Thomas Spence. "While the indictment named six people, authorities at the time seemed content to focus on Joe, the wealthiest and most prominent of the kidnappers," researcher Jerry Shields reported. Only Joe Johnson, said to be the gang's leader, was prosecuted. Found guilty, he was sentenced to thirty-nine lashes. Charges against the others were dropped.[7]

Patty Cannon was indicted again in 1829 along with her son-in-law and his brother, Ebenezer Johnson, on a twelve-year-old missing person case based on the discovery of human bones on her property and the testimony of a free black once in her employ. The Johnson brothers had left the area by the time of the indictment and were charged in absentia. The state had a weak case because the only evidence that Patty Cannon had actually committed the murders was the testimony of a black man who, according to statute, could not testify in court. Unfortunately for all, she died mysteriously in jail before going to trial, ending even this brief glimpse of her life.

Still, over the years and for a variety of purposes, researchers have compiled a fascinating but incomplete portrait of this "fiend in human shape."[8] How and why Patty Cannon became such a well-known public enemy is almost as interesting as figuring out what she did. Shields concluded that a simple explanation was that tales of her exploits, real or imagined, sold books and newspapers. Beginning in 1841, twelve years after her death, a work titled the *Narrative of Lucretia P. Cannon* was published in New York and her life became the stuff of legend.[9] The authors, probably ghostwriters, used newspaper reports of the arrest as the basis for a colorful and largely fictional tale. While the *Narrative* was "blatantly inaccurate in nearly every detail," Hal Roth would later write, it spawned several other books and many newspaper articles about Cannon.[10]

Her legend was embellished by two main groups, abolitionist propagandists and writers of gothic horror tales, both of whom demonized the female murderess. The propagandists, beginning perhaps with Lydia Maria Child's anti-slavery tracts in the late 1830s, bought attention to the horrors of the slave system, portraying the disease of the institution through contrast of innocent female slaves with abusive male slaveholders and overseers. Their intent was to persuade, in the strongest terms possible, a public not yet convinced. When interest was sparked, sales were good.

It was probable that the authors of the *Narrative* thought cruelties described by abolitionist lecturers, inflicted not by a male slave master but by a woman, made them all the more horrible and more exciting. Neighbors said that she ate her own baby to get the attention of and quell an excited crowd, they wrote. On another occasion, it was said, a crying baby so infuriated Cannon that she threw it in the fire and watched it die—the deed of a woman without a shred of human decency, let alone maternal instinct. They also wrote of whispered reports of her unusual strength. "She could stand in a half-bushel measure and lift five bushels of wheat (300 pounds) from the ground to her shoulders, a feat which can be achieved possibly by one man in twenty."[11] Unusual traits for one of the gentler sex.

These claims helped to expose the evils of those attached to the business of slavery. "We have reason to believe," Thomas King Carroll told his young daughter Anna, "that *all the wickedness*—this kidnapping of Negroes and making them steal and murder, is directed by a very bad woman named Patty Cannon" (emphasis in original text).[12] According to the *Narrative*, Cannon joined with Joe Johnson in the regular business of slave dealing, "a business that involved fitting out a slaver which went to Philadelphia and decoyed blacks on board, sent them to Cannon's head quarters and then to another slaver, to be transported South."[13]

The other promoters of the Cannon legend were those milking the popularity of gothic tales. Writers profited from the opportunity that the theatricality of slave settings gave to their work, providing yoked innocents as grist for their mill. Beginning in the late 1830s with Hawthorne's short stories, gothic horror tales were full of obsessed and tormented characters. These tales were meant to shock their audience and to address philosophical questions of humanity and society. Patty Cannon made a great gothic villain. Often described as handsome, witty, and engaging, robust with dark eyes and hair, and a Gypsy-like appearance, she was also depicted as a wanton creature, cruel and murderous. "Rarely in modern times," wrote J. H. K. Shannahan, a historian of the Eastern Shore, "do we find a woman so void of all human emotions and sympathies as this creature, who was at the head of as vile a gang of slave traders, cutthroats and murderers as ever stretched a gallows' rope."[14]

The published attention on Cannon increased her wickedness, as long after her death, reports of her crimes continued to surface and be embellished. Among the black population, her name was used as a kind of generic label for slave traders. Shannahan wrote with seemingly undisguised glee, "One had but to mention that Patty Cannon was coming and the darkey would turn as ashen as his color would permit and fly for his life."[15] Anna Carroll told Sydney and Marjorie Greenbie that terror would sweep through Kingston Hall "whenever there was a rumor of Patty's gang on the rivers."[16]

There is little question that Patty Cannon married into a gang that kidnapped and murdered people. Beyond that is much speculation and little real evidence of what she did. Obviously, Cannon's villainy is overdone. Reporter George Massey, who did extensive research on the tales, was not convinced by much of what he read. He concluded, "The woman was a tramp and a very vicious kind of person, but not nearly as wicked as she's been made out to be. And it turns out that Joe Johnson was the real leader of the kidnapping-highway robbery gang."[17] In this later view Massey is joined by Shannahan, Ted Giles, and Hal Roth, along with a thin paper trail of court documents, newspaper articles, and letters in which Patty Cannon was seldom mentioned. The legend has tarnished over the years.

As a final insult to convention, another longtime Cannon-Johnson researcher questioned the existence of the tavern. "I don't believe Joe Johnson had a tavern until George Alfred Townsend gave him one in his novel *The Entailed Hat*," Sharon Moore wrote, "and everything written after its publication has been polluted with legend over fact." The absence of a tavern, this place where traders met and captives were chained in the attic, would be a near-fatal blow to the exploits of "the woman of mystery."[18]

Was Patty Cannon a real person? The short answer is yes, but as historian Brenda Stevenson wrote of others, like "most women of the early colonial Chesapeake, she speaks to us only briefly and with too distant a voice to make her story clear."[19] Did she do the things she was accused of? Probably some of them, certainly not all.

Martha "Patty" Cannon, born around 1765, came of age in a society struggling with issues of freedom, enlightenment, and equality. Many slave owners in this slaveholding society saw the contradiction of their circumstance and freed their slaves. Others, believing God on their side, held on to their only liquid assets as long as they could. Most whites owned no slaves and did not care to think about the plight of enslaved competitors who seemed so alien (slaves did jobs without pay, gladly done by whites—with pay).

While her origins are unknown, recent speculation has emerged about Cannon's past. Local historian Bernard Medairy thinks she was the younger child of Levin Handley, an Eastern Shoreman who had a passion for horses and "an unbridled social life." The name Handley (spelled Hanley by Townsend) has been associated with Patty Cannon and may have been her maiden name. Some records exist for Levin Handley. In 1778, the governor of Maryland appointed Levin and his brother Handy to the Dorchester Militia. However, other members of the group objected due to the brothers' unsavory reputations and an inquiry was held. The commander of the militia wrote to the governor in June, stating "Capt. Levin Handley, a Militia Officer, whose character, if I am permitted to give my opinion, I think [is] too infamous for continuance in office."[20]

The governor ignored the recommendation. But in 1779 the Dorchester grand jury handed down indictments for stealing against Levin Handley. The first indictment was for stealing corn, a later one for stealing a cow, and in both 1780 and 1781 for the more serious crime of stealing slaves. Handley was found guilty of stealing slaves in 1781, a crime that carried the death penalty, and was sentenced to be hanged.

According to the press, Levin's sixteen-year-old daughter Martha Handley visited his cell on the morning of his hanging. Martha, it is thought, would later become Patty Cannon. Family members still in the area confirm that Martha was the girl's first name and "Patty" a nickname. At present, this is the only credible theory of Patty Cannon's origins. Suggestions that she was the daughter of an English nobleman cast out by his family, an alternative theory repeated in several publications, seem unlikely.

The whereabouts of Martha Handley after Levin's death are unknown. Further, there is no record of her marriage to Jesse Cannon or anyone else. The 1790 census lists a Sally Handley as living at Wilson's Cross Roads, later named Reliance. Roth speculates that Sally Handley may have been Levin's widow and thus Patty's mother. Medaary claimed that Patty had a brother also named Handy, who married a widow several years his senior, the aunt of Jesse Cannon. Both Sally Handley, a head of household, and Handy Handley are listed in the 1790 census of Dorchester County, Maryland. All of this serves to establish tenuous links and connections between the Handleys and the Cannons.[21]

Jesse Cannon's origins are also murky. Some think that he was the son of Levin and Elizabeth Cannon. Birth records also list a Jesse Cannon as the son of William Cannon who died in 1765. William may have made Levin guardian to his son, a fact that would explain both listings. Jesse Cannon was said to be a war veteran. His age would suggest a veteran of the Revolutionary War, but others suggest he was a member of one of the militias of the War of 1812, the war of the Eastern Shore. Two Cannons were listed in those war records, neither by the name of Jesse.[22]

Locals believe that Patty married Jesse Cannon, a mechanic, in the early 1790s, although it may have been earlier. The basis of the locals' belief may have been the age of the Cannon children. Patty and Jesse had at least two offspring, a daughter, Mary, and a son, Jesse Jr. Mary, said to be a local beauty, first married Henry Brereton, a slave trader. Brereton was hanged for murder in 1813.[23] Had Mary been born in 1790, she would have been 23 at that time, a young bride and younger widow. She then married Joe Johnson, who was also in the business of trading and kidnapping. Less is known of Jesse Jr. although testimony from Lydia Smith, a freed slave from Delaware, mentioned that at one point in a complicated kidnapping transaction, she was sold to the wife of young Jesse Cannon.[24]

With poor and missing records, a lot of guesswork goes into constructing a past for the Cannons. Eighteenth-century colonial Shore families were closely knit and had a rudimentary division of labor. Family members grew crops, raised livestock, and manufactured what was essential, surviving without generating a surplus and with little need for cash. This was the world of the parents of Jesse Cannon and Patty Handley, a world Jesse and Patty would only pass through.

Early on, the Eastern Shore was a place inhabited and patched together with the misfits and castoffs of other societies, citizens who spoke in a variety of accents and dialects. Three significant demographic patterns characterized the early Chesapeake: high mortality, a severely imbalanced sex ratio, and an immigrant-dominated population. Parents died young, and orphans and stepparents were common. By the mid-eighteenth century, life expectancies increased and the sex ratio became more balanced, thus generating a native-dominated population. A profitable slave-based tobacco and grain economy also flourished.[25]

Early deaths and serial marriages led to complex and truncated families. Blended families were the norm rather than the exception. In both Maryland and Virginia, orphans' courts were established "to oversee the care, placement and training of parentless minors and to guard material inheritances."[26] But on the Eastern Shore there were few strong public institutions, only individuals sustained by and sustaining each other. The harsh life led men and women to celebrate fully rites of passage (birth, marriage, death) with smoking, drinking, and playing of games of chance. The Patty Cannon persona, tavern keeper-bouncer, was no anomaly in the early eighteenth century.

However, by the mid-eighteenth century when Cannon was born, changes appeared in the accepted practices and women's roles became less ambiguous. The traditional farming and artisan culture began to disintegrate—many people were forced to become permanent wage earners;

others into the ranks of what historian Susan Branson called "capitalist-entrepreneurs." Women then occupied contradictory positions, as deputy husbands on the one hand, and hidden, undocumented laborers on the other. As Branson pointed out, "Old duties were exchanged for new ones that were defined by the developing ideology of 'separate spheres.'"[27] They had not yet reached the position of pro-slavery advocate George Fitzhugh that women had but one right (to protection) and one obligation (to obey a husband). But Shore society was moving in that direction and Cannon was clearly out of step with her times.[28]

Jesse and Patty Cannon, young and newly married sometime between 1781 and 1790, perhaps living on land rented from a family member (probably cousins Isaac and Jacob Cannon, said to be wealthy landowners), were in search of a more profitable pursuit than farming, particularly one that brought in cash. They needed money to purchase the inexpensive manufactured goods that filled the shelves of local shops and substituted for the handspun things once made by family members.

For many like Cannon, subsistence farming and artisan culture, celebrated in the past as symbols of the American republican spirit, clearly were less attractive and to be abandoned as quickly as possible. To follow a new way of life one had either to work for wages (if employment could be found) or (preferably) work for oneself.

Jesse Cannon's situation was similar to that of Thomas Coffin, a Nantucket ship captain whose life, unlike the Cannons's, was written down. Coffin's family was among the first settlers of the island and was employed in maritime trade.[29] In 1779 he married a local girl, Anna Folger, also from a well-known Nantucket family, about a decade before the Cannons's marriage. During her husband's long absences Anna Folger managed her family (which had grown by five) and ran the family shop. Over time Coffin did well enough to purchase a ship of his own but lost it in a dispute with the Spanish government over piracy. Wife Anna persuaded him to move to Boston where he became a merchant selling a variety of imported goods. Their youngest child was born in Boston in 1806. In 1809, Thomas purchased a factory that manufactured cut nails on the outskirts of Philadelphia and relocated his family once again, including his second child, Lucretia Coffin (later Mott) and his youngest, Martha Coffin (later Wright). It is both fitting and ironic that Lucretia Mott in later years became a member of the Pennsylvania Anti-Slavery Society, the society that exposed the kidnapping done by slave dealers. Lucretia Mott was also thought to be Harriet Tubman's first white abolitionist contact in the North. Lucretia's sister Martha Wright befriended Harriet Tubman in Auburn, New York.[30]

Young couples' prospects at this time reflected the complex mix of opportunity and possibilities that economists and politicians would later celebrate as characteristic of northern energy and inventiveness. Like Coffin, the Cannons, though they lived on the border, also had the option of migrating to the city. Baltimore and Philadelphia were nearby. Jesse Cannon was listed in some records as a mechanic, a catchall phrase that would have encompassed a variety of skills saleable in these port cities. Of course success was not guaranteed. But the drive toward upward mobility was clearly present in young Coffin and young Cannon. Thomas Coffin tried at least three different occupations—ship captain, shopkeeper, and merchant—before moving to Philadelphia. In 1813, the year Patty Cannon was first detained for assault, Coffin's cut-nail business failed and he went into debt. He died two years later. To keep the family going, his wife, Anna, "an independent, self-reliant woman," became a shopkeeper once again.[31]

The Cannons by contrast did not view migration to a city as a desirable option. Baltimore was not home. They chose instead to start a local business. Rural businesses were more vulnerable than urban ones because of the isolation and dearth of cash-paying customers. To survive, business owners had to take on more than one activity, like mail delivery and court seatings. And like the Coffins, Cannon family members had to work in the family business, dividing tasks according to member strengths and abilities.

Patty Cannon appeared to be an important partner who contributed to the family's prosperity. By most accounts, she ran the tavern and was said to take "pleasure in doing her own bouncing." Firsthand descriptions of her attest to her character. An article in the *Baltimore Sun*, source not stated, described her as "large and handsome, hair thick and black and black eyes that could flash and sparkle. She walked with a swaying, swashbuckling gait as she served drinks around to the patrons of the tavern."[32]

In isolated communities, the tavern owner was one of the leading community notables along with the merchant, the doctor, and the sheriff. "The tavern had an important part in activities of the whole Peninsula," Ted Giles wrote. "The tavern provided food, drinks, lodging, and sometimes various forms of recreation. The traveler, whether he had come by horseback, buggy, wagon, cart or stage coach, was glad to see the welcoming face of the tavern-keeper."[33]

Tavern work included supervising the cooking, washing, and cleaning on a somewhat large scale, as well as purchasing food, drink, and supplies; caring for lodgers; handling cash; and in Cannon's case in particular, the secreting of stolen captives in the attic, "a windowless dungeon twelve foot square, built of heavy oak." "Cash money passed from the pockets of the dealers to the stockings of Mrs. Cannon," Giles noted with a hint of sarcasm.[34] That Patty Cannon, a woman, ran the tavern was unusual but not unheard of and probably set up the foundation for her future notoriety (although several researchers have pointed out that contemporary newspapers never called it Patty Cannon's tavern). Running taverns was not something that proper women did.

At that time the Cannons were also engaged in smuggling. While Patty ran the tavern, Jesse's business combined slave dealing and river piracy. Like kidnapping, river piracy was a common local activity involving a variety of players and had a murky legal status. Beginning in the Revolutionary War and continuing to the War of 1812 the government licensed privateers, who ran privately owned and financed vessels "to attack the vessels of a declared national enemy, for profit." The British routinely sailed these waters and dumped goods to undermine the new government and the new economy. Captured goods were sold off mostly for the benefit—after fees—of the vessel owner who had taken all the risks.[35]

It is likely that river piracy without human cargo was initially an important part of Jesse Cannon's operations. Vessels of all sizes became so effective that the Royal Navy, vastly superior, was stymied. Privateers typically went after the lightly armed British merchant trade because of low risks and high profits. Their activities benefited the new U.S. government because British warships were drawn from the conflict to protect their merchant trade. In addition to licensed privateers, there were pirates who had no licenses and no authority and were technically criminals. But the new government benefited from their chicanery and winked at the infractions. Fortunes were made during this period, and even small, unlicensed operators such as Jesse Cannon and Joe Johnson could do well. It is known that Joe Johnson sailed a schooner from Cannon's Ferry to Baltimore and beyond. Over time, his cargo varied.

Kidnapping of blacks, freed and free, and reselling them into slavery was a business that evolved over time. It was illegal in both Delaware and Maryland, but prosecution of offenders was not common, as previously stated. Debates about the efficiency of slavery, the rights of slaves, and the rights of property owners all swirled around the early Republic, making a consistent policy almost impossible. Further, proving that an illegal act was committed probably would have exhausted the meager resources of most small communities. And states were divided as to the greater offense, kidnapping free people or the growing presence of free blacks generally.

Blacks free and freed were often despised because of fears of their potential influence on slaves and, after achieving independence in 1804 in Haiti, for their potential for murderous revenge. Pennsylvania abolitionist John Parrish noted with alarm in 1806, "We permit six hundred persons to be kidnapped in six months alone because people want to get rid of the free negroes."[36]

A slave-dealing business, because of its entanglements, often started out modestly, almost as a second job. A business could begin with "a plain farmer with 20 or 30 slaves endeavoring to earn a few dollars from worn-out land," historian Winfield Collins wrote. "He is in debt and hears he can sell his slaves in Mississippi for twice the value in his own state. He takes his slaves and goes to Mississippi. He finds it profitable and his inclinations prompt him to buy of his neighbors when he returns home."[37] Such a business could bring quick profit for those willing to take risks and to engage in devalued and dirty work. Herman Freudenberger and Jonathan B. Prichett found that while they could not say "how the slave traders in our sample started out, we know that relatively few could be characterized as slave holders," reaffirming the degraded status of the occupation. Most, they found, were professional traders selling slaves for their previous owners.[38]

As with any business, practices varied from those who maintained humane services to those whose captives suffered. The Cannon-Johnson gang was ruthless and cunning and soon outpaced its rivals in the ability to bring misery to the lives of African Americans on the Eastern Shore.

The growth of the cotton market in the early 1800s created a noticeable spike in the domestic slave trade. "In marked contrast to the unprofitability of slave labor in the older slave states," Collins wrote, "was their immense profit when employed on the fresh lands of the Southwest." A "good negro," he found, "healthy and between the ages of twenty and thirty could command from $800 to $1,200." By contrast, the average price of a "good negro" in Virginia was only $300. It was, Collins concluded, "an inducement to a certain class of men to engage in the business of buying them up and carrying them South."[39]

Maryland ranked third behind Virginia and North Carolina in states selling slaves west. In a typical piece published in the *Virginia Herald* in 1799 a trader wrote: "FOR SALE, A NEGRO MAN, ABOUT 38 years of age, very healthy and strong: he has principally since a boy engaged in hewing, sawing, planning and polishing furniture, and is well acquainted with taking care of horses, and hard labor in general. His present owner having no such employment for him is the cause of his being offered for sale."[40]

Over time, the volume of sales grew larger. In 1810, trader William Rochel advertised, "I have upwards of twenty likely Virginia born slaves now in a flat bottomed boat lying in the river at Natchez, for sale cheaper

than has been sold here in years."[41] Rochel's statement has several significant parts. First, he identified the Virginia origin of the slaves, suggesting a preference for native birth as opposed to African birth. Second,
the east to west (Virginia to Mississippi) migration of slaves is increasing
("cheaper than has been sold here in years") and profitable. And third,
the date, 1810, serves as a reminder that the closing of the African slave
trade in 1808, rather than causing "slave prices to fall to zero," spurred
a "spectacular long term increase in the value of slaves, growing demand
and limited supply."[42]

Of course some part of the western migration involved individual
slave owners, seeking to make their fortunes in the new land. Collins
found "a considerable immigration of slave holders with their slaves
between 1800 and 1815." A Marylander who had moved to Louisiana in
1817 reported to a friend, "In your states a planter with ten negroes with
difficulty supports a family genteelly; here well managed they would be
a fortune to him."[43] But not all were anxious to adapt to the new life that
was also filled with risks, especially when, with less effort, redundant
slaves could be sold.

As domestic slave dealing evolved, various forms of distribution
were created.[44] Brokers in southern cities bought slaves from the eastern
seaboard and sold them again outright or for a commission. Rural owners
in the East would sometimes attempt to sell "surplus slaves" on their
own through newspaper advertisements. In 1828, a notice appearing in
the *Charleston (Maryland) Telegraph* read: "Will be sold for cash or good
paper, a negro woman, 22 years old, and her two female children. She is
sold for want of employment, and will not be sent out of state." Such in-
state sales were less profitable but less prone to turmoil. Johnson argued
that "slaveholding ladies occasionally interceded on the behalf of the
people they owned," invoking the sacred bond between mother and child,
an appeal that "provided enslaved mothers one avenue of resistance."[45]

The long-distance trade, as Phillips called it, was more profitable
and open to all, but largely conducted by firms having "an assembling
headquarters with field agents collecting slaves for it, one or more vessels
perhaps for the coastwise traffic, and a selling agent at one of the centers
of slave demand." The field agents sometimes operated openly, "prowl-
ing about the streets of this place with labels on their hats exhibiting
in conspicuous characters the words 'Cash for negroes,'" the *Virginia
Northwestern Gazette* reported. Factoring in all costs, researchers have
estimated profits in trading to range from 15 percent to 45 percent.[46]

Established dealers used public jails, taverns, and warehouses to
collect slaves, while others had stockades of their own. The larger dealers were centered in major urban centers. Franklin and Armfield of

Alexandria, Virginia, housed their business in a brick residence, three stories high, on Duke Street. They were considered the leading traders in Maryland and Virginia, and "perhaps unequalled in all the South," with agents in Richmond and Warrenton, Virginia; Fredericktown and Baltimore, Maryland; and one Thomas M. Jones, on the Eastern Shore.[47] Their business thrived from 1830 to 1836; in 1834 they "were said to be sending from 1,000 to 1,200 slaves a year to the Southwest."

Slaves awaiting sale were stored in a "slave pen." Frederick Bancroft's description was to the point: "After a grated iron door secured by bolts and padlocks was opened, the caller was conducted from the yard back of Armfield's dwelling into another yard or court, covered on one side and surrounded by a high, whitewashed wall. This was the pen of the male slaves." The traders provided food and clothing for the slaves, telling Andrews that an attractive appearance increased the price. "Even the negroes, when they learned that they were to be sold, begged to be taken to him," Bancroft reported.[48]

The situation in the East New Market slave pen was not as hospitable. John Thompson, a slave from Dorchester who escaped to Massachusetts, wrote that "the pen was in a room on the second floor of a building." It had a long staple attached to the floor, "having four long chains attached to that. To these were attached shorter chains, to which the slaves were made fast by rings around their ankles." Men, women, and children, Thompson wrote, "were huddled in this room together, awaiting the arrival of more victims, as the drove was not full."[49] Sitting on a slave ship talking to another captive, Solomon Northup's companion remarked that "death was far less terrible than the living prospect that was before us."[50]

In season, Franklin and Armfield sailed twice a month, on the first and the fifteenth. The journey by sea from Norfolk to New Orleans averaged nineteen days. To protect their cargo, slaves were chained. Franklin and Armfield also made overland trips. "The inland journey," Johnson wrote, "could take as long as seven or eight weeks on foot, with the slaves covering about twenty miles a day." Smaller businesses sailed when the pens were full. English traveler G. W. Featherstonhaugh came across a slave coffle in the woods near the New River in Virginia and reported that he had "never seen so revolting a sight before, . . . female slaves standing or sitting, a great many little black children and two hundred male slaves manacled and chained to each other—prepared for the march."[51] Though less horrific, parallels of these journeys to the Middle Passage are obvious.

Six or seven members of the Woolfolk family on the Eastern Shore participated in the slave trading business, the most notorious of whom was Austin. His advertisement in the *Baltimore Republican* carried an index finger pointing to the words "300 NEGROES WANTED." Richard C. Woolfolk of Princess Anne, Maryland, offered cash for Negroes, the usual arrangement for traders, indicating in his advertisement that he needed six hundred or seven hundred for the New Orleans market. He promised the best prices. John Bull, also buying on the Eastern Shore, offered "the highest prices for slaves to go to the Louisiana market: for first-rate young men from 18 to 24 years of age, from $400 to 450; for women of the same age, $250 to $275, or $280, for first rate."[52] Frederick Bancroft's comments about these traders were instructive. "Such conditions excited the imagination and appealed both to very energetic men," he wrote, "and also to many that were too proud or too indolent to farm or lacked the talent, capital or inclination to earn a living at any ordinary business or labor."[53]

Smaller businesses, like the Cannon-Johnson one, had less of the veneer of respectability (Armfield offered callers a glass of Madeira) and were more likely to be labeled by their criminal intent ("gang"). Participants in their business included Jesse Cannon; his wife, Patty; their children, Mary and Jesse Jr.; Mary's first husband, Henry Brereton (sometimes called Brenton or Bruinton) and her second, Joe Johnson; and Johnson's brother Ebenezer. At the height of their power, the gang was said to have over thirty members.[54]

Their business had a much smaller margin of error. As historian Walter Johnson explained, "The itinerant and independent traders who bought slaves on their own account, traveled through the lower South selling as they went."[55] Male family members and some hired hands served as field agents and agents in Southern cities. Lack of capital probably forced "the gang" to improvise, unloading unruly and ailing cargo as a method of raising cash. With enough cash, a firm could engage in this "buy low, sell high" slave trade with impunity. From 1818 to the 1830s, Dorchester's circuit court records contain hundreds of bills of sale, legal transactions from slaveholders to traders.[56] And snatching vulnerable free labor added greatly to the profits.

All parties in the business were aided by the Fugitive Slave Act of 1793 that permitted slave owners to recover their runaway "property" at their own expense. The affirmation of the legality of returning fugitives opened the door to the abduction of free blacks. It was, said Don E. Fehrenbacher, "an invitation to kidnapping, whether the result of honest error or deliberate fraud."[57] Working in pairs, kidnappers could bring a free person into custody "as a suspected fugitive" and have the claim verified, often by bodily identification, by an accomplice. The alleged fugitive had no protection, Fehrenbacher pointed out, "against self-incrimination and no assurance he could testify in his own behalf."[58]

On the Eastern Shore in particular, the swelling number of blacks free or freed was met with general alarm. "There was little affection for free blacks on most of the Delmarva Peninsula," Hal Roth observed, "and few whites demonstrated any concern for their welfare."[59] Slave owners disliked free blacks, thinking they set a bad example for slaves, and nonowners feared their competition. Some free blacks prospered, but most lived on the edge of poverty, a condition that added to their vulnerability and to the hesitancy of some whites to intervene. "Their condition," E. A. Andrews wrote, "is pronounced to be worse than that of slaves in everything, except the consciousness of freedom."[60]

It was soon the case that marginal slave dealers dipped heavily into this free reserve. This was illegal—but free blacks had few rights and little recourse. Consequently their cabins were raided, they were plucked from the fields, and waylaid on country lanes. Free blacks had much to fear from traders. As Carol Wilson explained, "The crime was pervasive partly because of the potential for great profits from a successful kidnapping and sale of a free black into slavery, which made many kidnappers willing to take the risks."[61]

Kidnapping took several forms. The most obvious was forced abduction. Fugitive slaves and free blacks often put up fierce resistance to slave catchers, making it necessary for catchers to work in groups rather than singly. Gangs formed that raided fields where blacks worked, attacked traveling parties, and invaded cabins in the middle of the night. Unforced abduction through deception was another form of kidnapping. Victims were promised jobs, offered inducements such as entertainment or recreation and sometimes even marriage. They were then taken to vessels were they were chained and sent south. Some gangs hired blacks to perpetrate the scam. Children aged ten and older were particularly vulnerable to kidnapping. They put up less resistance than adults, were less likely to raise suspicions, and were easily sold in the South.[62]

Captives would be taken to boats on the Nanticoke, carried down the river to the bay, and then sold. "Johnson sailed a schooner from Cannon's Ferry to Baltimore, and stole all the Negro men he could hire and induce to go as stevedores in the hold of the vessel, and when he had gotten them there, would quickly put on the hatches, fasten them down, and sail for home and leave them in the care of Patty." Jesse is said to have taught Patty the business.[63]

The Pennsylvania Abolition Society provided traces of the Cannon-Johnson operation. In 1815, John Kollock, a constable in Georgetown, Delaware, wrote to the society about two sailors, Solomon Campbell and Jesse Leal of Salem (or Philadelphia), New Jersey, who used a small sloop to "fetch" blacks to sell as slaves in Carolina. They belonged, he wrote, to "a troupe of negro buyers" that included Jesse Cannon. Kollock found out about the troop when he rescued two boys from Philadelphia who had been kidnapped by Campbell and Leal. According to Kollock, the boys were enticed on board ship with the promise of peaches but instead had been taken to a tavern in Delaware in preparation for sale.[64]

In 1819, John H. Willits of Maryland was informed of the abduction of Sarah Hagerman, a free black girl who had been sold as a slave to Jesse Cannon. Willits approached the Maryland sheriff but was told that he could do nothing because Cannon lived in Delaware. Willits then sought help from the Maryland Abolition Society, which provided information on Cannon's business through his neighbor Hatfield Wright. Wright suggested that Willits first determine whether the girl was on the premises. He hired an agent for $5 who verified that she was there. Willits then tried to find a constable who could serve a warrant on Cannon.

Although apprehensive because of the gang's rumored violence, a constable was found and Willits and several recruits went to the house. There they found both Jesse Cannon and his son-in-law, Joe Johnson, armed and refusing to let them enter. Eventually the constable prevailed and they found several girls, but none fitting the description of Sarah Hagerman. In a strongly barred attic, they found five other women chained together, but again not the one they sought. They also searched a small hut and found two men, "much intoxicated and seemed quite happy." Frustrated, Willits abandoned the search, concluding in his report that he was forced to leave Sarah Hagerman "to an unknown fate." Authorities could do nothing about the others, as no known crime had been committed.[65]

Abram Luomony was a second victim of the gang whose case was reported to the Pennsylvania society. Luomony, a free black of Philadelphia, was hired by a boat captain to go to Cohansey Creek, New Jersey, for wood. At the mouth of the Broadkill (a river in Sussex County, Delaware that flows into Delaware Bay), the captain of the vessel sold Luomony. Luomony told authorities that "as a sailboat had passed under a bridge, a man called Johnson, possibly Joe Johnson, jumped off the bridge onto the boat. He tied and beat Luomony, robbed him of five dollars and a knife, and took him to an old house in the woods." Luomony managed to escape and sought help. Abolitionists in Delaware composed a letter detailing the events of his capture and had him deliver it to Philadelphia authorities. A warrant was issued for the captain, who was convicted and sentenced to one year of hard labor and one hundred pounds. Johnson was not charged.[66]

Jesse Torrey, a lawyer and anti-slavery pamphleteer from Maryland, described to a Congressional committee how he rescued a trio of freedmen in Washington who had been kidnapped in Delaware. One told him they had been chained in the basement of a tavern until a slave trader arrived and purchased them. They were taken across the bay to Annapolis and from there to Washington. Torrey said, "One of the trio, a man, had been pounced upon while hunting possums in the woods." The other two were a mother and her baby. They had been in bed in their cabin when three members of the Cannon-Johnson gang burst in and took them away. "One man held her down while another pulled a noose around her neck to keep her from screaming. The third assailant blindfolded her and she thought she was done for. Her only comforts were that the baby went with her and she had been able to bite off a piece of her blindfolder's cheek during the fray." In 1816, she successfully sued for freedom, but their purchasers, members of the Cannon-Johnson gang, were not charged; their penalty was loss of money, it was said.[67]

A celebrated kidnapping begun in 1826 and involving two dozen victims taken from Pennsylvania to Mississippi exposed more of their activities.[68] It started when Ebenezer Johnson, Joe's brother, tried to sell three boys (Samuel Scomp, Enos Tilman, and Alexander Manlove) and two women (Mary Fisher and Maria Neal, a woman slave who had been legally purchased) to John Hamilton, a planter in Rocky Spring, Mississippi. One of the boys told Hamilton that they were not slaves but free blacks stolen from Philadelphia. Hamilton notified a local justice of the peace. Ebenezer Johnson was questioned and produced a bill of sale. An agreement was made to keep the group at the Hamilton's until inquiries could be made. Ebenezer agreed and then disappeared.[69]

Samuel Scomp, age fifteen, was the oldest boy. He told authorities that he was an indentured servant from Princeton, New Jersey, who had run away to Philadelphia where a mulatto named John Smith, a member of the Cannon-Johnson gang, offered him work unloading a ship. Scomp accepted. On board, he was tied and put in irons by the captain, Joe Johnson. Nine-year-old Enos Tilman, the second boy, had been offered the same work and was also tied and chained. Alexander Manlove, the third boy, told a similar story.[70]

Mary Fisher, a free black from Delaware, told investigators that she had been gathering wood near Elkton, Maryland, when she was attacked by two men and taken to Johnson's house. Also taken were two boys, one of whom died on the later journey to Mississippi, and the other sold on the way in Alabama.

Although Mississippi was a slave state, some authorities were offended by the actions of slave dealers. They argued that "there is no community that holds in greater abhorrence, that infamous traffic carried on by negro stealers."[71] John Hamilton hired John Henderson, a lawyer originally from New Jersey, who wrote a letter to the mayor of Philadelphia, Joseph Watson, detailing the information. Henderson "suggested that if the statements of these unfortunate blacks proved accurate, they should be published" so that "the coloured people of your city and other places may be guarded against similar outrages." The mayor published the information. Thomas Garrett of Wilmington read of the kidnappings and wrote to Mayor Watson. "I find by our papers that thou hast received a communication from the state of Mississippi respecting several colour'd persons, said to be kidnapped, one of which is said to have lived in this place. There is a female of the name Charity Fisher who left this place the 6th day of last month, expecting to return in a few days that has not since been heard of by her friends." Jesse Green, of Concord, Delaware, wrote that Ebenezer Johnson had just returned from a slave-selling trip in Alabama.[72]

Four of the five captives on Hamilton's plantation were returned to the Philadelphia area. Mary Fisher, not wanting to travel by sea, remained in Mississippi. While indictments were issued against Ebenezer and Joe Johnson, among others, neither were arrested. John Smith, the mulatto, was eventually arrested and found guilty of two counts of kidnapping, fined $4,000, and sentenced to forty-two years in prison.

In the same year David Holmes (born in York, Pennsylvania, and the first governor of Mississippi) notified Mayor Watson that Duncan Walker (a lawyer and also originally from Pennsylvania) had taken a deposition from a slave named Peter Hook. Hook claimed to have been kidnapped by the Cannon-Johnson gang in Philadelphia in 1825. Hook's story was that a black man named John (probably Smith) invited him for a drink on a ship near the Arch Street wharf. Once onboard the ship he was tied and chained. Clement Cox and William Chase, two more victims, arrived the next night. The ship sailed to Johnson's home and the men were kept in the attic. According to Hook, several more blacks arrived in the next days. All but one were young boys.

Also chained in the attic on the other side of the room were two women: Lydia Smith, a twenty-three-year-old indentured servant sold to Ebenezer Johnson for $110, and Sally Nicholson. The entire group remained there for six months, awaiting buyers. Hook reported that they were severely beaten while at Johnson's house. They were then transported to Rockingham, North Carolina, where two more men joined them who had also been kidnapped from Philadelphia. In Rockingham two slave traders, Miller and Sutler, purchased most of the blacks from Johnson and sold them. Hook and three other boys were sold to a planter named Perryman in Holmesville, Mississippi.

In January 1827, Mayor Watson wrote to Holmes thanking him for the information and suggesting that he was drawing the noose around the "mazes of this infernal plot, by means of which, a great number of free born children, during several years past, have been seduced away and kidnapped." This was done, Watson said, "by a gang of desperadoes, whose haunts and head quarters are now known to have been, on the dividing line between the states of Delaware and Maryland, low down on the peninsula, between the Delaware and Chesapeake bays."[73]

Several states issued warrants for the arrest of the Cannon-Johnson gang. Making the case, however, hinged on the willingness of whites to vouch for the identity of the stolen blacks, something few were willing or able to do. The city council of Philadelphia authorized payment of a $500 reward for information leading to the conviction of the kidnappers. Walker wrote to Watson, "I can appreciate the difficulty you anticipate of identifying black children, by the evidence of white persons. But however onerous it may be on all hands, we must do our duty." He also wrote, "While our laws protect slave property, they will restore the free."[74]

Historian Carol Wilson argued that extensive laws passed by Mississippi and other Southern states reveal a desire to prevent free blacks from entering their borders, fearing their influence over the existing black slave population. She concluded, "Perhaps the efforts of southern citizens to return the victims of the Cannon-Johnson gang to their homes were an indication, not of sympathy for fellow human beings in trouble, nor of obedience to anti-kidnapping laws, but of the desire to expunge a group of people whom they viewed with distaste and fear."[75]

While these incidents provide evidence of gang activity, they also suggest the problems of prosecution. The Cannon-Johnson gang derived protection from a variety of legal devices. Local authorities needed to have a warrant to enter their premises and the warrant had to identify the person sought. The need for white corroborating testimony was often stymied by tales of the gang's violence. Many declined to get involved. And the gang sometimes had legal documents of sale, a situation that complicated the actions of local authorities, who did not have the right to remove slaves from their owners.

Still a gap remains between information on the atrocities committed by the gang and those specifically of Patty Cannon. "It is the writers—the newspapermen and novelists—and John Clayton who dwell on her as a fiend of unparalleled proportions," Hal Roth concluded.[76] Patty Cannon as gang member but not mastermind would have been something of an embarrassment for John Clayton.

John Middleton Clayton was one of the most distinguished politicians in the history of Delaware. Born in lower Delaware in 1796, he was educated at local academies and at Yale University and Litchfield Law School, also in Connecticut. His father was a tanner, miller, farmer, and slave owner whose business prospered and earned him a place of great respect in Delaware. While his son studied at Litchfield, however, the business began to falter, and by the time the son returned from his studies his father was all but bankrupt.

Clayton was in a desperate situation. Years later, he wrote a former classmate, "When I left Litchfield I came destitute of cash—nay literally penniless. Things were in a bad way. My father was as men of business say ruined—insolvent and made so by his own generosity in writing his name too often for some friends and dealing too much with Banks." He entered the law to recover. "I read hard," he wrote his friend, "but before I got through my course he died and left me with a large family by way of patrimony. Necessity compelled me to betake myself forthwith to the law—my only refuge."[77]

Clayton's father died in 1820; to satisfy his creditors, a sheriff's sale was held to auction off all his family's possessions.[78] Clayton worked incessantly at the law, took on desperate cases and developed a reputation of thoroughness and sometimes ruthlessness. His star rose in state legal circles. His biographer suggested, "When it was possible for any lawyer to win a case, to succeed, he was always the victor in the contest."[79]

In the early 1820s the Pennsylvania Abolition Society hired Clayton to assist Delaware Attorney General James Rogers in prosecuting Joe Johnson. Clayton was chosen for his considerable legal skills but not for his attitudes toward slavery or the black population. He thought slavery evil and freed his father's slaves but suggested "all had been industrious & happy while they were his father's slaves; but, once freed, several became heavy drinkers and died of their excess." He exhibited "anguish concerning the benefits of freedom," and "was never able to transcend the belief in white supremacy."[80]

However, black kidnapping was abhorrent to Clayton and he took on this case, as he did all others, with the intent to win. The decision against Johnson in the 1822 case was a sweet victory for Clayton. Biographer Joseph P. Comegys reported, "Others have told me how greatly he distinguished himself on that occasion; in fact the case is mentioned frequently for one particular feature of the trial—the fainting upon the stand of a false witness to prove an alibi, under the cross-examination the young lawyer gave him."[81]

In 1837, Clayton wrote about his involvement with and recollection of the Cannon-Johnson gang fifteen years before. "In 1822 at the April term in Sussex I assisted the Attorney General [James Rogers] and James Booth to prosecute Johnson . . . Johnson himself made a fortune at the business and easily escaped justice by removing from one county or state to another when pursued by an officer with a posse. . . . He was arrested at last in 1822 by the Sheriff of Sussex with a posse at the house of the notorious Patty Cannon. They had 15 or 20 negroes in chains hid about the premises and were surprised by the Sheriff."[82]

In 1829 the *Delaware Gazette* carried an article about the arrest containing two descriptive phrases referring to Patty Cannon. "This woman is now between sixty and seventy years of age, and looks more like a man than a woman; but old as she is, she is believed to be as heedless and heartless as the most abandoned wretch that lives." The article mentioned Joe Johnson as a man of some celebrity in the kidnapping business and suggested that he "for many years, carried on the traffic of stealing and selling negroes in which he was aided and instructed by the old hag, Patty Cannon." Clayton's 1837 account represents the first attempt to identify Patty Cannon as the gang's leader. Clayton, however, offers little in the way of direct evidence, revealing only that she was "a fiend in human shape," and "dressed like a man and carried a musket."[83]

Researchers found little evidence of gang activity between 1827 and April 1829 when Patty Cannon was arrested for the last time. Jerry Shields suggested that "with Joe leaving in 1826, and other members of the family having departed earlier, Patty evidently was not up to carrying on the family business alone."[84] Newspaper accounts record her as "visiting in prominent Dorchester and Caroline County homes, where she entertained her hosts and hostesses with gossip and amusing stories, and told their fortunes to supplement her diminished income." One report suggested that Joe Johnson heard about the $500 reward offered by the City of Philadelphia and "suddenly decamped, and has since been very cautious in suffering himself to be seen in that part of the country."[85]

Patty Cannon's luck ran out in 1829 when a local farmer, plowing fields that adjoined her property, came upon a chest filled with human bones. The chest was identified as belonging to Cannon and the bones believed to be that of a southern slave trader who had come into the area ten years before and disappeared. A search was made for other bodies. Three more were dug up, including that of a child with a fractured skull. Local authorities arrested Cyrus James, Cannon's servant and a "suspicious character."[86]

Under questioning James, a member of the gang (and some claim a black man "raised" by Cannon and out for revenge), provided testimony that twelve years before "Joseph Johnson, Ebenezer Johnson and Patty Cannon, had shot (a Negro trader from Georgia) while at supper in her house." He said they dragged the man out and buried him and that they had killed many others. He also stated that Patty Cannon shot a young mulatto child she believed was fathered by someone in her family and another child they had kidnapped. Based on the bones and James's statement, indictments were issued against Patty Cannon, Joe Johnson, and

Ebenezer Johnson. Only Patty was arrested. She was charged with three murders and the Johnson brothers one each. The case never came to trial because she "died in jail on the 11th instant."[87]

Even her death was something of a mystery. Patty Cannon died in the Georgetown county jail on May 11, 1829. The reported cause of death was poison, "administered by her own hand. The exact reason for her suicide is unknown."[88] There were also rumors that she died of natural causes or that she was assassinated. The local press at first reported that she had been taken to trial and plead guilty. This report was later retracted because of the impossibility of a trial at that time of year. All records of her arrest have vanished.

Several problems surrounded the prosecution of the case. The first concerned Cyrus James, who if black could not have testified against Cannon. Early records suggested that he was black, later ones that he was white. A second question concerned lack of evidence other than James's testimony. Who actually committed the ten-year-old murders could not be established. Reporter George Massey suggested that Cyrus James was "brain-washed and made up a lot of the tales about her." What Massey may have referred to was the considerable time that James was interviewed in custody before the charge was made. The bones were discovered on April 1; Cyrus James was arrested and brought before a justice of the peace in Seaford, Delaware, for questioning, but an indictment was not issued by a Sussex grand jury until April 13. Massey does not say that Clayton was behind an effort to coach James, if any occurred, but he did state that "Clayton had political ambitions and that he looked upon the Patty Cannon case as a chance to become conspicuous."[89]

• • •

George Alfred Townsend was born in Georgetown, Delaware, in 1841. Townsend was a newspaper writer who lived in New York and Philadelphia and wrote for over forty years. In addition to his daily columns, in 1884 he wrote his celebrated work of fiction on Patty Cannon called *The Entailed Hat.* A rumor survives that a longer version of the project, published by Harper and Row, had to be withdrawn "when prominent families in Delaware and Maryland objected to some of its revelations."[90] Townsend's book was the second fictionalized account of Cannon. The *Narrative of Lucretia P. Cannon* was the first.

Though a work of fiction, *The Entailed Hat* is a combination of both real and imaginary characters in real and imaginary situations. Prominent among them are Patty Cannon, Joe Johnson, Cyrus James as a white character, and John Clayton as hero.[91] Both the *Narrative* (1841) and *The Entailed Hat* (1884) documented Cannon's reputation for cruelty. When

the fictional Cannon was arrested, Townsend wrote, "Not agony nor re-
pentance nor hope of escape fluttered her cold heart, but only a feeling of
being ill treated and ungratefully deserted by her friends." According to
Townsends' tale, respectable people in the region forced by financial ruin
to deal with the gang "feared that Patty Cannon would make a minute
confession and implicate all who had dealt with her band." All blame falls
to the Cannons. Clayton, who in the novel is responsible for the capture
of Patty Cannon, forgives a guilty friend saying, "Rise up, friend, at least
your transgressions are washed in sincere tears." The fictional Cannon,
defiant to the end, announced in jail, "They shall never see me hang and
swallowed the arsenic she had concealed in her bosom."[92]

Part of the success of the fictional accounts of the Cannon gang is due
to the absence of anything else. For example, court records give little hint
of the composition of the gang and its leadership. The *Delaware Gazette*
article published at the time of her 1829 arrest refers to "Johnson and his
gang" and suggest that bones were found "on the farm where Patty Cannon and her son-in-law, the celebrated Joseph Johnson, Negro trader, lived
for many years." The article suggests that Patty Cannon was complicit
in the murders but does so only by her presence. That a woman would
participate in the murder of children would certainly shock a community
that knew her. But her portrait as "a woman void of all human emotions
and sympathies" is not suggested here. These were later inventions. No
trial was ever held and, as one writer later noted, "the actual perpetrator
of those horrible deeds, may be difficult to ascertain."[93]

Marjorie and Sydney Greenbie, in their biography of Anna Ella Carroll, suggest that by the age of nine Carroll's slaves were terrified of Patty
Cannon. That would have been 1823 and, if true, this would be one of
the earliest references to her villainy. The Greenbies, however, were fond
of "synthesizing" facts.

In the 1930s a newspaper reporter traveled the area to find tales of
Cannon. He was told, "She was one of Maryland's most spectacular renegades. . . . Her husband, equally disreputable, seems to have faded out
of the record about 1840, leaving his mate, who dressed like a man and
had the strength of Hercules, to carry on." The area resident then tells a
tale about a wonderful slave, Moses, who was abducted by Cannon. One
problem, of course, was that Cannon died in 1829.[94]

All of this leaves Patty Cannon with only the flimsiest of histories. Few reports connect her directly to acts of violence. More people
suggested that she ran the tavern. "Well-known for her hospitality on
the ground floor" is how one reporter described her. It is also generally
agreed that she was a "tall, handsome woman, well liked by the people
of Western Sussex." As the *Baltimore Sun* reported upon her arrest,

"Patty Cannon had done no kidnapping for several years. Seeing all her friends turned fiercely against her, however, she gave herself up to a Maryland constable." Researcher Jerry Shields has raised the question of why a hardened criminal would give up so easily. And, after 1822, why not start another gang if the old one had left? The kidnapping business was booming at that time, not in decline.[95] Surrendering in Maryland rather than Delaware made sense because of the differences in state laws. Cannon's lawyer was Josiah Bayly of Cambridge, Maryland (who quite possibly was paid $5 by Harriet Tubman to trace the will of Athow Pattison).[96] The Maryland constable who arrested Cannon was said to be Thomas Hicks, the same Thomas Hicks who persuaded Edward Brodess, Tubman's owner, to settle his dispute with Anthony Thompson, owner of Ben Ross and stepfather of Edward Brodess. Hick's career thrived with the 1829 arrest of Cannon. In that same year he was elected to state office in Maryland.[97]

Some said Cannon was tricked into walking into Delaware after surrendering, hence the indictments came from Delaware. Others suggested "a pitched battle between Patty's gang and a posse of lawmen occurred."[98] But there was no gang in 1829. There is something appealing, in a gruesome sort of way, in believing that the buxom, dark-eyed beauty lead a gang of male thieves and murderers while serving one more for the road to weary and unsuspecting travelers. It is, I suppose, yet another in a rather long list of reasons why Patty Cannon's villainy lives on. And the alternative, that Cannon was something of a victim, abandoned in the end by her daughter and son-in-law, not supported by the wealthy community she had served, in diminished circumstances, and dying alone in a Georgetown jail cell is not the stuff of epic sagas.

The real Patty Cannon died in 1829 and was buried in an unmarked grave. The Patty Cannon of legend was born after her death, bringing terror to slave quarters and black communities throughout the region, providing grist for the abolitionist propaganda mill and cracks in the mortar of the benevolent institution that allowed the selling of children from their parents, and wives from husbands—"the dark underside of the American Dream."[99]

2 | Maryland, My Maryland

Better the fire upon thee roll,
Better the blade, the shot, the bowl,
Than crucifixion of the soul,
Maryland! My Maryland!

Anna Ella Carroll was born in 1815 on a plantation called Kingston Hall near Pocomoke City in Somerset County, one of the two southernmost of the Eastern Shore counties and one of the most isolated. Her family's once-large holdings had begun to shrink through a combination of mismanagement, lack of foresight, and redundancy. Anne's father, Thomas King Carroll, was part of a poorer branch of a prominent western Maryland family. Charles Carroll, the patriarch of that family, had been "appointed receiver of Lord Baltimore's rents in 1691." His grandson Charles signed the Declaration of Independence.[1]

The western Carrolls were prominent in national affairs and devoted Catholics. Anne, raised as a Presbyterian at the dictates of her great-grandfather, a member of the wealthy Protestant King family, grew up to champion the anti-Catholic American Party. It was only one of a number of contradictions in her life. Balancing her many modern political interests while maintaining an aura of feminine gentility became something of an obsession with "Miss Anne." Though she belonged to Abraham Lincoln's inner circle of advisors, wrote political pamphlets at his request, and probably authored what became known as the "Tennessee Plan," her feats have remained in the background of history. Supporting testimony from a number of key administration players, after the fact, was insufficient to secure her compensation, let alone a place at the table.

Anna Ella Carroll was often hidden behind elaborate, self-constructed masks of gaiety and stubbornness. Described as "fair, petite and curvaceous," she was also said to be "aggressive, tenacious, occasionally ruthless and almost indefatigable." Most of all, she was a passionate, talented and flawed woman "at war with Victorian conventions" who grew deaf while shouting to be heard.[2]

Anne studied law at the feet of her father, a reclusive legal scholar educated at the University of Pennsylvania and its law school. Thomas King Carroll served in the Maryland House of Delegates from 1816 to 1817, was a county court judge from 1826 to 1829, and was appointed governor of Maryland in 1830, serving one year. His term, while undistinguished by legislation, earned him a place of esteem both locally and nationally. Thomas King Carroll was a Jacksonian Democrat and later a Whig. Fellow Democrat Jefferson Davis, among his admirers, tried on several occasions in 1860 to get him to join the Confederacy, offering him any position he desired. Thomas King Carroll, pro-slavery and pro-Union, always declined.

The value of his daughter's home-taught legal training and writing was widely recognized, though at times in a backhanded way. In 1862 A. S. Diven, a member of Congress from New York and a railroad man, wrote to Carroll about her pamphlet on John C. Breckenridge: "There is cogency in your argument that I have seldom met with," he wrote. "Such maturity of judicial learning with so comprehensive and concise a style of communication surprises me. Ladies have certainly seldom evinced ability as jurists—it may be because the profession was not their sphere—but you have satisfied me that at least one might have been a distinguished lawyer."[3]

While her father was governor, Carroll served in an unofficial capacity as his chief of staff and private secretary, drafting letters, arranging meetings, and lobbying constituencies. Unfortunately, her father's absence from Kingston Hall may have hastened its economic decline and when, at the end of his term of office, he was nominated for the U.S. Senate he refused, citing economic difficulties. Thomas King Carroll's debts eventually led him to sell Kingston Hall to a neighbor in 1837 and move to an estate called Warwick Manor, near Cambridge, Maryland. Carroll, now twenty-two, rented a house in Somerset and started a school for young ladies, not an unusual practice for "gentlewoman in straitened circumstances." As historian Janet Coryell suggested, it was an acceptable money-making activity within a "woman's sphere."[4] Somerset's economy declined as a result of the national economic crisis, forcing Carroll to close the school in 1843 and move to Dorchester County with her family.

Carroll left for Baltimore in the mid-1840s and worked as a promotional writer for railroad lobbyists and as an unpaid political operative for the Whig Party. While unusual pursuits for a woman, Carroll was restless on the Eastern Shore and loath, though she had many offers, to adopt the typical role of wife and mother. She had by then realized that it also fell to her to support her family and to protect them and her father, most of all, from his "misguided generosity."

It was one of the most exciting and crisis-ridden periods in American political history and her experience there had to be numbing. Many of the people she worked with at that time and later were friends of her father who valued the "ardent young worker for the party" and the clout of the Carroll name. Chief among them was Henry Clay, later architect of the Compromise of 1850, whom she always held in the highest regard. Others included Caleb Smith, a congressman from Indiana who would be instrumental in Abraham Lincoln's nomination; Thomas Corwin and Salmon Chase, Ohio Whigs who would later become Republicans; and William Seward, who would be the great friend and benefactor of Harriet Tubman. While Carroll disagreed with Seward's abolitionism ("wholly unrealistic"), she admired his strength of character and conviction. She also saw no contradiction, while not supporting abolition, in her own position that manumission was preferable to sending Maryland slaves into slavery in the Deep South.[5]

Desperate for money, Carroll embarked on an ambitious letter-writing campaign with the dual objective of securing employment for her father and a place for herself. Her mother died in 1849, leaving Carroll as her father's self-appointed caregiver. In April 1849 she wrote to John Clayton, foe of Patty Cannon and the newly appointed Whig secretary of state, pleading for a job for her father. "So high is my appreciation of yourself, so perfect is my confidence in the efficiency of your power to serve me, that I must trust to your kindness to excuse a daughter from making the effort to find a 'loved Father' a job," she wrote.[6] Thomas King Carroll was appointed naval officer at the port of Baltimore. The entire family then moved to Baltimore where Anne's younger brother Harry got a job as clerk to help with family expenses.

Buoyed by her victory, Carroll continued pursuing political appointments. She also quickened her pace of writing on national issues, first anonymously through letters to the editors and later as a political pamphleteer and lobbyist.

Carroll had to proceed with caution. The accepted political sphere for women of women's rights, reform, and abolition did not interest her. Her passions were the Union, the Constitution, and American political traditions, topics of which women were thought to be ignorant. Anti-slavery lecturer Sallie Holley wrote often of "the general distrust of women in politics."[7] Early on Carroll reasoned that her only path to influence in these areas was attachment to influential men.

In her first book, she explained this shadow stance, reflecting what historians have called the persona of the "republican mother," one who advanced the ideals of piety, virtue, and domesticity. "The privileged position of women as nurturer," Carroll wrote "allowed them control over the development of those who would control the future. God has given to woman to enlighten America and to America to light the world."[8]

Influential men became her "projects," and she provided advice and counsel, usually through letters, without being asked. Historian Janet Coryell finds a distinct pattern in her written appeals to men. Her letters were written with flowery phrases, began with flattery, included compliments to their intelligence, and ended with sentiment. These were typical expressions of a woman of her class and impediments she had to circumvent.[9] Though her methods might be offensive to more modern women, her goals would not be—she was charting a course in untested waters.

"So powerful were the cultural definitions of woman's role," historian Anne Firor Scott once explained, "so fixed the restrictions upon educational and professional opportunity that an ambitious woman had to become adept at appearing to conform to the cultural prescriptions at the very time she was seeking to defy them. Achieving women often spoke with pain of the deviousness they felt brought on by this necessity."[10] This was, at times, an all-too familiar description of Anna Ella Carroll.

Millard Fillmore, who in November 1848 was elected vice president under Zachary Taylor, was one of Carroll's first special projects. "Project" seems a more appropriate term than "friend" or "associate" because their correspondence was a bit one-sided and Fillmore, on occasion, sought the opinion of others about her veracity. For her part, Carroll often closed her letters to him with the phrase "your best little friend."

As many Whigs in her circle had hoped, Taylor left much of the policy making and political appointments of his administration to Fillmore. Taylor's attitude toward the struggle in Congress over the pressing issues of slavery and territorial expansion was vague. His desire to run the country like a military campaign was much clearer. On July 4, 1850, he became ill while drinking milk and eating cherries at a White House celebration. He died on July 9. Taylor's entire cabinet resigned forthwith and Fillmore, now president, appointed replacements. Daniel Webster, who somewhat late in the day had joined the Compromise of 1850, became secretary of state.

Attempting to involve herself in the 1852 campaign for Fillmore's renomination and to distribute largess to family and friends, Carroll wrote him often with advice and requests for favors. Her notes were written in phrases such as, "no selfish aspiration, no sordid interest, no political distinction has actuated me." She was careful not to obviously appear to quit the sphere to which she had been born, a sphere that imposed the noted limits on one of her class and sex. Her words had to first give reassurance and then win him over. So, in 1852 she wrote to Fillmore, "Honored Sir, it may look unique for an 'American lady' to be so heartily embarked in the interest of the political condition of the country, but I am sure it will be considered a pardonable offense."[11]

Comparing Fillmore to Pericles, Carroll observed in another letter that "only the spirit of partisanship had marred a universal acknowledgement of the exalted virtues, and undoubted patriotism, and the wise and just administration of the present National Executive." She also mentioned in this letter an article she had written in defense of Fillmore and ended with an appeal for a federal appointment for a friend.[12] At the end of May 1852 she warned him of traitors in his administration but concluded, "I do believe in spite of all their vituperation, their daily defamation and jealous and indefatigable exertions to bring ruin and disaster upon our cause, you will [win the nomination] by the voice of the American people."[13] The years between 1848 and 1852 were perhaps the most influential for Carroll and her Whig friends. The nation was at peace but disputes and disagreements within the party soon doomed it. Fillmore was passed over for the presidential nomination by Northern Whigs because of his support for the Compromise of 1850, legislation fiercely opposed in the North. (Sallie Holley never partook of communion in her favorite Buffalo church after her pastor allowed Fillmore—upon signing the Fugitive Slave Law—to return to his accustomed seat without rebuke.)[14]

In the months before the Whig nominating convention, Carroll wrote Fillmore to beware of Attorney General John J. Crittenden's "covert maneuvers," Webster's "great endeavors," and John Clayton's "ambitions to obtain the presidential nomination."[15] At the convention Fillmore lost to General Winfield Scott and Carroll switched sides. Thinking Scott's victory was due in part to the support of William Seward, she wrote to Seward in a congratulatory tone, "And where would have been prospects for success with any other name than Winfield Scott?"[16] Franklin Pierce, a Democrat from New Hampshire, won a decisive victory in the November election. Thomas King Carroll, naval officer of Baltimore, was once again unemployed. Carroll, in characteristic fashion, wrote to Democrat William Marcy, secretary of state under Pierce, on behalf of her father: "As a parent, as a gentleman, I appeal to you to sustain the efforts of a daughter, on behalf of a pure and exemplary Father."[17] But the elder Carroll remained unemployed.

Out of office, the Whig party split into two major factions. One side opposed, at the least, the extension of slavery into new territories and, at the most, supported complete abolition. The other, the side Carroll championed, feared the growing influence of foreign Catholic immigrants who, it was argued, voted as instructed by the Church in Rome. The slavery question for Carroll's faction paled by comparison. Theirs was to be an American Party (closely allied with the Know-Nothings), open to all, she argued, but one that carefully cherished the constitutional ideal of the separation of church and state.[18]

Toward that mission, in 1856 Carroll published her first book, *The Great American Battle,* which E. B. Bartlett, national president of the Know-Nothings, called "the textbook of the cause."[19] In the preface she wrote, "For the first time, I appear before the public. As a woman, I shrink with timidity and distrust. I have no affiliations with any principles which place her at variance with the refined delicacy to which she is assigned by nature. I have no aspirations to extend her influence or position—no political, religious, or personal animosities to resent." But in the text, she quickly got to the heart of the matter, casting flattery and timidity aside. "True Catholicism, as a spiritual faith has nothing to do with the corrupt manipulation of the new American vote. It is this enormous immigration that is making the trouble. Every year brings to our shores more than the whole number of Americans at the time when the Declaration of Independence was signed, and most of them are Catholics from lands which never had the first glimmerings of democratic government."[20]

Several things worried her. The first was that immigrant children be schooled "in our own school system" so as to be properly "Americanized" rather than left to the isolation of Catholic schools. The second was the voting process. "The other thing we can do is to clean up the ballot box, to watch the polls and cry aloud against every corrupt bargain for votes en bloc, and to take care that the government of the United States is not sold from under us by foreigners to traitors!"[21]

This was a new version of Carroll. No longer the reserved Southern lady hovering in the shadows, she is transformed into an articulate, angry, and somewhat bigoted orator working the crowd into frenzy. With a challenge to her own Catholic roots she wrote, "Is there an American Catholic so stiff-necked and hollow as not to shudder at the sight of that huge wheel which is bobbing over all our highways to enfeeble our sinews and put us under a torpid nightmare?" At the same time, she made it clear that she would not "interfere with their faith, which she would defend with her blood."[22] *The Great American Battle* found a large audience. In May 1856 she wrote her father: "The papers today announce a sale of 10,000 copies of *The Battle,* and the whole country is alive in its praise."[23]

While Carroll's anti-Catholicism was ingrained from childhood, she appeared by some accounts to hesitate before agreeing to take on the commission offered for her book. Her reluctance was logical because of her use of the Carroll name. Even after agreeing to write the book, Carroll was careful to separate native and foreign Catholics. Besides her obvious and somewhat desperate need for money, it was likely that Carroll was prompted by the turmoil within the Church at that time. Pope Pius IX (elected in 1846), after freeing all Italian political prisoners began a campaign, conducted over a number of years, that denied freedom of religion, rationalism, and Protestant worship in Italy, except for foreign visitors. Such ideas fueled Carroll's paranoia about the Church and its impact on American political traditions.[24]

Her compensation for writing *The Battle* was to be $1,000. In the same letter to her father she mentioned with some naivety, "My friends say that they will raise a fund and I shall have $1000 for my services. Every Whig is moving to have me relieved and to insure my efforts." However, further correspondence suggested that she was not paid as promised.[25]

Preparing for the election in 1856, she lobbied for the reemergence of Fillmore as the only individual on the Whig slate who could inspire national appeal—that is, transcend the growing North and South divisions. The Democrats, done with Pierce who had abandoned the Compromise of 1850 and, they thought, precipitated a civil war in Kansas over slavery and territorial expansion, nominated James Buchanan of Pennsylvania for president and John Breckenridge of Kentucky for vice president.[26]

Harriet Tubman's friend Thomas Garrett, observing the political scene, wrote his friend Eliza Wigham in England that he thought Pierce "was one of the most contemptible trucklers to the Southern interest of any man that ever held a responsible station in this country" and that Buchanan, if elected, would probably bring civil war. Garrett predicted that Fillmore would not carry a single state.[27]

Though Carroll had publicly condemned Buchanan ("who made the bargain with the foreign hierarchy") for his vote-getting schemes in prior elections, she was a longtime friend of the Breckenridge family, particularly of the vice president's uncle, Robert.[28] The bitter election, full of virulent anti-Catholicism, went to the Democrats. Buchanan's administration was only two days old when the U.S. Supreme Court delivered the *Dred Scott* decision affirming that blacks could not be citizens and thus had no rights that whites need recognize, infuriating the abolitionist community and further separating North and South.[29]

Despite philosophical differences with the Democrats, Carroll once again donned her role as Southern lady and became a fixture at administration social affairs. Past forty, her panic in being able to maintain her political influence by flattery, cajolery, and last-resort tears was palpable. Letters to political associates were more numerous, her pleas more desperate. Her beloved father's economic imprudence only added to Carroll's woes. Still, she remained a "gadfly" to the Democrats, warning those in the American Party about the Democrats' secessionist leanings and searching for yet another "national" candidate for the 1860 election.

William Seward was the front runner for the fractured Whigs at the beginning of the 1860 campaign season. In 1852, Carroll had written to him, "We of the South owe to you more than any other man the reputation we enjoy and the hopes with which we are inspired."[30] But in 1860, Carroll held two things against him. His abolitionism made him a decidedly sectional candidate and a liability to the national agenda that she believed was essential. And while governor of New York, his support of publicly funded Catholic education made him suspect to large segments of the former American Party. Behind the scenes Carroll worked for John Minor Botts, a slaveholding "Union" man of Virginia, formerly a member of the state legislature and the U.S. House of Representatives, who was antiabolitionist and "not particularly enamored of foreigners." She hoped that a divided convention would anoint him as a reasonable compromise.

While favoring Botts, Carroll saw the value of bringing the old Whig Party back together as the Seward campaign proposed. She would later write to Seward, again continuing her practice of not alienating any side potentially useful in the future, that he should have won the nomination. During the election season, however, she made no effort to support him, instead writing a piece in the *New York Evening Express* pointing out his liabilities. "We believe he would do nothing unconstitutional," she wrote, "had he the power to abolish slavery. But would the conservative men of all sections consent to try for President one who made these avowals?" Carroll also tried to influence Seward's ally Thurlow Weed against him. She suggested to Botts that Weed supported him when he did not, suggested to Weed that he abandon Seward, and all the while tried to keep Seward in her camp. It was a dangerous game, duplicitous in fact, but not unheard of in Washington. Unfortunately for her efforts, her political stock continued to decline.[31]

What she failed to anticipate at the beginning of the campaign was the ascendancy of Abraham Lincoln, who would pull most of the elements of the Whig coalition into the Republican Party. Lincoln's outsider status in the North-South divide and Washington circles gave him some currency with the public, although his personal style made him the subject of much scorn. The other leading candidate for the nomination was

Carroll's friend Salmon Chase, governor of Ohio. Biographer Marjorie Greenbie described him as "intense, high-minded and a representative of the abolitionists of the North."[32] It is not clear when and how Chase and Carroll first became acquainted but surviving correspondence suggests a close relationship after 1860. Carroll was also a friend of Chase's daughter, Katherine. But her assessment of the liability of an abolitionist stand affected her support of Chase.

At the Republican Party's nominating convention, members of the old American Party faction including Edward Bates, Caleb Smith, and Chase combined forces to influence the outcome. They objected to Seward because of his growing conservatism on the issue of abolition and his support of Catholic education. Thinking that Chase could not prevail, they threw their weight to Lincoln. Carroll, as a political operative—polling delegates, writing and passing notes—was obviously involved in some of these activities, as Bates and Smith were also her friends. But her association with Lincoln was not close at this time. Once elected, Lincoln did include many of her "friends" in his cabinet. Bates became attorney general, Caleb Smith secretary of the interior, and Chase secretary of the treasury.[33]

Appointed March 7, 1861, Chase wrote to Carroll four days later, "I will be pleased to see you tomorrow, at any time convenient to yourself after nine o'clock. I am not seeing anyone just yet on the matter to which you refer, but of course will see *you*. You have my grateful thanks for the great and patriotic services you have rendered and are still rendering to the country in this crisis" (emphasis in original text). It was a suggestive note, but the exact nature of these "great and patriotic services" is not known.[34]

In a crowded field, Lincoln's convention victory was hardly a mandate. It was, he said, "a convention that was two-thirds for the other fellow." After his election as president, Carroll turned her attention to writing in defense of many of his actions. She did so with some initial reluctance. In her rough draft of the pamphlet *The War Powers*, she described Lincoln as "a renegade Southerner, narrow minded, as all ignorant men are, [who] hates the South intensely, because he did not get its votes."[35] Still, long before the election, she had been writing about American political traditions and her passion for the Union, "the destruction [of which] would change wisdom for folly, light for darkness. . . ." Carroll and Lincoln shared this passion. This time, as Coryell suggests, "She made no apology for her intrusion into the political arena."[36]

In 1857 Carroll worked in Maryland to elect Thomas Holliday Hicks as governor. Hicks was a member of the American Party and a slaveholder, who "never lived, and should be sorry to be obliged to live, in a state where slavery does not exist, and I never will do so if I can avoid it." Hicks, like many nativist Protestants in Maryland, felt under siege. His world seemed to be crumbling and Catholic immigrants, thought to be influencing votes in Baltimore, the largest city, were deemed as good a source of the decline as any.[37] Hicks was also pro-Union.

In 1861, Maryland Democrats demanded that Hicks call a special session of the legislature to vote on the issue of secession. He refused, suggesting on more than one occasion that they "wait with calmness for the progress of events." He was under great pressure from the legislature, from public sentiment that on the issue of secession was decidedly mixed ("secession had a defiant minority"), and from grief at the death of a beloved child.[38] In April, federal troops passing through Baltimore were assaulted by a crowd of Southern sympathizers. Four soldiers and twelve citizens were killed.[39] Hicks responded to the pressure by calling a special session in Frederick, a city in western Maryland and a pro-union part of the state, rather than Annapolis, the capital. Maryland remained in the Union. Hicks always claimed that Carroll's support and aid made the difference. "When all was dark and dreadful for Maryland's future," he wrote to her in December 1861, "when the waves of secession were beating furiously upon your frail executive, borne down with private as well as public grief, you stood nobly by and watched the storm and skillfully helped to work the ship, until, thank God, helmsmen and crew were safe in port."[40] It was said that moving the vote to Frederick was Carroll's idea.[41]

• • •

There are several versions of the commencement of Carroll's military activities on behalf of the Lincoln administration. Marjorie Greenbie found among Carroll's papers a note that described herself "as an influence behind the scenes, but yet a real power, mighty for good in that great struggle." Carroll's official version, written at age seventy-five, suggests she wrote "an unpretentious pamphlet, which fell into the hands of Mr. Lincoln and so pleased him that he suggested its adoption as a war measure, and the satisfaction it gave so general that Governor Bates, then Attorney General, urged I should continue to write in the interest of the government."[42] Biographers Sidney and Marjorie Greenbie indicated that one of Carroll's first written works for the administration concerned the writ of habeas corpus. In April 1861, responding to the situation in Maryland, Lincoln had suspended habeas corpus at any point where there was rebellion. Many people objected, saying that only Congress had that right. Lincoln asked Attorney General Bates for an opinion. According to the Greenbies, "Bates asked Anne to write out her opinion, and submitted it, signed by her, with his own opinion, to President Lincoln." What survives is Bates's letter to the president dated July 5, 1861, and a later piece Carroll wrote in September.[43]

Carroll wrote that she accepted Bates's proposal "fired by enthusiasm in a noble cause." Soon after that she produced the *War Powers* pamphlet. Lincoln biographer Carl Sandburg noted that she was then invited to the White House on request of the president. "Her pamphlet," Sandburg wrote, "had elaborately defended the President's right of the writ of habeas corpus: one edition had been published under Seal of the Department of State and copies placed in the hands of all members of Congress."[44]

After meeting with Lincoln, she "went away and wrote an argument on *The Relations of the National Government to the Revolted Citizens,* which was published, given to members of Congress and put in general circulation." In that document, she passionately defends the Union and the Constitution. "Never were a people more jealous of liberty than our fathers were at the formation of the Constitution, and naturally so, too, as upon that Constitution depended the fruits of the independence which they had just achieved at the cost of so much treasure and blood." But, she continues, they also guaranteed "the right of the people to be secure in their person, houses, papers, and effects, against unreasonable searches and seizures, shall not be violated, nor shall any person be deprived of life, liberty, or property, without due process of law, nor shall private property be taken for public use, without just compensation." This, she also argues, was the basis of slaveholders' right of compensation.[45]

Carroll claimed that, on her own initiative, she planned a trip to St. Louis and upon mentioning it to Assistant Secretary of War Thomas Scott, was asked to survey attitudes in that city and report back. Later versions from the Greenbies would hint that Lincoln sent Carroll and Lemuel Evans on a secret mission. Nothing survives to support this contention, although the War Department did send Evans to Mexico to determine whether that country was supplying the Confederates. It was also suggested that Evans was sent to St. Louis to gauge Confederate strength and investigate a route for federal troops to go into the South.

Carroll and Evans were in St. Louis by October 1861. Both the Union and the Confederacy were preparing for war: they had to recruit, equip, arm, and train troops before anyone could think about battle strategy.

Early in the war, those in Washington thought that the Union would have a quick victory in the East and the war would end. What they had instead was quick and embarrassing losses. "With the exception of West Virginia," Lemuel Evans wrote, "six months after the beginning, the battle had been steadily against the union."[46]

The western front, an important source of rail and waterways that carried cotton, iron, manufactured goods, wheat, and corn, could not be ignored. But neither the Union nor the Confederates had an adequate naval fleet to protect it. Andrew Hull Foote, a Bible-packing temperance supporter, known for his "brimstone sermons and devout prayer," called the area "a wilderness of naval wants."[47]

Recruiting trained men was problematic for both sides. Confederate General Henry Morgan Stanley described his privates, "men of fortune, overseers of plantations, small cotton planters, professional men, clerks, merchants and a rustic lout or two," as very wanting. "The most singular characteristic was their readiness to take offense at any reflection of their veracity or personal honor." Before the battle at Belmont, Missouri, Union General Ulysses S. Grant complained that there were "many troops but in the greatest confusion, and no one person knew where they all were."[48] Chaotic responses were typical. In early September Confederate commander Gideon Pillow invaded neutral Kentucky, taking the city of Columbus, located near the confluence of the Ohio and Mississippi rivers. General Leonidas Polk moved in as well, on the western side of the Mississippi. Leaders in Richmond, Virginia, the capital of the Confederacy, were unhappy because no one had told them to do this, and President Jefferson Davis's administration was outraged. Tennessee Senator Gustavus Henry commented, "Whether it was altogether politic to take possession I need not say, but it will be ruinous to order (Polk) back."[49]

In November, General John C. Frémont ordered Grant to carry out diversionary tactics at Belmont, Missouri, a short distance below Cairo, Illinois. He was not to fight a battle but to harass the enemy so they would not bother Kentucky. Contrary to orders, a bloody engagement occurred. Grant, whose restless troops were eager to do something, attacked and drove the enemy out of town. With no other objective, he and his men then held a drunken victory celebration unaware that the fleeing Confederates had returned. They then had to fight their way out just as they had fought to get in. The press reported the events with undisguised alarm, describing Belmont as a "wholly unnecessary battle, barren of results, or the possibility of them from the beginning."[50]

The loss of life at Belmont greatly affected Carroll. Studying details of what happened there, she surmised that the problem was retreating with disabled boats upstream on the Mississippi. It occurred to her that pilots whom "military leaders would never think to ask" might have valuable suggestions about how to solve this problem. With the help of Lemuel Evans, she arranged to meet a pilot named Charles Scott. Scott told Carroll and Evans that there would be "death to every man who attempted to go down the Mississippi." Taking the Mississippi and plunging into the heart of the Confederacy had been an obvious goal of Union forces, but Carroll discovered, and Scott confirmed, a nearly impossible one because of the many peculiarities of the waterway. Searching for alternatives, Carroll asked about the Tennessee River because she reasoned, in a burst of inspiration, "It flowed the other way."[51]

She wrote at once to her friend Attorney General Bates explaining her idea. Bates was said to have passed her letter on to Assistant Secretary of War Thomas Scott. Both thought it impracticable, so Carroll prepared a more detailed plan and took it to Washington herself. Her plan read in part, "The civil and military authorities seem to be laboring under a grave mistake in regard to the true key of the war in the Southwest. It is not the Mississippi, but the Tennessee River . . . the river is navigable for medium-class boats to the foot of the Muscle shoals in Alabama, and is open to navigation all the year. . . . The Tennessee River offers many advantages over the Mississippi. We should avoid the most impregnable batteries of the enemy which cannot be taken without great danger and great risk of life to our forces. . . ."[52] Scott read the plan, listened to her arguments, and changed his mind. He next took it to Lincoln. Lincoln liked the plan, according to Carroll, while General George McClellan, not surprisingly, opposed it.

Action was taken in February when the gunboats were finally ready. Carroll's original plan was to go up the Tennessee, cut the railroad lines and then go south to Mobile, cutting the Confederacy in half and avoiding the Mississippi. At the same time she proposed surprising the South by taking Vicksburg from the rear. The taking of the Confederate forts Henry on the Tennessee and Donelson along the Cumberland were minor parts of her plan. In January, Lincoln, impatient with the progress of the conflict, issued War Order #1 directing the military to act by February 22, 1862. The order was impossible to enforce, illogical to impose, and ill-advised to issue, according to most military historians, but it gave life to at least part of Carroll's plan.[53]

The battle of Fort Henry was a great success. Seventeen thousand Confederate troops surrendered to Grant, who wrote his wife that it was the largest surrender in U.S. history. The battle at Fort Donelson was more difficult but ultimately successful as well. The Confederacy referred to these battles and the subsequent retreats as "disasters." The Northern press wrote as if it was the beginning of the end. The Lincoln administration, reeling over charges of corruption, cost overruns, and Secretary of War Cameron's poorly timed advocacy of emancipation, encouraged the premature enthusiasm. "The glory of our recent victories belongs to the gallant officers and soldiers that fought the battles," Edwin Stanton of the War department wrote to the *New York Times*, hoping to distract the press from the backstage military disarray.[54] Lincoln, meanwhile, happy that they were winning battles in the west, was desperately pushing his overly cautious eastern general to do the same.[55]

Thereafter Carroll would always believe—or at least contend—that it was her plan sent to the War Department in November 1861 that changed the course of the war. Coryell suggests that "Carroll, as a civilian and outsider," did not realize that what kept them from moving was not lack of intelligence but "supply shortages, battling commanders, lack of cooperation between army and navy and inexperienced troops and sailors."[56]

While Carroll's claim that the military had never before considered using the Tennessee River was certainly an exaggeration (one of her many exaggerations), the survival of her plan and no other and the support of many of the principals involved though long after the event should have lent greater weight to her assertions. In his memoirs Grant wrote that he considered the Tennessee in November—the same month Carroll took her plan to Washington—mentioning it to his command but was ignored. In January, he was told to prepare for a campaign, the architect of which he did not know.[57]

But the course of this war would not permit a single, quick, and simple victory. In April, farther south on the Tennessee River at Shiloh near the Mississippi state line, Confederate General Johnston, in charge of some 40,000 western forces, attacked Grant's position. With 36,000 troops on the Union side, a fierce battle ensued and the Union suffered heavy losses. At dawn the next day, with Union forces bolstered by 26,000 additional troops under generals Don Carlos Buell and Lew Wallace, the Confederates were forced to retreat. Grant, with so many dead, hardly saw it as a victory. He wrote: "It was a victory because it was not a crushing defeat."[58]

William T. Sherman, also at Shiloh, wrote to his brother: "I still feel the horrid nature of this war, and the piles of dead and wounded and maimed makes me more anxious than ever for some hope of an end, but I know such a thing cannot be for a long, long time. Indeed I never expect it, or to survive it." Over 13,000 men were killed or wounded on the Union side, 10,000 on the Confederate side, Grant wrote in his memoirs.[59]

Carroll was at this time hard at work attempting to influence Lincoln on the issue of compensated emancipation. Secretary of War Simon Cameron had been replaced by Edwin Stanton but the question of emancipation prematurely raised by Cameron hung heavily over the administration. Carroll realized the precariousness of Union support in the border states and feared the consequences of emancipation without compensation. But even more, she worried that such an act was unconstitutional. She wrote in the pamphlet: "Some wild theorists even allege that the power to wage this civil war against the insurrection carries with it the transcendent power of general confiscation over *all* the property situated in the States where the insurrection rages, as well as to strike down whatever State institution the Government may deem even indirectly opposed to the success of its aims" (emphasis in original text).[60]

The Greenbies suggest that in March Carroll and Lincoln devised a plan for limited compensation for Maryland and Delaware. Lincoln did in fact put forth a proposal in a special message to Congress in that month that read, "Resolved, that the United States ought to co-operate with any state which may adopt gradual abolishment of slavery, giving to such state pecuniary aid, to be used by such state in its discretion to compensate for the inconveniences public and private produced by such change of system." The resolution was passed by both houses but the border states, to whom it was directed, showed no interest in it. Abolitionists were unimpressed. "It is the most diluted, milk and water, gruel proposition that was ever given to the American nation," said Thaddeus Stevens.[61]

There is no record of their meeting or collaboration. Carroll did, as was her way, keep Lincoln informed of her position on this issue. In April she wrote, "Be not deceived, Mr. President, because the Union men of the South sustain you, in your efforts to suppress the rebellion and maintain the integrity of the Constitution that they will ever submit to the abolition of slavery, by the government." She warned him that a "reinforcement of at least fifty thousand fighting men" from border states were available to rebel forces if he supported any form of emancipation.[62]

The problem was that Lincoln listened to many people on this issue and ultimately charted a course that satisfied few—Carroll least of all. On April 16 he signed a bill ending slavery in the District of Columbia, providing for immediate emancipation, compensation of up to $300 for each slave of a loyal Unionist, and voluntary colonization of former slaves to colonies outside the United States. Republican members of Congress pushed the bill (Charles Sumner, Benjamin Wade, and Stevens visited Lincoln repeatedly) and border state delegations opposed it. In a letter to Horace Greeley in late March, Lincoln wrote, "I am a little uneasy about the abolition of slavery in the District, not but I would be glad to see it abolished, but as to the time and manner of doing it."[63]

In May Sumner introduced the Second Confiscation Act with the words, "We are at liberty to treat the people engaged against us as criminals or as enemies, or, if we please, as both." We must "pursue and punish them and blast them with the summary vengeance which is the dread agencies of war."[64] Carroll was quick to react. This position was false, she claimed in her second pamphlet, sometimes called "Reply to Sumner." Carroll argued that "war may exist between the General Government and a portion of the American people, but under the Constitution it never did and never can exist by armed resistance to its authority."[65]

The Sumner bill passed both houses of Congress. On July 12 Lincoln appealed to the congressmen of the border states to support his March plan for gradual, compensated emancipation as an alternative. On July 14 Carroll once again wrote to Lincoln in the strongest terms: "I do not now propose to argue upon the details of that bill, because, I have not succeeded in obtaining a copy; but I have read the synopsis, and understand the three leading points, to consist, in the confiscation of property—the emancipation of slaves—and arming them. . . . This bill will inaugurate a new policy, and change the whole morale of the war. It will no longer be regarded, as a war for the maintenance of the American Constitution, but as one, for the subjugation of the Southern States, and the destruction of their social system. And the judgment of the civilized world, will then decide, that the South is in a just struggle for Constitutional Liberty; against an arbitrary and revengeful government."[66]

Lincoln signed the bill on July 17, taking the unprecedented step of attaching to it the wording of a veto. His objections "centered on the extinguishment of real estate titles, regarding property, which was an unconstitutional forfeiture of property because it extended beyond the life of the guilty party, as well as on proceedings *in rem*." By now the only thing left of Carroll's strategies was colonization.[67] The Shiloh battle had been something of a wakeup call for the president and the public—with so many dead and a victory so precarious came renewed fears of a protracted war. Everyone was unhappy. Members of Lincoln's own party began to lobby not only for immediate emancipation but for greater Congressional oversight in the war.

Thomas Scott resigned his position in the War Department in June, depriving Carroll of her major ally. His replacement, Peter H. Watson, did not recognize her informal agreement with the department and was reluctant to authorize any new projects for her. By September Carroll was reduced to pressing for payment for work already done. She first submitted a bill of $5,000 and later revised it to $6,250, including the $1,200 promised from Scott. Watson paid her $750, which Carroll thought was an installment and Watson felt was the final payment. When she offered to write new pamphlets on emancipation, Watson wrote that she was "entirely mistaken in assuming that I have undertaken to employ you to write for this Department or to compensate you for writing." Carroll was surprised but not defeated and asked Watson to pass the request along to Stanton. "I cannot doubt that, could the Sec. give his attention to the proposition, he would at once concur in the utility of such a production as mine would be." Watson wrote back to say her request was rejected.[68]

Carroll tried to reestablish links with others in the administration and to attempt to receive the remainder of her payment. She also sought other work. In July she wrote to Lincoln, detailing the arrangements surrounding her writing and stated, "when I considered the time and labor the documents cost me, and its immense service to the country—for it was destined to stand as long as the Declaration of Independence—I thought $50,000 as being a small sum, and if so compensated, I would give it a very large circulation and continue writing for the government."[69] She waited until August to deliver the letter in person, had a short interview, and heard first not from him but through gossip that a woman had tried to hold up the president for $50,000. In great outrage, she wrote to him, "I am just informed, that at a public dinner table, in a Washington Hotel, a gentlemen, whose name I do not know, stated that the President had said, 'a lady demanded fifty thousand dollars for writing a document,: &c;' meaning, myself." Carroll wrote the president, she said, in an attempt to "forget the very disparaging manner in which it was represented" and to set the record straight. Her plan had been "to render efficient service to the Country, by going to Europe, and writing in its defense." The amount mentioned was to be used "in the circulation of my documents among millions; and to write and publish in Europe, during your Administration." She claimed that "many of the ablest men in the Nation" had been informed of and approved of her plan. While she did not mention Chase and Bates, both members of the cabinet, surely Lincoln would suspect them.[70]

Carroll also articulated her reasons for involvement in politics. "Mr. President, government, is something more than a machine, which requires simply the presence of a skilled engineer. It is an institution, which for the successful accomplishment of its ends; depends at last, not so much, upon the skill of the functionaries; as upon the temper and spirit of the people. . . . [It] is kept right, not by the officials of the Government, but by their leaders of thought, the independent thinkers, and actors of the day!" It is apparent that Carroll thought of herself as that independent thinker.[71] No reply from Lincoln survives.

The Greenbies suggested that Lincoln, as a kind of apology, asked her to work on the previously mentioned colonization plan. But the president then shifted his support from colonization to uncompensated emancipation. Pressed by the radicals in his party and convinced of gaining a military advantage, he issued a preliminary emancipation order in September stating that if the Confederate states did not return to the Union, all slaves within their borders would be free on January 1, 1863. Pressure from the border states, particularly from Thomas Hicks in Maryland (now a U.S. senator) kept slavery in Maryland, Delaware, Kentucky,

Missouri, and parts of Louisiana. Carroll's proposals for compensated emancipation had been ignored.

Increasingly dissatisfied with Lincoln and his policies, she began to cast about in late 1862 for a new candidate to support for president in the next election. The Republicans had done very badly in the by-elections that year and Carroll was confident that the right candidate could defeat Lincoln in 1864. Dividing her time between New York and Washington, her letters suggest she supported Salmon Chase, secretary of the treasury. The Greenbies argued for her continued support of Lincoln, but nonetheless suggested her view was "if it should be the Lord's will to replace him, who better than one (Chase) who was able to command power and dignity." She wrote her sister of her fears of Lincoln's "military despotism."[72]

The Chase candidacy suffered a severe blow in February 1864, when a letter written by Senator Pomeroy was distributed in the halls of Congress arguing that Lincoln could not win reelection and that Chase should be nominated. The letter was also leaked to newspapers, including the Washington *National Intelligencer*. Pomeroy represented a committee of the friends of Chase, including Carroll's friends Caleb Smith and Edwin Bates. No one has ever suggested that Carroll was a part of that group, although she met with Pomeroy on several occasions and sending out anonymous letters to newspapers was a favorite political ploy of hers. In any case, the tactic backfired and created an uproar within the cabinet, members against members. Chase's hopes for a nomination were crushed, even though he claimed no prior knowledge of the letter. Members of the committee later claimed that Chase had approved it.[73]

Chase wrote an apology to Lincoln, protesting his innocence and offering to resign. Lincoln accepted Chase's version of events, although with some skepticism. Later Carroll wrote Chase that "an irreparable mistake was committed" when he was passed over for the nomination in 1860. At the same time, she was careful not to abandon her ties to the administration, not ruling out the possibility of a comeback.[74]

In August 1863 advisors were still suggesting that Lincoln's chances of renomination were slim. In September, however, the long, hard-fought Atlanta campaign ended with the decampment of the Confederate forces and Sherman's dramatic possession of the city. The symbolic nature of this victory in the very heart of the Confederacy could not be overstated, though Sherman felt it was somewhat hollow. "The news of Sherman's success reached the North instantaneously," Grant wrote, "and set the country all aglow." It was followed by Sheridan's successful campaign in the Shenandoah Valley. "These two campaigns," Grant observed, "probably had more effect in settling the election of the following November than all the speeches, all the bonfires, and all the parading with banners and bands of music in the north."[75] Lincoln was reelected in 1864, benefiting from the view that the end of the war was near.

Carroll's life from the end of 1864 to 1867 is something of a mystery. She, with thousands of others, attended Lincoln's funeral in April 1865. The confluence of the war's end and the death of the president threw much of the country into shock. The violence and ruin in many parts of the South was on a grand scale, and Northern journalists rushed there to report on the destruction: barns and homes burned, livestock killed, bridges destroyed, and canals deteriorated. On the Eastern Shore, a Unionist described the plight of General Tench Tilghman and his family, who lived ten miles or so from the Carrolls: "This family, one of the oldest and most respectable, once very wealthy, are now reduced to that state which is even worse in my estimation than actual poverty, large debts, large pride, large wants; small income and small helpfulness."[76]

However, large parts of the rural South and most of Texas escaped physical devastation. In May 1865, President Andrew Johnson sent now U.S. Supreme Court Chief Justice Chase on a tour of the South, advocating black enfranchisement. Johnson's view (mirroring Lincoln's though harder on the planter class) was that "secession had been null and void, the states remained intact, and Reconstruction meant enabling them to resume their full constitutional rights as quickly as possible."[77]

Like many of her friends, Carroll soon soured on President Johnson. He was thought to be isolated, self-centered, and duplicitous. Like Lincoln, he wanted a restoration of the Union as quickly as possible. Unlike Lincoln, he wanted blame extended well beyond the high command. But Johnson's biggest battles were with the Radical Republicans who saw the war as a referendum on the rights of black citizens. The two years between Lincoln's assassination and the Congressional takeover of reconstruction were acrimonious ones in Congress, ending with Johnson's impeachment but not removal from office.

Few of Carroll's positions on these issues have survived, other than her obvious dislike of the man. In 1866 she drafted a pamphlet on Andrew Johnson: "He appears to have reasoned that by a general amnesty he could attach the masses of the South to his fortune, while by excluding the wealthy and political classes, he would invite them to personal applications for pardon whereby the mutual understanding could be reached." The pamphlet was not published. She was also said to be working on a biography of William Seaton of the *National Intelligencer* in collaboration with his daughter Josephine. The Greenbies suggested she was employed by the Department of the Interior at this time and that her financial situation was greatly improved.[78] She continued corresponding with the War Department to receive payment for her previously written pamphlets. Always close to her siblings, she moved in with her brother Harry for a time to save on expenses and proposed to William Seward that she be sent on a tour of the South "in some confidential capacity for the government," but to no avail. She also began lobbying the Republican Party to select Grant as the 1868 nominee.

Carroll decided to map out a systematic plan, with help from Lemuel Evans, now back in Texas, for compensation for her military efforts during the war. "Claims against the government for services rendered during the Civil War were heard by various committees throughout the 1860s and 1870s," the Greenbies pointed out.[79] This was the first time that Carroll raised this issue. In the past, the request for compensation had been for her pamphlets. One of the first people she wrote to was "My Dear General Grant." Carroll told Grant about the details of her Tennessee Plan and then asked, "Now, in the recital of facts which you are supervising, would it not be well to state the date when you drew up the plan for carrying the expedition into effect, and whether, to your knowledge, it had ever occurred to any other military man? And permit me to suggest the importance of your stating, in the work referred to, the date when the Tennessee became to your mind the plan of conducting the campaign in the Southwest, and to whom you communicated it, verbally or otherwise." Many assumed the idea was Grant's. Carroll hoped to get from him a denial that would validate her claim. Unfortunately Grant did not reply. Grant also did not deny Carroll's claims, accepting instead her support for his candidacy.

Late in 1868 Carroll went to Texas with Evans to observe the state's constitutional convention and to report to Grant. Evans was a leader of the "divisionists" at the convention with a plan to divide the state into three or more states. This proposal failed. Evans became ill at the convention's end and Carroll stayed to care for him. Gradually, he recovered. He hoped to return with Carroll to Washington as the senator from Texas. Instead, he was appointed chief justice of the Texas Supreme Court and presided there until 1873.

Back in Washington in early 1869, Carroll petitioned the Senate to award her compensation commensurate with her service. The year before she had withdrawn all her files from the War Department, probably for safekeeping. President Johnson fired her friend Edwin Stanton in 1868, precipitating the impeachment crisis. With fewer friends in power, she feared antagonizing the military in particular. Carroll started her petition in vintage style. "In pressing my claim," she wrote, "I cannot by any possibility detract from our brave and heroic commanders to whom the country owes so much and so far from opposing me I believe that as a class they would be grateful to see me or any one properly rewarded acc. to the part performed in this mighty drama." She strengthened her petition with favorable letters from Thomas Scott and Benjamin Wade along with copies of her pamphlets. Scott had warned her that "military men were tenacious and jealous."[80]

The petition had two readings but never moved out of the Senate. Senator George Vickers of Maryland suggested to Carroll that the explanation was "anti-Republican sentiments." Carroll blamed Massachusetts Senator Henry Wilson, a former Know-Nothing, whom she felt did little to move the petition forward. The committee told her they wanted more proof. Carroll added letters from Millard Fillmore, Reverdy Johnson, and Edward Everett. At the same time Evans wrote a pamphlet called "The Material Bearing of the Tennessee Campaign," that gave full credit to Carroll and outlined the critical nature of the military action. "The government was under the absolute necessity therefore of inflicting some decisive blow upon the rebellion in the next few months," he wrote, "not only to ward off foreign intervention and invasion, but to smother the spirit of secession in the Northwest, and prevent financial bankruptcy which, of itself, would destroy the nation."[81]

By May 1872 Carroll was convinced that she was getting somewhere with her petitions. Though not passed on, none had been rejected. "My enemies have fought me desperately to defeat me or rather my claim," she wrote her father. Still the summer passed without the bill going forward. She again reached out for public support with a new pamphlet, a new letter from her friend Benjamin Wade, and a letter from Kentucky Senator Cassius Clay, who expressed outrage that the claim had not been settled. Gerrit Smith wrote in response that "the country would be everlastingly disgraced if one of its wisest and ablest public servants went unpaid." Still nothing happened.[82]

Thomas King Carroll died in October 1873. "I lost the best Father, the most perfect of all the race," Carroll wrote Millard Fillmore. Though her father had been ailing for some time, it was a great shock to her and she took months to recover. But early in 1874 she was back at work publishing yet another explanation of her case.[83]

River pilot Charles Scott noticed publicized versions and made counterclaims. Carroll had always thought that her only hope was absolute concurrence in her views and that any opposition or even hint of opposition would hurt her case. When Scott went public, the *New York Times* "wondered if Carroll had bothered to press her claim while Halleck was still alive, since he was the obvious author of the plan." What the *Times* based this assessment on, other than public sentiment, was not known. Military records suggested that Halleck was late for the first battle, throwing doubt onto his authorship. Grant's public statements at the time hint that he did not know the plan's author, leaving Halleck, his superior, among the most likely of the military men. But Halleck's military ability was often questioned (he was called "irresolute" and a "military imbecile"). Grant suggested in his memoirs that Halleck thought travel on the Tennessee was "imbecilic." It is ironic that much of the inability to verify the claim rested on the disarray of the military—not on Carroll.[84]

In July 1876 Carroll and Scott appeared before a Senate hearing on her petition. As always, Lemuel Evans was at her side. Scott testified that he went to Washington in 1865 to ask General Grant for help. Scott, as one of the few Union pilots, worked for a lower salary and lost money during the war. After the war, he said, ex-Confederate pilots refused to work with him. He had, as part of his military compensation, received a certificate of validation that he traded for cotton. He hoped to sell the cotton duty free to make money. Not willing to simply rely on his friend Grant, he also called on Carroll and Evans, thinking them influential. According to Scott, Evans wrote out a permit giving permission to bring in not just the 1,000 bales Scott controlled but 10,000 bales duty free. Scott resisted but said Evans told him that everybody else was doing it. The scheme was to share the excess proceeds with Evans and Carroll. Scott said he refused and left. A few days later an article signed by Carroll praising Scott appeared in the *National Intelligencer.* Scott saw it and arranged to meet with Carroll and Evans again. They continued pressing their plan and again Scott refused.

Carroll's testimony, however, was very different from Scott's. She said he offered her one-fourth of the $30,000 he expected for the deal in exchange for her help. She refused. She did get him a copy of Treasury regulations governing the sale, she said. But she asked for nothing and received nothing. Carroll also claimed that she had not written the article, but that Evans had in order to "garner public support for her claim." Evans confirmed that he wrote the article because Scott "complained of the injustice done him."[85] Evans also admitted drafting a permit for Scott at Scott's request, but not in the terms Scott had outlined. Scott had no documentation to support his version and no records of meetings he claimed to have held. Scott got nothing in the end, not even compensation for the cotton.

Carroll got little except for the removal of Scott from the fray. And she suffered another setback in July 1877 when Evans, her faithful and constant companion, died. Again taking time to recover, Carroll was mostly silent during the ensuing months. Finally, in February 1879, the Senate Committee on Military Affairs issued a ruling on her petition, deciding against her. "There must have been," the committee report argued, "some unknown reasons for the omission, and important reasons underlying the non-action of these Congresses in these premises."[86] (In other words, if the claim had been valid it would have been decided before now.) The committee concluded that prior committees had deemed this account settled since Carroll, by her own admission, received $1,200 from Thomas Scott and $750 from Peter Watson (the two former assistant secretaries of war).

But even more implausible were the assessments of her military advice. "All civilized nations," the committee concluded, "honored the names and deeds of women like Florence Nightingale and Clara Barton because they are heroines who have risked their lives in the cause of humanity. But if they, like Carroll, applied for a monetary reward, why it would destroy much of the poetry and grandeur of noble deeds were a price demanded for kindred services, and achievements of this nature in the market as commodities of barter." Carroll, the committee concluded, should be satisfied with what she had already received. "The deficit should be supplied from the large store of gratitude which republics bestow upon their citizens."[87]

Two things hurt Carroll in 1879. The first was that the Senate committee was headed by Francis Cockrell, a former Confederate brigadier general and now Democratic senator from Missouri. Cockrell had anti-Republican sentiments and strongly opposed women's rights. He was determined to oppose the claim. Also against Carroll were members of the War Department who thought it "absurd that a woman's knowledge of topography and strategic lines led to the advance of the warriors." Former Assistant Secretary of War Thomas Scott warned Carroll of this attitude of the military.

But the blatantly sexist tone of the report did gain Carroll a new ally early in 1880—the National Woman Suffrage Association. Recording Secretary Matilda Jocelyn Gage published a pamphlet titled, "Who Planned the Tennessee Campaign of 1862? Or Anna Ella Carroll vs. Ulysses S. Grant," which summarized the case and explained "the injustice of man toward woman." Anna Ella Carroll, Gage wrote, "a young girl of Maryland, full of patriotic spirit, developed a plan that saved the Union." Grant was "feted, honored and re-elected" while Carroll, military genius, received nothing. "Had she not been a woman," Gage asked, "would she have met this injustice?"[88]

Historian Janet Coryell saw both irony and a double-edged sword in the movement's adoption of Carroll. The irony was that Carroll had never championed the women's movement. The double-edged sword was that the National Woman Suffrage Association supported Carroll, rather than the more conservative American Woman's Suffrage (which may have carried more weight). In 1871 and 1872 the national association was under strong public censure for the radical ideas of its member Victoria Woodhull.[89]

The Greenbies explain Carroll's alliance with that group because its president, Elizabeth Cady Stanton, was a cousin to Gerrit Smith, who was also a friend of Carroll's. Smith sent money to help Carroll free her household slaves (a feat she accomplished in 1860) and continued to correspond with her. Smith wrote in support of her claim, and the Greenbies hinted that Smith sent her money now and then to further aid her cause. Carroll also received support from the American Woman's Suffrage Association, which included the influential Blackwell family, also acquaintances of Carroll. Henry Blackwell was the husband of Lucy Stone, and his sister Sarah wrote one of the first biographies of Carroll.

The Greenbies do not mention Victoria Woodhull or the scandal that surrounded her. But it is interesting that in 1873 Carroll sent the association copies of her petitions and memorials with the words, "Thought this might interest you inasmuch as it may serve in some degree to furnish evidence in behalf of the cause you so ably represent."[90] Carroll, an avid reader, surely knew about the scandal. It was national news. One of the repercussions of the scandal was that many suffragists backed away from public discussions of issues of sexuality and women's rights. Carroll, on the other hand, whose relationship to Lemuel Evans was the subject of constant gossip, may have privately had more sympathy for Woodhull's situation.[91]

While the specifics of Carroll's reference to "the cause you represent" are unclear, both Stanton and Woodhull were strong advocates of a woman's right to divorce—a position they did not share with other suffragists. Beyond that were striking parallels in interests between Carroll and Woodhull. Woodhull was a writer, pamphleteer, and newspaper editor. Believing that "woman's ability to earn money is better protection against the tyranny and brutality of men than her ability to vote," she and her sister Tennessee Clayton opened a bank and brokerage house on Wall Street. Before becoming involved in the financial world Woodhull, like Carroll, had been a lobbyist and businesswoman who knew how to "penetrate all male domains." At one point she argued before the House Judiciary Committee that "women already had the right to vote as guaranteed by the 14th and 15th amendments."[92]

Eighteen years younger than Carroll, Woodhull was described as brilliant, attractive, and a frank speaker. At the age of fourteen she married an abusive alcoholic husband whom she later divorced. Woodhull denounced legal and religious arguments for enduring a bad marriage.

While claiming to be a "monogamist," she defended the right of others to choose their own lifestyles.

The press had a field day with her outspoken "strong mindedness." Cartoonist Thomas Nash lampooned "Mrs. Satan" in an engraving for *Harper's Weekly*. Religious leaders were appalled by her "brazen" assertions. But Woodhull somehow crossed a line when she published an article about the extramarital affair of Reverend Henry Ward Beecher, younger brother of Harriet Beecher Stowe. Reverend Beecher, considered the world's greatest orator, preached marital fidelity while having a longtime affair with one of his married parishioners. Unfortunately for Woodhull, Reverend Beecher, as one of the nation's most prominent clergymen, had a lot of clout. With the help of supporters, Woodhull and Clayton were arrested for using the U.S. mail to "utter obscene publication." Their case traveled through the courts for two years, landed them in jail for weeks at a time, and cost them thousands of dollars in legal fees and their businesses. In 1873, they were found innocent of obscenity and, in 1874, of libel. The husband of the parishioner, who had supplied the information, was never charged but received so much criticism for his action that he moved to France. Woodhull and Clayton moved to England, and Woodhull continued to support selected causes from a distance.[93] Carroll spent much time in New York and may have traveled in similar circles to Woodhull. It does not seem accidental that although probably frightened by Woodhull's flamboyant displays, Carroll wrote to the national association in 1873.

Carroll was called before the Committee on Military Affairs in 1881. Representative Edward S. Bragg, a former Union general, now headed the committee. On March 3, 1881, this committee found "the evidence unquestionably established Carroll as the author of the Tennessee Plan," and suggested that "the thanks of the nation" were due her as well as a pension. Republican President James Garfield took office in March 1881 and what must have been a jubilant Carroll corresponded with him immediately, mentioning the report. Garfield made a brief but polite response that gave Carroll, ever optimistic, hope that her cause was finally won. But Garfield was assassinated that summer, and in September Carroll had a paralytic stroke. Congress adjourned without passing the bill for her relief.

Partially recovered from her stroke by 1885, a lawsuit was begun on Carroll's behalf. It is not clear whether it was initiated by Anne or her sister Mary Carroll. The lawyer, R. B. Warden, argued before the U.S. Court of Claims in spring 1885. Judge Charles C. Nott delivered the court's opinion. "It may be true," he wrote, "as the claimant alleges, that she was the first to conceive this idea, the first to enunciate it, the first to bring it to the attention of the government; and it may be and unquestionably is true that the strategic movement described in her letter was subsequently accomplished; and yet it may likewise be true that the plan thus successfully carried out originated with the military officers of the United States as well as with Miss Carroll, and, so far as the government is involved, was substantially their plan and not hers."[94]

Carroll lived in Washington from 1885 until her death, and was cared for by her devoted sister. They were at times destitute—although Mary Carroll had a job at the Treasury Department and they were sometimes sustained by contributions from suffragists. Mary was nearly fired in 1892 because of her frequent absences from work and her excuse of "nervous prostration." In December 1893 she sent a despairing letter to President Grover Cleveland. "Today I have not marketing for tomorrow. I have no means even for required medicine from day to day and am well nigh desperate." Her job was restored and the sisters struggled on until February 1894 when Anna Ella Carroll, without hearing or voice, rested her case.[95]

3 | Harriet Tubman, Called Moses of Her People

What made a most pathetic impression upon me was her broken teeth, which had been partially knocked out with a stone in her own hands, because of a toothache, while hiding by day on her latest escape.
—*William Lloyd Garrison*

Harriet Tubman was twenty-seven when she got her first taste of freedom. Slipping through the woods and marshes of the Eastern Shore, she arrived in Pennsylvania through a combination of cunning and the kindness of strangers. Freedom was said to be everything to Tubman. "There are two things I've a right to and these are Death or Liberty. One or the other I mean to have. No one will take me back alive; I shall fight for my liberty, and when the time has come for me to go, the Lord will let them kill me."[1]

Offering in exchange a bed quilt, which she had made and valued, Tubman received information about two contacts and directions to safe houses from a neighborhood Quaker rumored to aid fugitive slaves. Her journey begun, she traveled alone in the night, helped at times by others in the Underground Railroad network and most often by her own initiative and resourcefulness. Upon reaching free soil—Pennsylvania—for the first time, she was overcome. She would later recall, "When I found I had crossed the line, I looked at my hands to see if I was the same person. There was such a glory over everything; the sun came like gold through the trees, and over the fields; and I felt like I was in Heaven."[2]

Reality soon brought Tubman back. She had no family, no friends, and no money. "I was," she said, "a stranger in a strange land; and my home, after all, was down in Maryland; because my father, my mother, my brothers, and sisters, and friends were there." The decision to leave the Eastern Shore was one of the most difficult of her life. She left not only family and friends, but the only world she knew. "Every slaveholder seeks," her Eastern Shore neighbor Frederick Douglass wrote, "to impress his slave with a belief in the boundlessness of slave territory and of his almost illimitable power." But when Tubman's owner Edward Brodess died, leaving many debts, rumors rapidly circulated that his slaves would be sold to pay them. Tubman knew it was time to leave. She tried to get others—her husband—her brothers—to go with her but they were unwilling or afraid. So she set out with only her fears and her faith to keep her company.[3]

Harriet Tubman was born to Harriet (called Rit Green) and Benjamin Ross, near Cambridge, Maryland. The exact place and date of her birth are unknown. As Douglass explained, "By far the larger part of the slaves know as little of their ages as horses know of theirs, and it is the wish of most masters within my knowledge to keep their slaves thus ignorant."[4] Harriet told Franklin Sanborn, her biographer, that she thought she was born in 1820 or 1821. Some historians have listed her birth as early as 1819, others as late as 1823. In 1979, local historian John Creighton found that Anthony Thompson paid $2 to a midwife in 1822. Creighton and others believe Harriet was the child delivered by the midwife.[5] She was named Araminta and called Minty by her family, giving herself the name Harriet, after her mother, later in her life.

Tubman has had many biographers and chroniclers, yet the woman beneath their layers of interpretation is often elusive. Tubman, at heart a private person, perhaps intended it to be so. Phrases like "a very affection-ate nature," "a great simplicity of character," and "profoundly practical and highly imaginative" have sometimes been used. Sympathetic scribes often seemed more content to employ racial features as a signifier to explain her character to their audiences. "She is the grand-daughter of a slave imported from Africa," Franklin Sanborn wrote in 1863, "and has not a drop of white blood in her veins." George Garrison, son of William Lloyd Garrison, called her "a little woman of black complexion and African stamp." Helen Tatlock, a friend of Tubman who was interviewed by biographer Earl Conrad, said she was "a magnificent looking woman, true African, with a broad nose, very black and of medium height."[6]

None of these descriptions do justice to the richness of expression and the searing gaze staring out at us from several photographic portraits that have survived. Tubman's longtime friend Ednah Cheney was perhaps closest when she noted, "She has needed disguise so often that she seems to have command over her face, and can banish all expression from her features, and look so stupid that nobody would suspect her of knowledge enough to be dangerous; but her eye flashes with intelligence and power when she is roused." Cheney also remarked upon Tubman's little-mentioned love for beauty and art. "I never left her alone a little while in my room but I found her standing in admiration before a cast or a picture, and she was overwhelmed with delight at the present of a little statue. She said she had visions of these things when in the woods."[7]

Historians agonize over the questions of "voice" and point of view in these reflections because Tubman could not read or write. How much can we accept as faithful recollections and narrative, and how much of what was written was infused with the recorder's bias? Dialect was often used as proof of authenticity—statements said to be in Tubman's own words— but the result was nevertheless often stilted and unconvincing. To wit: Tubman, upon reaching free soil, saw "such a glory ober eberything, de sun came like gold trou de trees, and ober de fields." The best resolution seems to identify the recorders and point out the variations and discrepancies, as historian Jean Humez did in her recent biography.[8]

Tubman's first "biographer" was Franklin Sanborn, a native of New Hampshire who taught school in Concord, Massachusetts. A Harvard graduate, Sanborn was active in the New England abolitionist community and one of the so-called "Secret Six" who aided John Brown. He was also editor of a Boston anti-slavery newspaper called *Commonwealth*, and it was in this newspaper in 1863 that the first biographical article about Tubman appeared. Ednah Dow Cheney was the second biographer. Cheney was a childhood friend of Sanborn's wife and a woman who shared his political views. In 1865, Cheney wrote an article called "Moses" for the *Freedmen's Record*, the journal of the New England Freedmen's Aid Society. Sallie Holley was a third author of biographical information about Tubman. Holley's letter appeared in the *National Anti-Slavery Standard* in 1867. Holley, graduate of Oberlin, came to the abolition cause through her father, Myron Holley, a member of the Liberty Party. She was a close associate of Wendell Phillips, William Lloyd Garrison, and Gerrit Smith, and dedicated herself to speaking for the cause of slavewomen. It was Holley who speculated that $40,000 would not be too high a price on Tubman's head, a hypothetical figure that has often been repeated as fact.[9]

The fourth and most extensive early biographer was Sarah Bradford, who wrote *Scenes in the Life of Harriet Tubman* based on interviews she conducted with Tubman in 1868. Bradford, daughter of a lawyer and judge from Albany, New York, married a lawyer and moved to Geneva, New York. When her husband left her and moved to Chicago, Bradford, needing to support her family, ran a school for young girls and wrote children's books. Friends in Geneva and nearby Auburn introduced her to Tubman. Unlike Sanborn, Cheney, and Holley, Bradford was not part of the anti-slavery intellectual community. Her motives for taking up the cause of Harriet Tubman, other than their friendship, are not as well known. Many have complained about the product. Historian Jean Humez attributed Bradford's awkward writing style, constant self-censorship, and protection of Tubman to her culture of middle-class Anglo-American respectability. Bradford was very meticulous about the truth of her writing, observing at one point, "Much has been left out which would have been highly interesting, because of the impossibility of substantiating by the testimony of others the truth of Harriet's statements."[10]

Bradford wrote two versions of her biography of Tubman. She characterized *Scenes in the Life* (published in 1869) as a hurried project because of other commitments. *Harriet Tubman: the Moses of her People* (published in 1886), clearly written to help Tubman with her financial difficulties, was presented in the more characteristic vernacular of the day.[11]

Beyond the issues of style and voice, a rather consistent and compelling portrait of Tubman arose from the various biographical works—a result, no doubt, of the power of Tubman's own input. Despite all the trials, she had strong roots and personal agency. Harriet's great luxury in life was to be closely acquainted with both of her parents and many of her siblings. She was particularly close to her mother, called nervously sensitive by some, who nursed her somewhat rebellious and sickly child back to health on numerous occasions. Tubman recalled in one interview, "I used to sleep on the floor in front of the fireplace and there I'd lie and cry and cry. I used to think all the time, 'If I could only get home and get in my mother's bed!' And the funny part was she never had a bed in her life. Nothing but a board box nailed up against the wall and straw laid on it."[12] The home itself was said to be "a sagging cabin with buckling walls and a narrow clay-daubed chimney."[13]

Frederick Douglass, a neighbor in Talbot County, was not as lucky. He never knew his father and only remembered seeing his mother four or five times in his life. "It is a common custom, in the part of Maryland from which I ran away," he wrote, "to part children from their mothers at a very early age."[14] Douglass thought this was done to blunt the natural affection of a mother for her child. The infant was frequently given over to a woman too old for field labor, while the mother was hired out. Why was Tubman's situation so different? Her good fortune, it seemed, was partly due to her owner Edward Brodess's family connection to the wealthy Anthony Thompson. It is also possible that Douglass failed to realize that owners kept families together to discourage runaways.

Tubman's family was a tangled web of enslaved property. Athow Pattison, a local farmer and Revolutionary War veteran, owned her mother,

Rit. Anthony Thompson, "a wealthy and prominent landholder," owned her father, Ben Ross. Pattison, who died in 1797, bequeathed Rit to his granddaughter Mary Pattison and also stipulated in his will that she be freed at age forty-five, a common Chesapeake practice. Rit was probably born between 1785 and 1789, which would have made her at least forty-five by 1834. In 1800, Mary Pattison married Joseph Brodess and had a son, Edward, in 1801. In 1802, Joseph Brodess died; one year later, his widow Mary Pattison Brodess married Anthony Thompson, enslaver of Ben Ross. Because of the changes, Rit's legal status became even more entangled.

Ben and Rit, now owned by the same family, "married" as in the custom of the time and began having children. Bearing children was sanctioned both in the eyes of the slave community and by religious practice. Offspring of enslaved women were owned by the mother's enslavers, making it a practice condoned and encouraged in the "big house" as well. Yet, as Anna Ella Carroll once commented, slave increase could descend into a quagmire for owners depending on their resources as "year by year there were more mouths to feed, more bodies to clothe, an ever-increasing army of simple, devoted people coming to maturity and looking to their masters, as to God, for everything."[15] Historian John Hope Franklin, on the other hand, had a somewhat different interpretation, calling this increase "slave breeding, one of the most fantastic manipulations of human development in the history of mankind."[16]

Slave women were encouraged to become mothers by the age of thirteen or fourteen, "in much the same way that experiments were carried out to discover new crops to grow on the exhausted soil." It is believed that Rit had nine children. Her first, Linah, born around 1808, would have made her slightly older than the average new mother, depending on her year of birth. A second child, Mariah Ritty, was born around 1811 and a third, Soph, by 1813. By 1816 she had Robert and then Harriet in 1822. Ben was born in 1824, Rachel in 1825, Henry in 1830, and her last child, Moses, in 1832.[17]

Edward Brodess claimed ownership of these children through the estate of his mother, Mary Pattison Brodess Thompson. During 1823 or 1824, he apparently took Rit and some of her children to live with him on his farm in Bucktown, about ten miles away from Ben Ross's home.[18] It was here, several years later, that Harriet began her first work activities, caring for her brothers. "The next thing I member," she said, "was when I was four or five years old, my mother cooked up to the big house and left me to take care of the baby and my little brother. I used to be in a hurry for her to go, so as I could play the baby was a pig in a bag, and hold him up by the bottom of his dress."[19]

In 1825, Brodess sold a sixteen-year-old slave named Rhody to Dempsey Kane, a slave trader from Mississippi. Historian Kate Larson believed this slave was actually Mariah Ritty, Tubman's older sister. This sale, assuming it was Mariah, was illegal because it was "a slave for life sale," whereas Mariah, according to the terms of the Pattison will, also would have been free at age forty-five. Brodess's wife Eliza inherited slaves from her father, all of them "slaves for life," causing confusion in the situation of the slave girl Rhody, whose identity (was she one of Edward's? or one of Eliza's?) was almost impossible to prove in court.[20] Slaves would have had to have very good lawyers indeed to extricate themselves from the web of slave case law.

At this time and continuing into the 1830s Ben and Rit had an "abroad marriage," living in different places and visiting each other, perhaps as seldom as once a week. Still, a real affection existed between the two, and the couple lived together faithfully, according to Franklin Sanborn. "There were seldom courtships or preliminaries to marriage among blacks. Women were often forced to cohabit with men they hardly knew because their masters wanted them to become pregnant," he wrote.[21]

In this respect, Rit had a better situation. Ben was a valuable slave, who became a "timber inspector, and superintended the cutting and hauling of great quantities of timber for the Baltimore shipyards."[22] Rit, who was about the same age as Edward's mother, may have worked as a cook in the big house for some part of Edward's life and enjoyed the benefits of a longtime, faithful servant. Because of this Ben and Rit seem to have had some influence over Thompson (Edward Brodess's guardian until 1822), and afterwards over Brodess himself. In Brodess's case, "benefit" is perhaps too strong a word because the actual circumstances of his generosity involved persuading him to retrieve a sick or injured child from the harsh treatment of cruel temporary employers he selected. And there were several. Edna Dow Cheney explained that Harriet "seldom lived with her owner, but was usually hired out to different persons."[23]

At the age of six, Tubman was taken from her mother and her babysitting chores and sent to live with James Cook and his wife, a weaver. As Tubman recounted the circumstances, "I nursed that there baby till he was so big I couldn't tote him any more, and I got so mischievous about the house that they put me out to learn to be a weaver."[24] In addition, Cook trapped muskrats and taught her to watch the traps by wading through water up to her armpits. Tubman was less fond of weaving than of muskrat trapping. Never fond of Mistress Cook, she also rebelled against the indoor lifestyle that was the fate of a weaver, who was expected to sit for hours at a loom and make cloth for the family for whom she worked. Her labors with the Cooks were curtailed by frequent illness—on one occasion, ailing with measles, she grew very sick. Rit then stepped in and persuaded Brodess to let Harriet come back home to recover.

At age seven, Tubman was sent away to take care of another baby. "I was so little I had to sit on the floor and have the baby put in my lap." One morning, while her mistress and her husband quarreled, Harriet stood by waiting for instructions and near a bowl of sugar lumps. Never having tasted something that looked so wonderful, little Harriet grabbed a lump. Unfortunately, her employer turned and saw her. Chased with a rawhide whip, she managed to escape and run to the shelter of a pigpen at a nearby farm. "And there I stayed from Friday until the next Tuesday, fighting with those little pigs for the potato peelings and other scraps that came down in the trough. The old sow would push me away when I tried to get her children's food, and I was awfully afraid of her," Tubman recalled. By Tuesday she was so starved, she returned to her mistress and a severe beating. Thomas Garrett wrote that "she was whipped so often that the back of her neck was covered with scars so deep they were visible for the rest of her life."[25]

At the age of nine, Tubman was once again employed as a child nurse and general house-worker. Her task was to clean all day and care for the baby at night. Her mistress was particularly cruel and whipped her five or six times a day, according to Tubman's nephew Harkless Bowley. She was also so starved at this job that she was unable to perform her chores to the satisfaction of her employers and was sent home.[26]

In later years, Tubman had a somewhat charitable interpretation of these early experiences. "They don't know any better, it's the way they were brought up," she explained. "Make the little slaves mind you or flog them, was what they said to their children, and they were brought up with the whip in their hands." But she also told Benjamin Drew, a reporter, "Now I've been free, I know what slavery is. I have seen hundreds of escaped slaves but I never saw one who was willing to go back and be a slave. . . . I think slavery is the next thing to hell."[27]

Rit was thought to have had five children before Harriet and nine in all. Two, perhaps as many as three, were sold south. "We were always uneasy," Tubman told Drew. "Every time I saw a white man I was afraid of being carried away." She also told Bradford of memories of two older sisters who "had gone no one knew whither" and that she had "seen the agonized expression on their faces as they turned to take a last look."[28]

The obvious and dramatic cruelty of family separation inherent in slave sales is well documented. Perhaps less so was the additional burden of legal wrangling that seemingly underpinned every legal transaction. This was particularly so for Ben and Rit and their family. "The law was an ass," is perhaps an appropriate explanation. In June 1820, for example, the orphans' court of Dorchester County authorized Anthony Thompson to build a house and barn on his stepson Edward Brodess's property near Bucktown. The buildings were to be constructed under the supervision of Brodess's uncle Gourney Pattison. Thompson, who was Edward's guardian as well as his stepfather, carefully conserved Brodess funds. One can assume that the plan was at first agreed upon by all sides. When completed, however, the cost exceeded Brodess's means and he was unwilling to pay, forcing Thompson to take him to court for compensation. The court directed the Cambridge sheriff, probably Thomas Hicks, to make Brodess, who had so far refused, appear before them. Brodess first appeared in April 1824, four years after the fact. In court, Thompson claimed that Brodess owed him over $1,800. Brodess agreed to pay but continually stalled. Finally, in 1827 the court ordered Brodess to pay immediately.[29]

Brodess, with the help of some of his Pattison relatives, appealed the decision before the appeals court in neighboring Talbot County, arguing that the Dorchester orphans' court had exceeded its authority in allowing Thompson to build on the land in the first place. The appeals court agreed with Brodess. Thompson lost the case, all effective communication between the two was presumably ended, and the situation of the Brodess slaves—the real victims of this family feud—was made even more precarious.

Edward Brodess's financial instability was only one in a series of nightmares that befell Tubman. In her teens, she was hired out as a field hand. One day, probably in 1834 or 1835, a slave of a farmer named Barrett left his work without permission and went to the village store. The overseer pursued him, threatening to whip him when found, and Harriet followed, fearing trouble. Finding the slave, the overseer called on Harriet and others to tie him up in preparation for punishment. She refused, and as the man ran away, placed herself in the door to hinder pursuit. The overseer grabbed a two-pound weight and threw it at the fugitive. It missed him but struck Harriet in the head and nearly killed her.[30]

Once again, Rit had to nurse her ailing child back to health. Harriet's recovery was long and difficult. Biographer Earl Conrad visualized her appearance as "disabled and sick, her flesh all wasted away. She lay on a pallet, or more correctly a bundle of rags in a corner of the room, and through dulled eyes she watched the movements of her family about the small, box-like place."[31] Her injury was lifelong, "causing her to fall into a state of somnolency from which it is almost impossible to rouse her," it was reported on many occasions. Brodess tried to sell her, but no one wanted her. "Dey say dey wouldn't give a sixpence for me," Tubman told Bradford.[32]

Though not a rapid recovery, Tubman relied on a strong religious faith and her love of the outdoors to heal. Because of her injuries, a deep slumber could occur without notice three or four times a day, and many people on the plantation thought she was half-witted. Tubman realized that she could use this perception to her advantage, feigning illness and being able to live and work essentially on her own terms. Many others before her had used this ploy. As Frederick Douglass explained, "Ignorance is a high virtue in a human chattel and as the master studies to keep the slave ignorant, the slave is cunning enough to make the master think he succeeds."[33] Through her tragic injury, Tubman learned an important lesson. As Deborah Gray White observed, "bondswomen, like bondsmen, were adept in inventing schemes and excuses to get their own way."[34]

Edward Brodess, whose relationship to Tubman was strained by his financial woes, went back to hiring her out as she recovered, when he found he could not sell her. Brodess's growing family and poor management skills plagued him throughout his life. He married Elizabeth Keene in 1824. Their first child, John E., was born in 1827 and a second in 1829. A third child, Richard, was born in 1831 and was listed in the 1850 census as age nineteen. Five other children were listed, the youngest a girl aged seven.[35] Creating offspring seemed to be a Brodess specialty; making a profit was not. But in any case, small farmers were more vulnerable than the large planters to financial reverses due to poor weather or insect infestations, and when such events occurred, the liquidation of slave property was often the only option. Selling slave children was a quick fix.[36]

According to Bradford, Tubman recovered enough to able to work as a field hand "following the oxen, loading and unloading wood, and carrying heavy burdens." She loved the outdoors, the strenuous labor, and remarkable power of muscle that she developed as a result. "Her feats of strength often called forth the wonder of laboring men," Bradford observed.[37] It was the perfect preparation for her future escapes and rescues.

Anthony Thompson, Brodess's stepfather, died in 1836. In his will, he freed his enslaved man: "Ben, to serve five years and then free." He also gave Ben ten acres of land in Poplar Neck "for and during of his life time peaceable" with a privilege of cutting timber on any part of "my land for the support of the same."[38] Ben Ross was soon to be a landowner with a source of income. He would also be free in five years, but his family would not, a special kind of hell invented by American slaveholders for their favorite slaves.

In Dorchester, as in most of the South, children's legal status derived from their mother. Ben Ross headed a family of slaves. His "impotence" was more than psychological. As historian Barbara J. Fields observed, "The division of family members among a number of small slaveholders multiplied by that number the danger of a family's disruption by the financial mischance or simple human mortality of an owner."[39] Slave-women like Rit, who could bear children, represented at the same time an asset to her owner and a danger to her children. In good financial times, owners tended to promise to avoid the disruptive practice of child sales. But in bad times, anything was possible.[40] Slave families in these circumstances lived in fear that such a disaster was just around the corner.

Though Ben Ross's manumission was scheduled for 1841 by the terms of Anthony Thompson's will, the 1840 census suggested he may have been considered free before that. Sometime between 1836 and 1841, Ross was awarded the land. Anthony Thompson had two sons, Anthony Jr. and Absalom, both of whom became doctors. Anthony was the executor of the will and in 1836 had the responsibility of dividing the forty-three slaves (ten men, eight women, and twenty-five children) his father owned. None of these were Ben Ross's children with Rit—although in 1843 he was able to purchase for $10 the freedom of two of Thompson's slaves: Maria Bailey, listed as "delicate," and Aaron Manokey, "a cripple."[41]

Harriet would have been twenty-one in the year of her father's manumission. Not yet married, she worked with him in the area of Peters Neck, hauling timber along the canal.[42] It is assumed that Ben Ross worked for either timber supplier Joseph Stewart or John D. Parker.[43] Stewart's mercantile, farm, shipbuilding, and lumbering businesses required the labor of many people—slaves and freemen—with varying levels of ability, from highly skilled blacksmiths to ship carpenters and sail makers, sawyers and timber inspectors, stevedores and drivers, and farm laborers.[44] Ben Ross worked as a timber inspector and supervised cutting and hauling timber for the Baltimore shipyards, a skilled job. Few women worked in this area. Harriet's employment may have been arranged by her father. She worked first in Stewart's house, but afterwards again outdoors. While little is known of the relationship between the Ross family and the Stewarts, the fact that many of the Ross children took the name Stewart when freed may suggest a degree of respect.

In 1844 Harriet, aged twenty-two or twenty-three, married John Tubman, who worked for Stewart on occasion. As a free man, John Tubman had far greater mobility than Harriet, including the ability to search for the best employment. Kate Larson believed that he worked, as needed, for several farmers and timber harvesters during that time.[45] Though it was a somewhat late marriage in terms of child-bearing, Harriet's "advanced age" and John's freedom apparently raised no concerns. Unions between slavewomen and free men were not generally encouraged although the potential benefits of such unions (children or the reduced likelihood of flight) were recognized. "Slaveholders might deplore the mingling of slaves with free blacks; they might heap anathema upon it and even try periodically to prevent it. But their needs conflicted with their fears," Fields noted.[46] As indicated, had Harriet had children, they would have belonged to Brodess.

Tubman's great love for her husband John, with whom she shared a cabin for five years, "the only deeply physical love of her life," was apparent even after she escaped. "The proof of her affection," Conrad wrote, "is in the fact that two years after her escape she underwent all of the hazards of a journey back into the slave country to see him and bring him North."[47] He did not go with her, however. Early biographers, in emphasizing John's disloyalty in staying behind and choosing another wife, gloss over the complexities of the situation, including Harriet's expressed feelings about "my old man." In an interview conducted in 1911, Tubman was asked to state her name. "'Harriet Tubman Davis,' she replied. The interviewer asked, 'Shall I write it with or without Mrs.?' 'Any way you like,' said Harriet, 'just so you get the Tubman.'"[48]

His love for her was also evident. "That John Tubman chose to marry a slave woman despite a surplus of free black women to choose from suggests that he too was deeply attached to his partner," historian Catherine Clinton argued.[49] And Larson added, "It was a bittersweet moment for a free man such as John Tubman to marry Harriet. He must have loved her deeply, for he had forfeited many rights incumbent upon the marriage of a free couple." His children would be owned by another.[50]

The period between 1844 and 1849 was an unsettled one for Harriet and her brothers and sister and their children. Brodess's debt grew with every passing year. Rumors abounded about impending sales, and on more than one occasion Brodess was forced to admit he would not sell his slaves or at least not sell them off of the Eastern Shore. Concern grew stronger that they were all on the market. Tubman said she first prayed for her master to be changed, softened and converted. Later she changed her prayer. "I began to pray oh Lord, if you aren't ever going to change that man's heart, kill him lord, and take him out of the way."[51]

Tubman, always frugal, had been able to save money with her "hiring out" arrangements. Her arrangement with Brodess was a $50 to $60 yearly payment. What she earned in excess was hers to keep. Using the oxen, she hired herself out plowing fields and hauling timber. According to Sanford, at one point, she bought a pair of steers for $40. The plan, Larson thought, was to earn enough money to purchase her freedom.[52]

She also hired a lawyer for the sum of $5 to clear up the ownership dispute in Mary Pattison's will. Rit thought that she was in fact free, having reached age forty-five, according to her understanding of the terms of Athow Pattison's will. Tubman also believed "as there was no provision for Ritty, in case of her Mary's death, she was actually emancipated at that time."[53] Mary Pattison had died sometime before 1810. Conrad attributed Tubman's interest in the legal niceties to information she learned from John Tubman, whose mother had purchased her freedom. The lawyer advised Harriet that "any of Rit's children would, by the terms of the will, no longer be slaves when they reached the age of forty-five. A codicil further provided that any of Rit's children born after her forty-fifth birthday were free born." Tubman probably felt that the family situation could be clarified by the court.[54]

These circumstances, however, turned dire with Edward Brodess's sudden death. With his many debts, Tubman feared that it was just a matter of time before his slaves would be sold to pay them, a custom that superseded all prior arrangements. The slaves had been promised that his will provided that none of them would be sold out of state, but even in this Tubman was not convinced. She began to have dreams of escape. In one, in particular, she dreamed she was "flying great distances over fields and towns, looking down over rivers and mountains like a bird." She would "see a line, and on the other side of that line were green fields, and lovely flowers, and beautiful white ladies, who stretched out their arms to me over the line, but I couldn't reach them no how."[55]

In 1847 Tubman, who had been hiring herself out to various employers, went to work for Dr. Anthony Thompson. Thompson, educated at the University of Maryland Medical School and also a Methodist minister, lived in Cambridge at that time on a fourteen-acre farm and preached of slaves' duty to their masters and "stinted on their food and clothing." This Thompson was not beloved by his slaves. Unlike his father, the younger Thompson fell on hard times and sold off slaves to pay his bills. In an interview with William Still after his escape, Ben Ross said Dr. Anthony was "a rough man towards his slaves" and one who had been "pretending to preach for twenty years."[56]

Edward Brodess died in March 1849.[57] In July, his wife Eliza and her agent and neighbor John Mills petitioned Dorchester County's orphans' court to order the sale of several of the estate's slaves to accommodate debts. Brodess's will had only given Eliza "use and hire of his slaves" until her death, after which all of his estate would go to his children. In anticipation, the court ordered the sale of all his personal property in June, "negroes excepted." The petition also proposed the sale of Ben and Rit's twenty-year-old granddaughter Harriet, daughter of their oldest child Linah who had been sold many years before. Granddaughter Harriet had a two-year-old daughter named Mary Jane. The auction was scheduled for July 16 but was put off. Tubman told Bradford that for years "she never closed her eyes that she did not imagine she saw the horsemen coming, and heard the screams of women and children, as they were being dragged away to a far worse slavery than they were enduring there."[58]

Larson believed that Tubman's legal inquiries may have postponed the auction of Linah's daughter Harriet. But still in need of money, Eliza Brodess arranged another auction of Brodess slaves, scheduled for September 10, this time involving Kessiah, aged twenty-five, a second daughter of Linah, and Kessiah's children, James Alfred, aged six, and Araminta, an infant. Kessiah was married to John Bowley, a free man working in the shipyard in Cambridge. Bowley and his brothers were shipbuilders and blacksmiths, part of the network of free blacks who provided information and support for the Eastern Shore black community. As wage earners, they may have tried to raise cash for a private sale, a legal practice. The court-ordered auction was scheduled and then rescinded. Despite pending court actions, if Eliza Brodess had completed a sale, it could not have been rescinded. Once sold, slaves were gone.[59]

Around the same time, perhaps also encouraged by Tubman's inquiry, Gourney Pattison, grandson of Athow Pattison and Edward Brodess's uncle, filed suit against Eliza Brodess and John Mills claiming ownership of Rit and any of her children. They discovered that Athow Pattison neglected to specify in his will what would happen to his slaves upon reaching the age of forty-five, although freedom was surely his intent. Gourney Pattison argued that in the absence of a clear directive Rit and her children should revert to the Pattison estate. He also asked for all wages that Brodess had collected from Rit after age forty-five. The case was dismissed in August 1849.[60]

During the course of these suits Dr. Anthony testified about the matter of ownership. He supported the Brodess-Mills claim and at the same time provided information about Tubman's family, stating, for example, that "Rit was the mother of Linah, Soph, Robert, Ben, Harry, Minty and Mose. Linah and Soph were sold out of state. Mose and Minty since the death of Edward Brodess have run away from the possession of his widow." He also added that "all of the children were born while their mother Rit was under 45 years of age, except Moses the youngest, he may have been born after. . . ."[61] Thompson's recollections, in the absence of other documentation, were sufficient to dismiss the case—but as the only hard evidence are hardly adequate substantiation of the existence of a slave family. He remembered only seven children of Rit, leaving out Mariah, sold in 1825, and Rachel, born about that time. Reliance on the memory of one young man to establish not only ownership but life history itself was another of the absurdities of the slave system.

Slaves greatly feared being sent to the South. "All over Maryland," historian Catherine Clinton wrote, "slaves dreaded the 'Georgia Traders,' the appellation given to any slave buyer who appeared."[62] Tales of mistreatment were common. One Eastern Shore newspaper "felt compelled to assure its slave-owning readers, blacks who were 'sold south' really were better fed and better treated and led more useful lives."[63] But Frederick Douglass had another explanation for the fear, suggesting that slaves were more attached to place than free people. "The slave is a fixture; he has no choice, no goal, no destination; but is pegged down to a single spot, and must take root here, or nowhere." The idea of removal is "attended with fear and dread."[64] While some slaves were sent south as punishment, a majority were not discipline problems but small children—many boys in particular—sold without their mothers. It was akin to being sent into oblivion.

When Tubman escaped, she left her husband John behind. She had tried to persuade him to leave with her but he refused. Two years after her first escape, she returned to lead him into freedom and he again refused. John Tubman had by this time taken another wife, Caroline, a free woman, causing Harriet much anguish. Because of their disunion, John Tubman, the "faithless man," was generally dismissed by Harriet's interviewers.[65] Sarah Bradford indicated that Harriet told her that John teased her about her fears that she would be sold and threatened to turn her in if she tried to escape. (Bradford, who was scrupulous in verifying facts about Harriet, was herself abandoned by her spouse and may have inserted some of her own resentments into Harriet's tale.) Franklin Sanborn's version, the only contemporary male version, was slightly different. He wrote, "With money in her purse, she traveled back to Maryland for her husband, but she found him married to another woman, and no longer caring to live with her. This, however, was not until two years after her escape, for she does not seem to have reached her old home in her first two expeditions." The women biographers failed to mention the time lapse; the male made little mention of her anger and grief.

Tubman said little about "her old man," suggesting that she did not think it was anyone's business but her own.[66] As Earl Conrad later pointed out, "Harriet was always notably silent about the matrimonial phase of her life, and it is the only chapter upon which, apparently, she was hesitant to speak." It was common practice if after two years of marriage a slave wife did not become pregnant to replace her.[67] Solomon Northup reported in his narrative, for example, of Critty, a slave "forced to take a second husband when her first marriage did not produce children," and then "sold to a trader when it became apparent that her unwillingness or infertility could not be overcome." Critty's "anguish was intense," and she soon "died of grief."[68] The Tubmans lived together, childless, for five years before Harriet escaped.

John Tubman, then, was probably more victim than villain. His ties to family and friends in Dorchester and his steady employment surely made him reluctant to seek another, perhaps more hostile world off the Eastern Shore. Even in Maryland, vagrant free blacks could be bound or sold for renewable terms by a magistrate's court. (It was also rumored that the only time Harriet returned to Maryland after the Civil War was to attend the trial of the man who killed John Tubman on a back road just outside of Cambridge.)

Tubman and her brothers Ben and Henry ran away for the first time in September 1849. Clearly, they thought it only a matter of time before their extended family would be separated. Shortly after this, an ad appeared in the *Delaware Gazette* on October 3, 1849. It told of three runaways: Harry, aged nineteen; Ben, aged twenty-five; and Minty, aged about twenty-seven. Minty was described as "of chestnut color, fine looking, and about 5 feet high." A reward of $100 was offered. Ben and Harry (Henry) were Tubman's brothers. Having escaped, the two brothers panicked at the dangers before them, resolved to return, and "in spite of her remonstrance dragged her with them."[69] Still plagued by bad dreams, Tubman left again in early October.[70]

Once in the North Harriet's goal, quickly arrived at but almost impossible to achieve, was to make a home there and bring her family to freedom. She went first to Philadelphia, a gathering site for fugitives and ex-slaves, and secured work as a domestic servant—cooking, cleaning, and scrubbing. She changed jobs whenever she could to raise her wages and spent little of her earnings.[71]

Early on, Tubman made the acquaintance of the Vigilance Committee of the Pennsylvania Anti-Slavery Society and its major employee, William Still. Born in New Jersey, Still was the youngest son of a black family who had escaped the Eastern Shore before he was born. He began working for the society in Philadelphia as a janitor in 1847. Recognizing his skills of observation, contacts within the black community, and interest in the fugitive cause, his employers eventually hired him to record histories of escapees. Still, known as the scribe of the Underground Railroad, took a special interest in Tubman. "Harriet was a woman of no pretensions," he wrote. "Her success was wonderful. Time and again she made visits to Maryland on the Underground Rail Road, and would be absent for weeks at a time, running daily risks while making preparations for herself and her passengers."[72]

Tubman schooled herself in the activities and causes of the Pennsylvania society, a group that opposed not only slavery but colonization and the 1850 Fugitive Slave Act. They, in turn, wrote letters for her to her family in Maryland. Her first rescue involved a niece, Kessiah, and Kessiah's two children, who were about to be sold at auction in Cambridge. Tubman's efforts in this and other rescues involved not only cunning and courage but capital as well. Some people had to be paid to help, others to look the other way. It is only a matter of conjecture how many times Tubman returned to set her people free. Nineteen, a number used by many including Sarah Bradford, seems unlikely. Though its significance pales in the light of the sacrifice, most historians now agree that Tubman made from ten to thirteen trips, and brought out nearly seventy slaves.[73]

Tubman found work as a domestic and cook in hotels and private homes in Philadelphia and in Cape May, New Jersey, saving every penny she could. From the beginning she was involved in the network of black abolitionists who kept in touch with and aided fugitives. As Larson noted, "Tubman relied heavily upon a long-established, intricate, and secretive web of communication and support among African Americans to affect her rescues. Among the black conductors on the road to freedom from Cambridge were Samuel Green from New Market, Samuel Burris from Camden, Delaware, and Robert Loney on the Susquehanna. The collective efforts of free and enslaved African Americans operating beyond the scrutiny of whites along the various routes to freedom were crucial to her success."[74]

Tubman found freedom but not necessarily safety. As the activities of the Cannon-Johnson gang attested, Philadelphia was a favorite center of slaveholders and a place for slave catchers to "retrieve their property."[75] It was also a city hostile to the growing number of free blacks who competed with white laborers in the newly industrialized setting and were blamed for poverty, crime, and other urban problems.[76]

In 1850, William Still extended Tubman's contacts to the abolitionist group. "Conductors" included not only Thomas Garrett, her lifelong friend and supporter, but also John Hunn of Middletown (with whom Garrett would later be charged for the crime of aiding a fugitive);[77] John and Hannah Cox, whom Sallie Holley claimed were the first conductors across the Pennsylvania line; Isaac and Dinah Mendenhall, Garrett's inlaws; and Lucretia (sister of Martha Wright) and John Mott. As Tubman explained to Sarah Bradford, she was "obliged to come by many different routes on her journeys." Presumably she had to rely on many different conductors as well. Garrett constantly worried for her safety.[78]

Included in this network, Larson discovered, were John Tubman's brothers, Tom and Evans, who worked as stevedores on the docks in Baltimore. Also working there were members of the Bowley family and the Manokeys, Eastern Shore families having strong contacts to the Ross family. Their work-related travel between Baltimore and Cambridge gave them access to family news on both shores.[79]

A few months later, in early 1851, Tubman went back to Baltimore to bring Moses, her youngest brother, and two others to freedom. Later that year she made her first return to the Eastern Shore, a more dangerous journey than Baltimore for Tubman. This was the trip to bring back her husband John. It is not clear whether she waited because of the danger or some other circumstance. He refused to leave. She returned again in December and may have spoken with John Tubman one last time; then she brought out eleven other people.

This group traveled to Philadelphia, New York City, Albany, and Rochester, New York. In Rochester, they may have stayed with Frederick Douglass for a time. Douglass was always very protective of the identities of fugitives, fearing reprisals. He wrote in his 1881 autobiography, "On one occasion I had eleven fugitives at the same time under my roof, and it was necessary for them to remain with me until I could collect sufficient money to get them on to Canada."[80] While it is not known how often Tubman and Douglass associated prior to her escape, given their mutual ties to watermen it is likely that they were familiar with each other's abolitionist activities. The timing and size of this group suggests they were the same. In 1855 Tubman and her party reached their final destination, St. Catherine, Canada.[81]

Tubman remained in Canada for several months and considered it her residence off and on until 1857. "The first winter was terribly severe for these poor runaways," she reported to Sanborn. "They earned their bread by chopping wood in the snows of a Canadian forest; they were frost-bitten, hungry and naked." In the spring she returned to Philadelphia and worked again in Cape May during the summer to earn money for her next rescue. She constantly needed cash in all her trips; her personal contributions were more significant than usually noted. Tubman hated to borrow money and did so only as a last resort. In fall 1852, she left Cape May, New Jersey, went into Maryland and brought out nine fugitives.[82]

Three of her brothers, Robert, Ben and Henry, and one sister, Rachel, remained on the Eastern Shore. Twice between 1852 and 1854, Tubman tried but failed to rescue her brothers. "We started to come away," Henry told an interviewer in 1863, "but got surrounded and went back. After we went back, we concealed ourselves, and a white gentleman offered to buy us as we were, but our mistress says, 'If I can't keep them, I'd rather see them sold to Georgia.'" The mistress was Eliza Brodess, whose financial troubles had continued but whose enmity was apparently stronger. "After the gentlemen saw she wouldn't sell us to him at any price," Henry stated, "he sent us word, 'Boys, I can't buy you. If you can get away, get away.'" They did not get away, nor did Eliza Brodess sell them.[83]

Tubman continued to worry about the fate of her brothers and sister and devised an elaborate plan for their rescue. First she employed a friend to write a letter to Jacob Jackson, a free man living near her brothers who could read and write. Jackson was under suspicion of aiding fugitives, so Tubman had to proceed with caution. The note said to "tell my brothers to be always watching unto prayer, and when the good old ship of Zion comes along, be ready to step aboard." It was signed William Henry Jackson. When the "self elected postal inspectors," as Bradford called them, read the note they could not make it out and called Jacob Jackson in to explain it. "I can't make head nor tail of it," he told them and went off to tell Tubman's brothers that she was coming.[84]

The rescue finally occurred in late 1854. "We had heard that we were to be sold," Henry recalled, explaining the perils of such escapes. "We made ready to go away, but we couldn't get away; and our sister was out in Pennsylvania and came down after us when she heard we were going to be sold, but we wouldn't go. After she had gone away, our hearts mourned that we didn't go with her. Just after that, we heard we were to be sold again, and she came in good season." (Good season was a term for Christmas, a time when slaves were given time off.) Ben and Rit waited all day for the arrival of their children. Rachel, who lived on the Brodess farm, did not come and, some speculate, was not allowed to attend. According to Tubman, "[We] sent two strange men up to the house to try and speak to 'Old Ben,' their father, but not let their mother know of their being in the neighborhood." Ben Ross came out, heard their story, and gathered provisions for his children. When the group set out at last, Ben tied a blindfold over his eyes and walked with them for some miles. After the holidays, a search was made for the missing brothers. Anthony Thompson told the "man-hunters" to ask the parents. Rit told them that her children did not come to visit for Christmas and Ben said in all honesty that he had not seen them. Thompson concluded, "Well, if Old Ben says that, they haven't been round."[85]

Eliza Brodess, having lost so many of her "assets," went to court against John Mills, thinking that he had actually sold the fugitive slaves behind her back. She asked the court to direct Mills to provide a full accounting of the sales. Mills died before the decision came down in 1859. But his administrator, Polish Mills, told the court that "John Mills never having had the negroes in possession had [only] put one negro Kissy up for sale and she ran away."[86]

Poor Eliza—but perhaps not dumb Eliza—sold Rit, now nearly seventy, to Ben Ross in 1855 for the sum of $20. The document of sale stated that "Ritty was slave for life and that she was age 55." This was false information that Brodess may have wished to be put on record as it would affect her ownership claims of Rit's children and grandchildren.[87]

• • •

Tubman made more trips in 1856. In one, Josiah "Joe" Bailey (described by Bradford as "a noble specimen of a Negro"), a valuable slave offended that his new owner insisted on a whipping as a mark of submission, decided to leave. Joe submitted to the whipping but went to Ben Ross that night to find out about the next time "Moses" was coming. About a week later, Tubman arrived and Joe, his brother William from another plantation, and several others left. Thomas Garrett was asked to help in the escape. Garrett, realizing that bridges in Wilmington were closely watched, engaged two wagons and several white bricklayers. The group went across the bridge singing and shouting and the guards let them pass. At nightfall, the wagons returned. The bricklayers were on top, the fugitives hidden below. Once again, the guards let them pass.[88]

In 1856, Reverend Samuel Green, an ex-slave who had purchased his freedom, traveled to visit his son who had escaped the Eastern Shore and was happily settled in Canada. Upon the elder Green's return to Maryland, "a party of gentlemen" raided his cabin and found a map of Canada, several railroad schedules, letters from his son, and a copy of Harriet Beecher Stowe's novel, *Uncle Tom's Cabin*. Reverend Green was arrested for possession of materials that could produce "discontent." The charge against him stemmed from a rarely enforced 1841 act of the General Assembly that stated, "If any free black knowingly receive or have in his possession any abolition handbill, pamphlet, newspaper, pictorial representation or other paper of an inflammatory character which could create discontent or stir up to insurrection the people of color of the state, he or she shall be deemed guilty of felony." If found guilty, the prison term was ten to twenty years in prison. The statute itself had wide latitude in interpretation. Politicians saw the difficulty of measuring "discontent" created by a pamphlet. In Green's case, the prosecutors argued that the schedules, map, and letters constituted a real plan to stir up the "people of color." The court was not convinced, ruling that these materials were "not in and of themselves incendiary." The prosecutors then filed new charges citing possession of the book *Uncle Tom's Cabin* (possession of which was alleged to be illegal) as the incendiary act. Green was found guilty on that charge and sentenced to ten years in the Maryland State Penitentiary.[89]

The story of Green's arrest and conviction was carried in the national press. Outrage was expressed throughout the country that possession of a best-selling novel was a crime. Even the *Easton Gazette*, sympathetic to the sentence, expressed the opinion that the case should be understood in context. "That Green was convicted simply and solely for having *Uncle Tom's Cabin* in his possession is certainly true, but it is equally as true that he never would have been arrested upon that charge but for his well ascertained agency in the escape of our slaves."[90]

Eastern Shore slave owners did not back away from their stand. There had been a constant flow of runaways—singly and in groups—and they wanted it stopped. They met in Cambridge in November 1857 to consider how to better protect their interests. Their anger clearly focused on the free black community, which in Maryland at this time numbered over 80,000. They drafted a document referencing two existing Maryland laws and a proposal they hoped to enact. The first was a 1715 law prohibiting a slave from traveling more than ten miles from his home without permission and a written pass. The second directed the state to pay $6 for the recapture of fugitive slaves. The third was a provision to remove or reenslave all free blacks. James Stewart, a lawyer turned politician, argued "the negroe is in his happy element on a sugar or cotton plantation, and will laugh to scorn the mistaken views of the Abolitionists."[91]

Tubman sensed that her parents might be in real danger.[92] On March 8, 1857, a party of eight—six men and two women from the Cambridge area—attempted to escape. A reward of $3,000 was offered for their arrest. A black man entrusted with their care betrayed them for a share of the money and they were captured and placed in a Dover jail. According to William Still's account, in the confusion of the arrest, the eight managed to escape by jumping out of windows and fleeing to Camden, Delaware, to the home of William Brinkley, a free black and a railroad associate of Tubman's. Brinkley wrote Garrett asking for help. Garrett had the eight removed and hidden until they were finally taken to Wilmington. Clearly, a number of people were involved in this rescue, but chief among the suspects in the hiding of the eight was Harriet's father, Ben Ross. It was rumored that he was to be arrested.[93]

Tubman, sensing something was wrong, left Canada for New York City and attempted to get $20 from contacts there. Though at first refused, eventually she received $60 from "people sympathetic." She arrived on the Eastern Shore in June and began a trip with her parents. She had an old horse and built a "primitive" cart with old chaise wheels. Tubman somehow got this vehicle with her parents in it to a train station and with Garrett's help, got them to Canada.[94]

Ben and Rit were miserable in Canada and complained constantly. The Canadian winter was hard on them, so Tubman wanted to move them farther south. In 1859 she chose Auburn, New York—a station stop on the Underground Railroad and an area filled with anti-slavery activists, and also the home of William Seward, whose anti-slavery stance was well known. He arranged in secret for Tubman to purchase a house and land from him. Acting in conscience, Seward took a great risk, particularly as one seeking higher office, because Tubman was a fugitive and the transaction violated the 1850 law. [95]

Tubman made her last rescue in December 1860. Her sister Rachel and her two children were still in Maryland. Tubman attempted to rescue them on several other occasions but failed. Thomas Garrett explained to his friend Mary Edmondson, "Harriet has still one sister and her 3 children yet in slavery. She has tried hard this summer to get them all away together, but two of the children are separated some twelve miles from their mother, which has caused the difficulty, her sister refusing to leave without bringing all her children away."[96]

When Harriet arrived, she learned that Rachel had died. "For want of $30 dollars," Edna Cheney wrote, she had to leave the children behind. "Thirty pieces of silver; an embroidered handkerchief or a silk dress to one, or the price of freedom to [two] orphan children to another!" Even with all of Tubman's glorious successes, this single failure weighed heavily on her.[97]

Tubman did bring out Stephen Ennets (owned by John Kaiser), his wife Maria (owned by Algernon Percy), and their three children, Harriet (age six), Amanta (age four), and a baby (three months). Along the way she collected two others. Martha Wright learned of this rescue and wrote to her daughter, "We have been expending our sympathies [probably a reference to the death of Tubman's sister] as well as congratulations, on seven newly arrived slaves that Harriet Tubman just pioneered safely from the southern part of Maryland."[98]

• • •

Harriet Tubman first met John Brown in Canada. Brown was a deeply religious man who believed that slavery was a sin against God. Born in Connecticut, he joined the abolitionist movement early and engaged in various schemes to liberate slaves. In November 1850 he wrote his wife, "It now seems that the Fugitive Slave Law was to be the means of making more Abolitionists than all the lectures we have had for years. It really looks as if God had his hand in this wickedness also."[99] Like many abolitionists, Brown was outraged by the passage of the Kansas-Nebraska Act of 1854 that nullified the Missouri Compromise of 1820. Under this act the Kansas Territory was created, a part of which might eventually join the union as a slave state, something prohibited in the 1820 Compromise. Abolitionists felt that Southern slave owners had taken control of the federal government and were forcing their views upon the North. With funds secured by friends such as Gerrit Smith, who also helped Carroll free her slaves, John Brown went to "Bleeding Kansas" with a guerilla force and participated in the uprisings there.[100]

Brown, having finished his work done in Kansas ("I have been trembling all along lest they might 'back down' from the high and holy ground they have taken," he wrote a friend in 1857), turned his attention in 1858 to a plan to create a separate government for ex-slaves in the Appalachians.

To provide funds and support for his cause, Brown persuaded a group of six wealthy abolitionists (known as the "Secret Six") to help him. They included Gerrit Smith, Franklin Sanborn, Thomas W. Higginson, Theodore Parker, George Stearns, and Samuel Howe. Brown had other supporters as well. Lewis Hayden, a black minister from Detroit, raised $600 for Brown. Frederick Douglass, with whom Brown had at least one meeting in Rochester, New York, and Reverend Jermain W. Loguen, a black minister and abolitionist of Syracuse, were aware of some parts of the plan. Douglass strongly recommended that Brown meet Tubman to get her involved.[101]

Brown and Loguen went to Canada to meet with fugitives settled there in hopes of raising an army for his cause. There, with financial help from Gerrit Smith, he first met Tubman, who impressed him greatly. "I came here direct with J. W. Loguen the day after you left Rochester," he wrote his son. "I am succeeding to all appearance. Beyond my expectation. Harriet Tubman hooked up with his team at once."[102]

For the next several months Brown traveled in Canada raising money and recruiting others to work with him. He traveled to Chicago for a few weeks to raise more cash. Tubman "busied herself among ex-slaves, seeking recruits to fight at the old man's side." Brown was back in Canada in the second week of May where a convention was organized. Brown was chosen commander in chief, and John Henry Kagi, war secretary, and a provisional constitution was adopted. But Hugh Forbes, a member of Brown's group and a "military adventurer," revealed the plan to Senator Hugh Wilson of Virginia. Had it not been for Forbes's betrayal, the raid would likely have occurred soon after the convention. As it was, plans were put off and many recruits began to drift away.[103]

While Douglass eventually declined to become directly involved, "General" Tubman planned to join Brown. Several things plagued her at the time—her recurring illness, which incapacitated her for long periods, and her constant need for money to continue her efforts to rescue her family. With the raid delayed, Tubman returned to Auburn to be with her parents and later, in the winter, went to Boston to raise funds.

Franklin Sanborn explained, "She left New England with a handsome sum of money towards the payment of debt to Mr. Seward. Before she left, however, she had several interviews with Captain Brown, then in Boston." Tubman again returned to Auburn for but a short time, then went to New England "to do 'missionary' work for Brown: to win the support of prominent anti-slavers and to find recruits."[104]

Correspondence suggested that in spring 1859 Tubman was still very much involved. Edwin Morton, a tutor in the home of Gerrit Smith, revealing knowledge of the plan, wrote to his friend Franklin Sanborn, "I suppose you know where this matter is to be adjudicated. Harriet Tubman suggested the 4th of July as a good time to raise the mill." At the same time Brown wrote to Sanborn with the idea of sending him or someone with Tubman to Canada. Sanborn then wrote to his friend Reverend Higginson, "He [Brown] is desirous of getting someone to go to Canada and collect recruits, with H. Tubman, or alone as the case may be & urged me to go but my school will not let me." Higginson, for whatever reason, did not go.[105]

By June 20, 1859, Brown was in Washington County, Maryland, and Jefferson County, West Virginia, trying to muster his men. It was clear that July 4 was too early. But Brown made plans. In early July he rented a farm near Harper's Ferry that served as his headquarters. In August Brown's son, his chief representative in the North, wrote his father that he was still hopeful that Loguen, Douglass, and Tubman might be drafted. The problem was that Tubman could not be located. It was not until late August that Frank Sanborn wrote to Brown stating that Tubman was in New Bedford and very ill. That fall Brown met with Douglass, who had decided not to join him at Harper's Ferry.[106]

Disappointed, Brown continued his hunt for Tubman. Having recovered somewhat from her illness, she may have traveled as far as New York or perhaps Philadelphia. On October 6, Brown made a hurried trip to Philadelphia and met with a group of black leaders in a last attempt to get them to join with him. Tubman may have been at the meeting, though it is unlikely. An Eastern Shore rumor, widely circulated, was that Brown, disguised as a woman, traveled through the town of Trappe and attempted to pick up recruits. Kate Larson speculated that this might have been Tubman, placing her much farther south than other published reports. Sallie Holley reported that John Brown's wife stayed at Lucretia Mott's home during the time of the raid. Tubman, a frequent visitor, may have been there as well. It was known she was not at Harper's Ferry.

On October 16, 1859, Brown and his men struck the federal arsenal at Harper's Ferry. Brown's plan was fairly simple: capture the town, steal the weapons, and cross the nearby Potomac into the western Maryland hills. They did capture Harper's Ferry, but things went horribly wrong as they tried to transport the weapons. "Brown's entire operation depended upon the hope that hundreds of slaves in the surrounding Virginia countryside would rise up on his request to join the fight and help his small band overcome overwhelming odds." Instead, poor advance work and planning produced a forty-eight-hour armed struggle in which a number of the band members were killed. The raid failed; John Brown was captured and eventually hung by the Commonwealth of Virginia. In the time between his arrest and his death, public opinion transformed Brown from madman to martyr. His last written words were, "I, John Brown, am quite certain that the crimes of this guilty land will never be purged away but with blood. I had as I now think vainly, flattered myself that without much bloodshed it might be done." These were prophetic thoughts. After this, Tubman always talked about Brown, the Old Man, as the true liberator of her people.[107]

Douglass captured abolitionist community sentiment toward John Brown in writing of their last meeting:

> Captain Brown urged us both (Shields and Green) to go with him, but I could not do so, and could but feel that he was about to rivet the fetters more firmly than ever on the limbs of the enslaved. In parting he put his arms around me in a manner more than friendly, and said: "Come with me, Douglass; I will defend you with my life. I want you for a special purpose. When I strike, the bees will begin to swarm, and I shall want you to help hive them." But my discretion or my cowardice made me proof against the dear old man's eloquence—perhaps it was something of both which determined my course.

Twenty-two years later, on the very spot where the raid began, Douglass observed, "If John Brown did not end the war that ended slavery, he did, at least begin the war that ended slavery."[108]

• • •

The year 1860 was, in the words of Franklin Sanborn, "the mad winter of compromise when state after state and politician after politician went down on their knees to beg the South not to secede. Mr. Seward and many of the most patriotic of the country went over to the side of compromise." Seward's growing conservatism was motivated in part by his political ambition. He believed that his "Irrepressible Conflict" speech delivered in 1858 had cost him the nomination for president. He negotiated a position in Lincoln's cabinet, felt that he would be the behind-the-scenes leader of the country, and planned to be the Republican nominee in 1864.[109]

At the urging of friends and supporters, Harriet Tubman went to

Canada after the Harper's Ferry raid. Even Seward was believed capable of betraying his friend. Sanborn felt the "suspicion an unworthy one," but added, "so little confidence was felt in Mr. Seward, by men who had voted for him and with him, that they hurried Harriet off to Canada, sorely against her will." She remained there until spring 1861. When war broke out she rushed to New England to raise cash for an expedition to Maryland to bring out the last of her family.[110]

Her exact whereabouts were unclear. William Welles Brown wrote that long before General Benjamin Butler declared slaves "contraband of war," Harriet Tubman hung about the fringes of the Union army. Earl Conrad also indicated that Tubman followed Butler's army as it marched through Maryland. Butler, a former Massachusetts politician, commanded a post at Fort Monroe, Virginia, and was allied with the New England anti-slavery forces. He offered to use his troops to put down what a news report called "a stampede of slaves" from Cambridge, Maryland—an offer that brought him censure. To regain his standing, when Confederate forces approached his camp with a flag of truce requesting the runaways, Butler cited international law, declaring that the slaves were now "contraband of war" and refused to give them up. Lincoln's administration, struggling particularly with the issue of emancipation, at first did not discourage Butler's temporary solution because it "freed secession slaves" and gave cover to border state Unionist slave owners. They wanted time for public opinion in the North to be swayed to the idea of fighting a war to end slavery.[111]

Fort Monroe, on the western shore of the Chesapeake at the mouth of the James River, was a magnet for escaping slaves, and their number rose dramatically. Volunteers were brought in to oversee the "contraband," supplying them with food, clothing, and work, and Tubman may have helped unofficially. After August, enactment of the first Confiscation Act officially permitted ex-slaves work as manual laborers, cooks, and washerwomen.[112]

Tubman was in New England in late 1861 when news came of the fall of Port Royal, South Carolina. With its capture, the Sea Islands and their rich plantations and slaves became part of the Union Department of the South. Within the Lincoln administration, Salmon Chase decided that Port Royal represented a unique opportunity to test whether released slaves could become free laborers. The force of his personality persuaded a reluctant cabinet and president who were skeptical of this "experiment." Freedmen's aid societies immediately formed and recruited volunteers to go to the Sea Islands.[113]

To execute his plan, Chase sent his longtime friend Edward Pierce from Massachusetts to Port Royal to lead the experiment. Pierce landed in South Carolina in March 1862 with people and supplies. Other volunteers from the North were already there. Disagreement and conflict emerged from the beginning, particularly surrounding the large group of ex-slaves, not yet free, who did not know what they were supposed to do and a contingent of white Union soldiers who needed food and supplies but did not want to participate in an experiment with "peculiar" black contraband. (They called this the period of great confusion.)[114]

Tubman wanted to go to Port Royal from the first, but getting there was a complicated matter. Volunteers needed authorizations and transport passes. In April, Tubman finally secured a pass. In May, she left for Port Royal with the idea that she would be a valuable person to operate within enemy lines to procure information and scouts.[115]

Union General T. W. Sherman controlled the Sea Island area. At first he issued an order of protection for whites living there. But local residents were not reassured and Sherman soon reported to his commanders "that every white inhabitant has left the islands." With the exodus, cotton gins were destroyed, houses looted, and cotton houses burned. "The masters themselves were responsible for a large amount of the destruction," but they were ably assisted by plantation slaves and federal soldiers, Sherman reported. It was also a problem that the Union army, needing food, left many in the slave community to starve. Conducting any experiment in the midst of such chaos was doomed to failure.[116]

By the time Tubman reached Beauford, South Carolina, on the mainland, General T. W. Sherman, who was blamed for many of the conflicts, was replaced by Major General David Hunter. The War Department felt that Hunter had a better understanding of its anti-slavery views, even though these views were still in formation. Hunter met Tubman and liked her. He found that he valued her aid, because over time "she was one whom northerners could understand." Tubman was asked to serve as liaison between the white and black communities, but it was a vaguely defined job from which she was forced to make her own way. The military allowed her the privilege of drawing rations as an officer or soldier, but as historian Charles Wood explained, "The freed people, becoming jealous of this privilege accorded her, she voluntarily relinquished this right and thereafter supplied her personal wants by selling pies and root beer."[117]

The Port Royal experiment took place under the scrutiny of the press and government workers. "Flooding into the islands were military officers, Treasury agents, northern investors and a squad of young teachers and missionaries known collectively as Gideon's Band," historian Eric Foner wrote. Each group had its own ideas about how to proceed and what was important, and often these were at cross-purposes. The Gideonites—young, enthusiastic, wealthy, and incompetent—were the least powerful. The influential—members of private enterprises and the Treasury under Chase—were the ones who proposed employing the ex-slaves as paid workers. The experiment was underway. They hope to learn, Foner noted, "how the freedmen adjusted to the end of slavery."[118]

Tubman had a variety of duties, she explained to Emma Telford in 1905. "The [Christian] commission had been set up by the YMCA to distribute supplies of clothing, food, books and other items to the Union soldiers."[119]

She received $200 from the government, the only compensation she ever got, and used part of it to build a wash house. Apparently black women supported themselves by washing for the officers of the gunboats and the soldiers.[120] Soon, however, Tubman's chief duties were in nursing. "Among other duties which I have," she wrote to Franklin Sanborn, "is that of looking after the hospital here for contrabands. Most of those from the mainland are very destitute almost naked. I am trying to find places for those able to work, and provide for them as best I can, so as to lighten the burden of the government, as much as possible, while at the same time they learn to respect themselves by earning their own living." While this sentiment is vintage Tubman (she had after all worked almost from the moment of her escape), it is also a prime statement of the free labor doctrine of Chase. In December 1861 Northern papers reported, "The cotton upon these islands is being picked by contrabands, under the direction of our officers. About two million dollars of cotton has already been seized."[121]

Tubman spent long hours at the hospital. She washed the wounded with cold water from blocks of ice and kept the flies away. "I'd begin to bathe their wounds,' she told Sanborn, 'and by the time I'd bathed off three or four, the fire and heat would have melted the ice and made the water warm, and it would be as red as clear blood.'" Acknowledged for her nursing skills, Tubman was sent during this time to Fernandina, Florida, where men were dying of dysentery. She prepared a medicine from local roots that had a very good success rate in curing the illness.[122]

In December 1862 Tubman's friend Reverend Thomas Higginson (now Colonel Higginson) arrived in South Carolina as an aide to General Rufus B. Saxon, a military governor of the Department of the South. Higginson's assignment was to organize the first "officially sanctioned" black regiment. Previous experiments with black regiments in Louisiana had met with mixed results. The problem was not so much the ability of the men as their reception by fellow white soldiers. General Hunter had also attempted to build a regiment of black soldiers in South Carolina, an effort Lincoln overruled. But heavy losses at Fredericksburg, Vicksburg, and Stone River forced the issue.[123]

In early spring 1863 Tubman organized a scouting service for the Department of the South under Hunter. Tubman's unit was directed by Colonel James Montgomery, an expert in guerilla tactics and a veteran of the Kansas uprisings. Like Higginson, Montgomery formed a group of black volunteers. Tubman and Montgomery had in common a friendship and respect for John Brown and they became comrades. Tubman's scouts and river pilots, nine in all, were local men who knew the terrain. She sent them out to learn the enemy's whereabouts and movements and their strengths and weaknesses—advance information crucial to any military exercise. Tubman did her job well.[124]

Hunter wanted to use the scouts to harass the Confederate forces guarding Charleston and Savannah, hoping to stymie enemy movement in the southeast. Along the way they collected contraband from the surrounding area. The Department of the South also sent small parties up the rivers to break up rebel batteries and destroy their defenses. These trips were hazardous and exhausting for the soldiers and the weather was fierce at times. Yellow fever and dysentery, diseases little understood within the military, were widespread, and Tubman was forced to divide her time between the roles of guerilla fighter and nurse.

Early that summer, Tubman conducted her most famous raid up the Combahee River (referred to by locals as the River Jordan). Tubman had several objectives in this raid, among them to find and remove torpedoes placed in the river by the rebels, and to destroy rail lines and bridges to cut off supplies. Confederate investigators would later complain that the scouts provided good information and did a good job "as to the character and capacity of our troops and their small chance of encountering opposition."[125]

Montgomery, Tubman, and a party of about 150 black troops in three gunboats started up the river in June. They were immediately spotted by Confederate lookouts but because of their small numbers the Rebels could do little more than warn the others. Union gunboats moved up the river without opposition, dropping off bands of soldiers at various points to liberate blacks on nearby plantations and set fire to Confederate property. The plan was Tubman's though official records give it to Montgomery. "As the gunboats passed up the river the Negroes left their work and took to the woods," she reported, "for at first they were frightened. Then they came out to peer, like startled deer, but scudding away like the wind at the sound of the steam-whistle." One can only imagine what they thought, seeing these soldiers of color, armed and moving quickly on the river. "The word was passed along that these were Lincoln's gunboats come to set them free." The celebration was instantaneous and glorious. Overseers, who had been keeping the people back with whips and guns, ran away. The plantation slaves flocked to the boats. Montgomery later recalled that so many tried to hang on, they could not move. To make their getaway he asked Tubman to start a song of thanks, which she did. When the freed people raised their hands in praise, the boats were able to slip away. Tubman's account was more charitable. "There were women with children clinging around their heels, hanging onto their dresses, or running behind, but all rushed at full speed for Lincoln's gunboats. Hundreds crowded the banks, with their hands extended toward their deliverance, and most of them were taken aboard the gunboats to be carried to Beaufort." Nearly eight hundred people were rescued. "'I never saw such a sight,' Tubman recalled, 'we laughed and laughed and laughed.'"[126]

Hunter was so pleased with the expedition he wrote to Secretary of War Stanton extolling the virtues of the black troops as well as his brilliance in commanding them and proposed a continuation of warfare through the swamps and inlets of the area. At the same time he was a little taken back by Montgomery's aggressive guerilla tactics and warned him to spare "household furniture, libraries, churches and hospitals" and added that he hoped the Colonel would not destroy crops growing in the ground "without mature consideration."[127]

The more immediate problem was feeding and caring for the contraband. Taken to Beaufort, South Carolina, they formed a large refugee camp. A dozen or so wooden buildings housed the refugees; each room had a fireplace, an opening for a window, and a double row of berths along the wall. It was rough and crude and a new life in freedom.[128]

On the very day that Montgomery and Tubman returned from Combahee, the 54th Massachusetts Infantry Regiment, the first regiment of free Northern blacks, arrived in Beaufort. The regiment was handpicked, the brainchild of Massachusetts Governor John A. Andrew, and included two sons of Frederick Douglass and a grandson of Sojourner Truth. They were commanded by Robert Shaw, Harvard educated and a principled white abolitionist. On June 10, 1863, Montgomery, Shaw, and their companies steamed up the Altamaha River to Darien, Georgia. Tubman did not accompany them. The troops, after firing a few shots, landed unopposed and, over Shaw's protests, looted houses and burned the town. Montgomery's philosophy was that "Southerners must be made to feel that this was a real war." The Northern press condemned the "plain of ashes" and the "invasion of Yankee negro vandals."[129]

Embarrassed by what took place at Darien, Shaw pleaded with General Quincy Gillmore (Hunter's replacement) to let his troops, who were disciplined and ready for action, play a part in Gillmore's plans to gain control of the outlying batteries south of Fort Sumter. He hoped to separate himself from the "blatant disregard for civilian safety" and to redeem his troops who were blamed for the "invasion."

In July 1863 the 54th Massachusetts led by Shaw attacked Fort Wagner, a Confederate stronghold that had seventeen artillery guns, thick walls ringed by a moat, and 1,500 Confederate soldiers inside. The first action was to be diversionary and the Union troops held their lines firmly. They then withdrew to Morris Island, site of the main attack. With little means of transport on a marshy terrain, their journey "took two awful days in which they had no sleep, no rations and very little water." Picked because of their resolve as much as their strength and courage, the 54th Massachusetts troops saw the battle as some kind of referendum on their abilities.[130]

Unfortunately for them, Gillmore grossly underestimated Southern strength. "Their onslaught failed for lack of timely reinforcement, but the soldiers fought on," historian Willie Rose indicated. The 54th Massachusetts refused to retreat, choosing instead to die. "Men fell all around me," Lewis Douglass, son of Frederick, recalled. "A shell would explode and clear a space of twenty feet, our men would close up again, but it was no use, we had to retreat, which was a very hazardous undertaking. How I got out of that fight alive I cannot tell." Union losses were horrific: 1,500 dead, wounded, missing, or captured compared to only 174 Confederate casualties.[131]

Historian Albert Bushnell Hart, who interviewed Tubman, felt it was this battle she described as, "And then we saw the lightning, and that was the guns; and then we heard the thunder, and that was the big guns; ant then we heard the rain falling, and that was the drops of blood falling; and when we came to get the crops, it was dead men that we reaped."[132] Tubman was there after the assault to bury black soldiers and to nurse the wounded. It was said that the dead and wounded whites were sent to Hilton Head and Clara Barton and the blacks to Beauford and Harriet Tubman. But in defeat, the racial separation was not mentioned as the Northern press celebrated "dark-skinned heroes who fought the good fight" and blasted the Confederates who stripped Robert Shaw's lifeless body and threw him naked on a pile of dead black soldiers. The Northern public reacted with shock and outrage.[133]

Montgomery, temporarily in charge of the 54th Massachusetts, accompanied them and two newly arrived units, the Eighth U.S. Colored Infantry Regiment and the First South Carolina Colored Volunteers into battle at Olustee, Florida, thirty-five miles west of Jacksonville. It was February 1863 and another costly defeat "with honor" for the Department of the South and the last for Montgomery, who later resigned his commission in September. Fighting at this battle was Nelson Charles (later

Nelson Davis), who had just arrived, having been recruited in Philadelphia. Davis was a private in Company G and, according to the Tatlock statement, a "magnificent physical specimen," not yet thirty years old. Davis would become Harriet Tubman's second husband.[134]

Tubman ended one of her letters to Sanborn with mention of her parents. "I have now been absent two years almost, and have just got letters from my friends in Auburn, urging me to come home. My father and mother are old and in feeble health, and need my care and attention. I hope the good people there will not allow them to suffer, and I do not believe they will. But I do not see how I am to leave at present the very important work to be done here."[135]

Tubman finally decided to go north in spring 1864. In February she ran into George Garrison, son of William Lloyd Garrison, who wrote his brother of the meeting. "She no sooner saw me than she recognized me at once, and instantly threw her arms around me, and gave me quite an affectionate hug." She told Garrison she wanted to go home but General Quincy Gillmore would not allow her to do so because of her valuable services as spy, nurse, laundress, and cook. Appealing to his brother about her difficult financial situation, William Garrison commented that he thought "she had a chance of making a good deal of money here, and can easily get fifty times more work than she can do." Exhausted, Tubman obtained a certificate signed by Surgeon Henry Durrant of the hospital and General Rufus Saxon. She relied heavily on these documents in order to move about freely.[136]

The spring of 1864 was one of the bloodiest periods of the war and individuals attempting to travel were in great danger from war-weary renegades. After reaching Auburn, Tubman once again fell ill and was bedridden for some time. During this period she formed her friendship with Sarah Bradford, who had already befriended Tubman's parents.

Sometime in June, Tubman was sufficiently recovered to go to Boston in search of food and clothing. In July the *Commonwealth* carried a notice about her visit and her needs. Tubman stayed with Dr. Rock, a black Boston abolitionist who had helped to recruit men to serve with the 54th Massachusetts. She also met Sojourner Truth, who was on her way to Washington to meet President Lincoln. Tubman expressed no interest at the time in meeting Lincoln, although Truth persuaded her that Lincoln was a friend.

It was not until early spring 1865 that she began planning to return to the South. In February, Lincoln decided to create a black army with black officers and Tubman was called upon to help in the efforts. The idea originated with Tubman's friend Martin Delany, who had long been urging the Lincoln administration to make more use of the slave and ex-slave population. Confederates hatched a desperate plan at the time (never implemented) to arm slaves and force them to fight Union troops. Delany proposed a network of black soldiers who would travel surreptitiously throughout the South gathering recruits and undermining Confederate action. Lincoln agreed and Delany was made the first black major in the U.S. Army.

While Tubman conferred with Delany and others in Washington, she decided instead to get involved in nursing services in the Washington area. By this time William T. Sherman had marched through Georgia to the coast and had turned northward toward Richmond. Grant and a force of over 125,000 soldiers were approaching from the west. Tubman was persuaded by members of the U.S. Sanitary Commission, a private organization, to go to the James River Hospitals in Hampton, Virginia, where there was pressing need for nurses. Tubman went and remained there until July 1865. Abuses in the hospital were legion, and Tubman next traveled to Washington to complain to officials in the War Department. "And so great was the confidence of some officers of the Govt. in her," Charles Wood wrote in his report, "that Surgeon General Barnes directed that she be appointed 'Nurse or Matron.'" A directive from Barnes in Tubman's possession stated: "I have the honor to inform you that the Medical Director Dept. of Virginia, has been instructed to appoint Harriet Tubman 'Nurse or Matron' at the colored hospital Fort Monroe, Va." It was signed, "Very Resp. Your Obt-servant, JH Barnes."[137]

Apparently Secretary of State Seward, while recovering from an attempted assassination, recommended this action. Tubman received a pass dated July 22, 1865, permitting her to proceed to Virginia on a government transport, free of cost. Before leaving Washington, she spoke to Seward about a claim against the government for back pay. She received only $200 for all her services. Seward suggested she obtain confirmation from General David Hunter and had a note sent to him. According to Earl Conrad, nothing profitable came of the attempt. Neither Seward nor Hunter secured any funds for her.[138]

Nor did the appointment as nurse come through, so Tubman did not stay long at Fort Monroe, returning instead to Washington, "and thence home—to devote herself, since the country's need had ceased, to her aged Father & Mother." With the war at an end, Tubman felt she must return to Auburn. She boarded a train with a hospital nurse's pass, which entitled her to half fare. Missing her connection, she got on the wrong train and the conductor refused to honor her ticket, stating "We don't carry niggers half fare." The conductor pulled on her arm and when she resisted, called three men for assistance. Tubman was thrown into the baggage car. "The car was filled with emigrants," she said, and no one seemed to take her part. The only words she heard, accompanied with fearful oaths, were, "Pitch the nagur out!"[139]

Tubman returned to Auburn in 1865, ill from the train incident. On the way there, she stopped in New York seeking medical assistance. Friends in Auburn, hearing about the train incident, thought she could sue and went about preparing a case for her. They thought a settlement in her favor would provide financial security. Rich Republican friends, flush with military victory and emancipation, also gave generously of money, food, and clothing. In addition, the Freedman's Association of Boston paid her a salary of $10 a month to help freed men and women. On the suggestion of a nephew in South Carolina, Tubman used some of her money to support two freedom schools.[140] But these times would not last.

From Cambridge, Maryland, came the news that her husband, John Tubman, had been murdered. John Tubman had argued over ashes with Robert Vincent, a white man, one morning. At about five o'clock that evening, John was walking down the road when Vincent passed him in a vehicle. Vincent stopped, asked if he was the same man with the same views as in the morning. John replied that he was, whereupon Vincent shot him dead. Vincent went on trial for murder. There was no doubt about his guilt. There were, in fact, two witnesses: Rebecca Camper, who witnessed the argument at her house; and John Tubman's thirteen-year-old son who, while standing in the woods, watched the shooting. But both witnesses were black and the jury was all white and all Democratic. "The Republicans," the *Cambridge Intelligencer* wrote, "have taught the Democrats much since 1860. They thrashed them into at least a seeming respect for the Union—They educated them up to a tolerance of public schools. They forced them to recognize Negro testimony in their courts. But they haven't got them to the point of convicting a fellow democrat for killing a Negro." The jury found Vincent not guilty. John Tubman left a widow and four children.[141]

• • •

The years after the Civil War grew increasingly difficult for Tubman. Living in Auburn with members of her family, she had no visible means of support. Her fame as "Moses" and war spy made her home a refuge for the sick and abandoned of the war but not a magnet for financial enterprise. People came to her for help; she gave what she had. One of those who lodged with her was Nelson Davis, of the Eighth U.S. Colored Infantry who fought at Olustee, Florida. Davis was twenty-one years old when he enlisted and at some time later became sick with tuberculosis. He lived in the Tubman household for several years and worked as a sort of handyman. In 1868, among family and friends (including William Seward), they married. Harriet was in her late forties, he was twenty-five.[142]

There was some unkind speculation about this relationship. Some argued that they wed so that Tubman could care for Davis—a strange assessment that probably said more about her biographers. He was often ill, and able to work only sporadically, but their marriage lasted nearly twenty years. They went into the business of brick-making when he was well enough and adopted a child, at the request of the child's dying mother.

Tubman's parents also lived with her and were, by most reports, difficult. Frequently hungry and increasingly infirm, they expected Harriet to provide for them. She told Emma Telford of being so overwrought by their complaints on one occasion that she locked herself in a closet. Later, she came out, went to the local market and talked enough merchants into giving her leftover food that she was able to make soup. Tubman's deep religious conviction and stamina somehow carried her family through the hard times. Sometimes they ate, sometimes not.

Sallie Holley reported that Tubman visited Gerrit Smith in November 1867. "She wants Mr. Smith to help her get her claim allowed against the government. She has a letter from William H. Seward to Maj.-Gen. Hunter, dated 1865, in which Mr. Seward says, 'I have know her long, and a nobler, higher spirit, or truer, seldom dwells in human form.'" Noble thoughts—but insufficient to ease her condition.[143]

Ben Ross died in 1871. Thomas Garrett also died that year, and Seward in 1872. One by one Tubman's family, friends, and financial backers were beginning to leave her. Desperate for money, she got involved in an unfortunate gold swindle in 1873. It began when her brother John Stewart (formerly Robert Ross), who lived in Auburn, was approached "by two strange colored men, who introduced themselves as his friends, giving the names of John Thomas and Stevenson." The men told Stewart that they had found a large sum of gold, $5,000 in gold pieces, in South Carolina during the war. As black men, they were afraid the government would seize it if they turned it in. For $2,000, they would sell the pieces to someone who could handle the transaction without suspicion. Stewart said he did not have the money but would ask his sister. Tubman was convinced and "the strangers took lodgings at her house, Stevenson remaining three nights, and John Thomas, two." Tubman called on various bankers and capitalists in Auburn to aid in the exchange. Most refused. Anthony Shimer, a local politician who had known Seward for many years, agreed to put up $2,000 for the gold. Arrangements were made and Tubman, carrying the cash, went with the men into the woods where the gold was buried. They dug up a box and demanded the cash. Tubman refused, asking to see the gold. The men said the box was locked and they had forgotten the key. After much discussion, they told Tubman to guard the box while they went for the key. "She examined the trunk, after they left, and found it to be only a common box. She had seen a trunk full of gold and silver buried in Beauford, S.C., during the war, and had that in mind when this affair came up—the reminiscence aiding her most sanguine imagination in the present instance."[144] In examining the box, however, she found no key hole. Though suspicious for the first time, she waited for the men to return. They did not and her suspicions turned to fear, "thinking," she said, "of stories about ghosts haunting buried treasures." Distracted, she searched for something to open the box and, finding a rail, worked with such frenzy that "she sank down grasping for the box, and lost all consciousness." When she came to, she was bound and gagged and the money was gone.[145]

Shimer, of course, wanted his money back. The authorities were brought in and for days the local press carried stories of the "gold swindle." Anthony Shimer, a risk taker, received a lot of scorn for his participation and ultimately was the big loser.[146] Tubman survived by a combination of her prior standing in the community and racist assessments that it was to be expected—black people could be easily fooled, which was why they needed protection and control.

Still without funds Tubman pursued a variety of activities. She cleaned for the Wright family and others in the community and she sold produce from her garden door to door. Sarah Bradford's book on Tubman, though hastily done, brought in over $1,500. Tubman used some of these funds to settle her debt with the Seward family.

Tubman never lost her yen for political activism and got involved with the National Woman Suffrage Association—the same organization with which Anna Ella Carroll became allied. In doing so, Tubman separated herself from Frederick Douglass and Francis Watkins Harper, who argued that a ballot for black men was more pressing, for the time being, than one for women. Abolitionists feared that women's rights would overshadow the rights of blacks. Tubman's position on the issue of black men versus white women was not clear. But like Carroll, her motive was in part networking and her sense of loyalty. Tubman was a longtime friend of Susan B. Anthony, who had, from her home in Rochester, aided fugitives en route to Canada. In a 1911 interview, Tubman said, "I belonged to Miss Susan B. Anthony's association." When asked if she really believed women should vote, she replied, "I suffered enough to believe it."[147] Whenever she was able, Tubman attended local suffragists' events. In 1888 she spoke at a nonpartisan society for political education for women. The group reported, "Her recital of the brave and fearless deeds of women who sacrificed all for their country and moved in battle when bullets mowed down men, file after file, and rank after rank, was graphic. Loving women were on the scene to administer to the injured, to bind up their wounds and tend them through weary months of suffering in the army hospitals. If those deeds do not place woman as man's equal, what do?" Listeners paid rapt attention to the brief speech, the *Auburn Daily* said.[148]

Tubman's private woes continued. Her mother died in 1880. In 1882 or so, her wood-frame farmhouse burned down. Her brother John Stewart died, and her husband continued his decline with tuberculosis. Davis, who had rebuilt the house, died in 1888. But Tubman's public beneficence and sacrifice also continued as she planned to establish the John Brown Home for Aged and Indigent in Auburn.

Tubman appeared at several suffrage conventions in the 1890s. In 1896, the *Rochester Democrat and Chronicle* reported, "Certainly the most picturesque, if not the most interesting incident of the afternoon's meeting was the appearance on the rostrum of Susan B. Anthony, the veteran worker of political emancipation for women, leading by the hand an old colored woman. Miss Anthony introduced her as Mrs. Harriet Tubman, a faithful worker for the emancipation of her race, who had reason to revere President Lincoln." The reporter described Tubman as an old woman in a cheap black gown, black coat, and big black straw bonnet without adornment. Her face was black, and old and wrinkled, he said, though "marked with honesty and true benevolence." He concluded the article with the comment, "This old woman who can neither read nor write, has a mission, which is the moral advancement of her race. She makes her home in Auburn, but depends on the kindness of friends to assist her, by a dollar now and then, or a bed, or a meal, as she travels from place to place."[149]

In 1901, Bradford wrote to Sanborn about Tubman's horrible state. "I have been to see Harriet," she said, "& found her in a deplorable condition, a pure wreck, [mind?] & body—surrounded by a set of beggars who I fear fleece her of every thing sent her." Bradford took charge of money sent to Tubman and allocated it as needed. "If I could only get her into a home where she would be well cared for I should be so glad, but she will not leave her beloved darkies." Several years later Ellen Wright Garrison wrote in a slightly more optimistic manner, "We stopped on our way home to make a carriage call on Harriet Tubman. We drove into her yard & such a leaking rummage heap as it was! Quantities of old dry goods boxes (for kindling) old cooking utensils sitting on the ground, old wagons & an old buggy in rags & tatters & dozens of other things & I counted five homely cats, four puppies & and their dusty Ma, a dirty pig & lots of chickens besides 2 white children eating apples & looking very much at home."[150] Tubman, she said, "came out of the kitchen looking quite well & brisk & when she saw Fanny she said 'O my lord!' and clutched her hand with rapture—We gave her ten minutes or so & then Fanny pressed a bill upon her & we tore ourselves away."[151]

Early in 1899, a bill was introduced in Congress to pay a pension to Tubman for her service as a nurse. To this point, the only money she received was $8 per month as the widow of Nelson Davis. After discussion within Congress, and objections from a South Carolina congressman, it was settled that Tubman would receive $20 per month.[152]

In 1908, with a U.S. flag draped about her shoulders, a band playing, and a crowd gathered around her, Tubman dedicated her home for the aged, named not for John Brown, but for herself—the Harriet Tubman Home. In her words of welcome, she said, "I did not take up this work for my own benefit but for those of my race who need help. The work is now well started and I know God will raise up others to take care of the future. All I ask is united effort, for 'united we stand: divided we fall.'"[153]

Contributions from friends allowed Tubman to stay in a hospice in her last days. J. Osborne wrote to Emily Howland that Tubman was thin and weak—though the last time she saw her she was, "bright and talkative very clear in mind, told me what she wanted me to do with her gold pieces, which were given to her by Mrs. Osborn & her children, in case she didn't live very long." The note was dated February 19, 1913. Tubman died March 10, 1913. In a *New York Herald* interview in 1907, she seemed to sum up her half century after the war (the fifty years not included in the celebratory children's books), when she commented, "You wouldn't think that after I served the flag so faithfully I should come to want in its folds."[154]

4 | Political Economy and Marginalization

> As Harriet grew older she became a marvelous specimen
> of physical womanhood, and before she was nineteen years
> old was a match for the strongest man on the plantation.
> —F. C. Drake, 1907

In 1862, J. E. Cairnes, a professor of political economy at the University of Dublin, wrote one of the last works on the subject of American slavery before its demise. Historian Ulrich Phillips was critical of Cairnes's methodology, saying it was "short on data," "partisan," and that he drew "the bulk of his data from traveler's accounts," suggesting that his "picture of the Southern non-slaveholder was the most extreme of his grotesqueries."[1] Cairnes's flawed research nevertheless presents a tantalizing economic description of social strata in the South before the war. "The constitution of a slave society," Cairnes wrote, "resolves itself into three classes, broadly distinguished from each other and connected by no common interest—the slaves on whom devolves all the regular industry, the slaveholders who reap all its fruits and an idle and lawless rabble who live dispersed over vast plains in a condition little removed from absolute barbarism." Nonslaveholders, he added, follow a "life alternating between listless vagrancy and the excitement of marauding expeditions." Civilization, he concluded, in a harsh indictment, could not progress under slavery.[2]

Cairnes echoed Adam Smith's view that the economic cost of slavery was excessive because of its "lack of zest, frugality and inventiveness."[3] A number of political thinkers in the United States, William Seward and various factions of the Whig, Free Soil, and Republican parties prominent among them, adopted similar views of the political and economic costs to workers of slavery. Neither Cairnes nor the American thinkers had women in mind in making their critique. Women were on the margins of U.S. society, both North and South, and considered at best irrelevant, at worse helpless and dependent. But as pro-slavery advocate George Fitzhugh warned in 1854, "There is something wrong with woman's condition in free society, and that condition is daily becoming worse." Fitzhugh feared abolitionism, feminism, and Northern democratization, all of which he thought would destroy the status quo and institution of marriage, both essential to keeping women in their place.[4]

While few at that time were as extreme in their fears as Fitzhugh, his views and those of Cairnes may provide a context in which to examine women's labor before the war. Historian Jeanne Boydston uses the word "anomalous" to describe positions that female wage earners occupied in the transition to capitalism. In precapitalist systems, working women "became a logical inconsistency," she wrote, "an oxymoron." Many believed, in fact, as historian Alice Kessler Harris explained, "When women strode bravely into the work force, they landed in its lowest places, without coercion, with their full consent and understanding and even encouragement."[5] Yet somehow along the way the accepted domestic sphere imploded as Fitzhugh feared, and their consent "vested women with unaccustomed responsibilities."[6]

This chapter examines the work choices of the mismatched Eastern Shore trio: Cannon, the nonslaveholder; Carroll, the slaveholder; and Tubman, the slave. Though they did so at different times, all three entered the wage-labor market, an unusual choice for women, but for the obvious reason of the survival of their families and for the less obvious reason that no other option seemed acceptable. In so doing, they all managed to violate basic gender norms by doing men's work instead of what women ought to do.

In a society only beginning to industrialize, a preferred path to mobility begins by working for someone else, then having one's own business, and eventually hiring others. The goal is to quit the wage laboring class. These rational economic steps, it is believed, are the building blocks in the creation of a middle class. The work is hard and time consuming but in the end brings upward mobility and the hope of advancement to the hard-working poor.[7] Before the war, the white North was well on its way to this model of development. The white South, on the other hand, comprised mainly of slave owners and the poor, had few opportunities for a middle class, little hope of social advancement for those at the bottom, and hence a lack of progress.

Explanations for the backwardness of the South centered on the institution of slavery, in much the way Cairnes articulated it. Nobody worked except the slaves—nobody wanted to work and therefore little got done. In 1835 William Seward visited Virginia and wrote in some despair, "An exhausted soil, old and decaying towns, wretchedly-neglected roads, and in every respect, an absence of enterprise and improvement, distinguish the region through which we have come, in contrast to that in which we live. Such has been the effect of slavery."[8]

By contrast, as Eric Foner points out, the idea of the dignity of labor was always a theme of importance in the antebellum North. Max Weber's connection of the New England Protestant ethic, work hard for the night is coming, to the rise of capitalism is part of this intellectual history. Over time, it was argued, "the key ingredient in producing a robust capitalist economy above the Mason-Dixon Line was the rise of a fluid, free labor force, an ingredient notably absent in the South." The antebellum South did not produce commercial agriculture and supplied few resources for technological innovation. Nonslaveholding whites were despised because they had to work—they were little better than slaves, it was said—to support themselves.[9]

Free laborers in the North could work for wages as an artisans or even as unskilled workers and, over time, acquire enough money to start their own business or buy land. It was an economic view that mirrored the antebellum Northern economy "centered on independent farms and small shops."[10] The capacity for growth and development in the North was so marked that "white artisans and unskilled workers fled to northern cities from the South," it was said, "to escape the depressed wages caused by competition from slave hires."[11]

The Chesapeake economy was on the middle ground between North and South, a geographic and political terrain that was one-third slave in 1790 and less than one-sixth by 1850.[12] It managed its transition to free labor over many decades, having the largest free black population in the country by 1810. At the same time it had a substantial white majority, so whites filled many of the jobs "free coloreds" did in other slave societies. Because of this, "free blacks though they constituted an essential element of the work force" had a problematic position in society.[13]

For many decades, production of tobacco kept enslaved blacks on the Eastern Shore at work throughout the year. With the collapse of the profitability of this crop, a change in the demand for labor occurred. While diversification into cereal crops like wheat was achieved, fewer workers were needed and many of those had greater value as commodities. The Carroll family, most affected by the change, saw their wealth gradually eaten away. They had too many slaves for the kind of crops they were forced to grow. Surplus slaves had to be sold. The Rosses were surplus slaves and though promised otherwise, were likely to be sold south. The

Cannons's small farm, though not affected by tobacco failure, could not compete with commercialized agriculture slowly making its way across the Eastern Shore. For all three, changes had to be made.

Patty Cannon: Transition from Agriculture

The individual household in the agricultural South in general and on the Eastern Shore in particular was the fundamental unit of production and reproduction. In an idyllic historic portrait, the colonial/new republic wife was a "strong, sturdy goodwife producing household necessities and plying her crafts."[14] Patty Cannon, as a child and young woman, was familiar with this life.

The problem for the Cannons was that the new economy was mired in conflicting and sometimes contradictory directions and policies. "In so complicated a science as political economy," Thomas Jefferson wrote in 1816, "no one axiom can be laid down as wise and expedient for all times and circumstances, and for their contraries."[15]

It was a time of financial bust and boom, and the new nation struggled with war debt, a lack of credit, and an absence of consistent economic policy.[16] Patty and husband Jesse were in search of a profitable business. Growing a business depended on money. As Alexis de Tocqueville observed, in the early republic there was the importance "not only of work itself, but work specifically to gain money."[17] There were both legal and illegal ways of obtaining cash. The legal ways included growing crops and selling them, making things and selling them, and working as a wage laborer. Wage laborers included skilled and semiskilled artisans, mechanics, day laborers, and farm hands. Skilled artisans probably made enough to accumulate savings, but farmhands did not.

Accumulating cash from legal activities was a slow process. Illegal activities were more lucrative but had more risk. In the Chesapeake, some watermen like Jesse prospered in the perilous and dangerous business of patrolling the waters, dismantling blockades introduced by the wars, and highjacking cargo. Jesse had a small boat and stole cargo when he could.

The Cannons gradually entered into the kidnapping business. Stealing slaves and reselling them, a crime for which Patty Cannon's father was hung, was too dangerous for most gangs. Capturing fugitives was less dangerous but paid less. The practice of manumission of slaves at the time of the Revolutionary War elevated payment for such work. In the years that followed, historian Ira Berlin pointed out, "The number of free Negroes increased manifold, so that by the end of the first decade of the nineteenth century there were over 100,000 free Negroes in the Southern states."[18] In 1820 nearly 9 percent of the black population was free.

The Cannons's slave-dealing business began sometime in the 1790s and continued until Patty Cannon's arrest in 1829. While businesses varied in the part of slave dealing they concentrated on, it is likely that differences were a matter of degree. The Cannons specialized in kidnapping.

Slave dealers were not viewed favorably in society. D. R. Hundley, a planter from Alabama, noted, "Preeminent in villainy and a greedy love of filthy lucre stands the hard-hearted negro trader. . . . Some of them, we do not doubt, are conscientious men, but the number is few. Although honest and honorable when they first go into the business, the natural result of their calling seems to corrupt them; for they usually have to deal with the most refractory and brutal of the slave population, since good and honest slaves are rarely permitted to fall into the unscrupulous clutches of the speculator."[19]

The local community considered the Cannon-Johnson gang to be particularly violent and thereby granted them a greater wall of protection. While operating for over thirty years, authorities detained the gang on only four separate occasions, according to local records. And only once was a member, Joe Johnson, found guilty. In 1826, he was sentenced to jail for kidnapping and given thirty-nine lashes. The judge spared his ears. For the rest of the time, the gang ran their business without public scrutiny.

Slave dealing was a good business. By the 1820s, traders "with saddle bags heavy with money, stopped at plantations and offered high prices for slaves, it was said. Many Virginia and Maryland plantations were thus becoming human stock farms, breeding for the cotton fields." Austin Woolfolk, a slave trader with an office in Baltimore, paid $22,702 to slave owners for sales of their people in Talbot County and slightly less from Dorchester in the year 1825.[20]

Because of the demands of their other businesses, Jesse Cannon and Joe Johnson probably left Patty to run the tavern, as part of the "mixed economy" of a rural family. On the Eastern Shore "the inns are almost invariably poor; for nobody goes to a tavern that can rely upon good introduction, acquaintance, or even fair appearance," it was said.[21] It was unusual but not unheard of that a woman, especially one as strong as Patty, would take on this type of responsibility. The more usual occupations for women were seamstresses, laundresses, milliners, and bakers.

The tavern sat squarely on the line between Delaware and Maryland, so that when authorities from one state came for a member of the gang, he or she had only to go into an adjoining room to be out of their jurisdiction. The two-room attic was built to house captives and contained devices to prevent them from escaping. One room was windowless and its double door had heavy iron locks. J. H. K. Shannahan, quoting a witness, said, "It was sealed with a two inch white oak plank, with ring bolts fastened securely into the ceiling and walls, to each of which a chain was attached."[22]

Patty Cannon's responsibilities were twofold: running the tavern and caring for the kidnapped blacks while other gang members went in search of prey, and bribing local sheriffs, judges, and other officials. While the bribes were not recorded, her care of the fugitives in the attic was mentioned on more than one occasion. Robert B. Hazzard of Sussex County, Delaware (five years old at the time of Cannon's death), who remembered tales of the gang from his parents, gave a particularly detailed description. According to Hazzard, Joe Johnson sailed a schooner from Cannon's Ferry to Baltimore and "stole all the Negro men he could hire and induce to go as stevedores in the hold of the vessel, and . . . [would] quickly put on hatches, fasten them down, and sail for home and leave them in the care of Patty."

Hazzard's father explained, "One of the men Joe Johnson stole and brought from Baltimore was leg ironed and put in the loft or stairs of Patty Cannon's house. The room was over her cookroom and had a trapdoor. It was in February and on a bright and pleasant day she left the house and was out so long that he took the opportunity to get away. He lifted the door, let himself down, and fell upon the floor: got out and went to Seaford, ironed as he was." Hazzard's father came upon him, took him to his home, broke off the chains, healed his feet, and sent him back to Baltimore, Hazzard reported.[23]

Such remembrances would make Patty Cannon a more behind-the-scenes player in the kidnapping activities and would explain why those rescued rarely mentioned her. They talked frequently about Joe and Ebenezer Johnson and Jesse Cannon but almost never about Patty Cannon. She was better known for running the tavern. But local author Shannahan believed that "while Johnson was the working head of the gang, it was Patty's fertile brain which devised the many subtle schemes by which they worked."[24]

For dealers in general, justification for their activities, both legal and illegal, lay in the belief of the rightness of the institution of slavery, the notion that all blacks were basically slaves to begin with, and concern for the growing number of nonslave blacks. On the Eastern Shore, slaveholders eager to sell surplus slaves to a slave-hungry west added to the profit. It was a good time to be in the slave-dealing business.[25] And for nonslaveholding whites like the Cannons, it was one of the few lucrative areas of employment.

The area's large population of free blacks made them perfect candidates for abduction. Working alone in a field, traveling along a road, or any of a number of other activities could become occasions of capture. Children were the most vulnerable to being overpowered and taken away. Both children and adults were lured by false promises of jobs. Occasionally even romance was used as a pretext for kidnapping.[26]

A web of circumstances conspired against the free black population. Slave catchers hunting fugitives for slave-owning clients were required to produce little evidence, thereby encouraging the practice of kidnapping. If kidnapped at an early age, children could grow up never knowing they had been free. But even with the knowledge of their former free status, once in the South they had little recourse. One can only guess at the number of free blacks who were labeled fugitives. The result was a terrible practice that went unchecked.

Levina Johnson, though not rescued, sent a letter to her family providing details of her capture. "I was kidnapped by Jacob Purnal, Joseph Johnson & Ebenezer Johnson," she said, "at the Cross Roads the division of Maryland and Delaware. I am now in Augusta Georgia owned by John Filpot. I was brought to Georgia by the above named Johnson & Sold to Mr. Filpot, myself & two children." She wanted her family, particularly her husband and brothers to know where she was and wrote "I once was Free but now am a slave. I wish to inform you all that I am still striving to get to Heaven." The latter, no doubt, is a reference to her wish to escape.[27]

In going to work at the beginning of the nineteenth century, Patty Cannon joined a violent gang of thieves and murderers. Nothing is laudable or excusable about what they did to innocent people. That she participated in some of the more horrific gang activities seems a given, although in a more peripheral way than her husband and son-in-law. But what seemed to condemn her most of all was not her gang activities but her physical prowess.

She was nearly sixty when bones were found on her property in 1829. Many neighbors expressed surprise that she would have been involved in murderous activities. Still, the later villainy that attached to her always had more to do with gender violations (such as accusations of poisoning her husband, or killing babies, or seducing men and beating them up) than with her work (kidnapping free people and selling them into slavery).

Irrespective of her guilt, perhaps it was the belief that these deeds were done by a woman that threatened the constructed agency of slaveholders and the system itself. Owning slaves was about being successful, male, and strong. As historian Walter Johnson explained, young men "bought slaves to make themselves frugal, independent, socially acceptable, or even fully white." Parts of the ideological imperatives of that culture—"whiteness, rationality, honor and patriarchy"—were threatened by this other side.[28] Given all the goodness and responsibility that society associated with owning slaves, how else to understand Patty Cannon than as an evil "other," a mean and crazy gypsy woman who murdered innocents for no reason.

Anna Ella Carroll: Slaveholder and Political Operative

Anna Ella Carroll could have married. She did not. Instead, she invented the occupation of political pamphleteer-lobbyist, one that made use of her writing skills and her extensive reading, particularly in the law. It was a bold act, one ahead of her time and for which "women had no business."[29]

Politics was regarded as the privilege and responsibility of men in nineteenth-century America. After all, men voted, women did not. Women, not even permitted to speak in public, were expected to remain in the private sphere of home and family. Carroll never did that. Time after time she involved herself with politicians and campaigns: arranging meetings; writing letters, articles, and pamphlets; giving advice and counsel; working with lobbyists and businesspeople. Often she submitted her work with the expectation of payment; too often she waited in vain. But never did she think of herself as violating community norms.[30]

Carroll began her working career at age nineteen, starting a girls' school sometime around 1837. Girls' schools themselves were a relatively new phenomenon. Carroll's school on the Eastern Shore was very small. She taught history and geography and hired an assistant to teach French. Seeking employment became necessary because of her family's declining finances, a burden Carroll took up as the eldest child. Teaching was an acceptable occupation for one of her sphere in "embarrassed circumstances." What family resources were available went to educate her brother Tom, nine years her junior, who it was hoped would become a doctor.[31]

Carroll had to close her school when economic panic settled in the region and prevented parents from paying even the modest fees for their children's education. The panic also brought the collapse of Kingston Hall. Thomas King Carroll was able to arrange sale of home and many of its slaves to a neighbor, and the family moved to Warwick Manor on the Choptank. He was forty-seven at the time and sought a lucrative political appointment to supplement his remaining income.[32]

With her father's consent, Carroll decided to move to Baltimore, a city of over 100,000 people, to seek economic advancement. Of course, marriage would have been the surest route to success but Carroll's involvement with men already married seemed to get in the way. Employment opportunities for women were few and further restraints were placed on a single woman without means. In Carroll's case, her father put her under the care of his friend Reverend Robert Breckenridge, of the Kentucky Breckenridge family, pastor of a Presbyterian church in the city. Breckenridge provided protection, support, and counsel for Carroll in her father's absence. Breckenridge apparently held great influence over Anne as his two crusades (colonization of slaves and anti-Papist teachings) became her ardent concerns as well.[33]

According to Sidney and Marjorie Greenbie, Thomas King Carroll had a second requirement for his daughter: a safe and respectable place to live. Anne needed to find a boarding house run by a lady of similar social background who, in turn, was very selective of her tenants. Breckenridge recommended such a house, so Anne and her slave Leah, another of those protections, moved there.

Baltimore, one of the largest cities in the United States at that time, was home to the country's first railroad, the Baltimore and Ohio. Charles Carroll, last living signer of the Declaration of Independence and distant relation of Anna Ella, laid the cornerstone at its opening in 1828. The nascent railroad industry hired "scribblers" in lieu of public relations officers whose job was to copy articles and pamphlets for public distribution. Anne's first job in the industry was to do this writing for the rail companies. As she explained to the Greenbies, her work—done at her rooms, not in an office—was considered respectable employment because she "did not sully her skirts." Wearing a veil to hide her face, she would travel to a place of business, "give her name in a low voice," and be admitted into an inner office to receive her work. Anne made all of her connections through her father's influence and her distant relationship to the prominent Carroll family.[34]

Carroll's job skills improved over time and she became especially known for her ability to acquire information from diverse sources and to succinctly record it. With her income increasing, she persuaded her father to sell some of his slaves to her so that they would not be seized in any judgment against him. His still-weak financial situation left such sales a strategy of last resort. The plan was that the slaves would remain with him; Anna would pay $400 for each slave when she could afford it, and then free them as the law permitted. The arrangement was mostly a loan to her father with the slaves as collateral. It was a clever pact because it was less likely that the slaves would be seized in judgment against her— and neither she nor her father liked the alternative of selling the slaves outright. But the satisfaction of the debt still required resources.[35]

By 1843, Carroll was actively involved in the presidential candidacy of Kentucky senator Henry Clay, a good friend and close ally of Reverend Breckenridge. She considered Clay a mentor. An even closer relationship developed between Breckenridge and Carroll, both of whom worked on the Clay campaign and for the Whig Party. Carroll's family worried about the friendship because Breckenridge was a married man.[36] Clay lost the election in 1844 to James Polk by a few thousand votes, and many Whigs, including Carroll and Breckenridge, felt that voter fraud was the cause.[37] Carroll blamed future president James Buchanan of Pennsylvania for the loss because she believed Democrats used the immigrant vote to win the election. (Buchanan, a Democrat and political opportunist, was among the first to use that strategy.)

Perhaps out of concern for his daughter and her reputation as well as his financial situation, Thomas King Carroll accepted a post in Baltimore in 1845. He left some slaves at Warwick Manor to manage the land and moved his family to rented quarters. Robert Breckenridge left town very soon after. He accepted a position as president of Jefferson College in Pennsylvania and for the next twenty years had no contact with Anna, even when their paths occasionally crossed.[38]

Carroll still wrote for the railroads and worked a great deal for R. J. Walker, a friend of her father's who had also attended the University of Pennsylvania law school. After graduation Walker went to Mississippi and amassed an empire of slaves, plantations, and land. Walker was an early pioneer of the railroad industry, becoming president of the Atlantic and Western Railway. A Democrat who had freed his slaves in 1838, he was a friend and advisor to Carroll as well as her employer. The Greenbies suspect it was Walker who advised her on the plan to buy her father's slaves.[39]

Walker became secretary of the treasury in Polk's cabinet. As a member of the administration, Walker and his wife entertained often and Carroll was on many of their guest lists. It was at their home that she met his young protégé from Mississippi, Representative Jefferson Davis, and Buchanan, who had become secretary of state.[40]

Carroll now lived in Washington, at 347 Pennsylvania Avenue, the boardinghouse of the Misses Polk, Washington gentlewomen with wide political acquaintances particularly among the Whigs. Their brother Joseph worked in the Treasury Department. She was in her thirties and in addition to writing took on an informal role as confidential secretary and hostess for many leading political figures, all friends of her father. The first was said to be Thomas Corwin, a Whig senator and a married man from Lebanon, Ohio, whose family remained behind. Corwin was in his fifties, attractive, charming, and deeply devoted to his wife and family. According to the Greenbies, Carroll served as an escort, hostess, and keeper of his calendar. If Corwin could not be found, people contacted Carroll.[41]

As Thomas Corwin's hostess, Carroll befriended Indiana congressman Caleb Smith (a friend of Corwin's), and Virginia congressman John Minor Botts, both of whom became useful allies. At the same time she somehow managed to maintain her friendship and employment with R. J. Walker. Walker would later become disenchanted with Davis, who was pushing for secession if expansion was not allowed, a position with which Walker did not agree. Carroll's apparently successful insertion of herself into this political jumble was admired.

In May 1846 a national crisis emerged in the form of a war with Mexico. At the center of the crisis was the hope of southern Democrats like Jefferson Davis for the expansion of slavery into newly settled western territory and the fear of the Whigs like Thomas Corwin that they would succeed.[42]

Both Corwin and Henry Clay were angry at the Whig Party's selection of "war-hero" Taylor and thought Winfield Scott was the better candidate. As a compromise, they helped select Millard Fillmore of Buffalo, New York, as the vice presidential candidate. At Whig Party gatherings at Corwin's, Carroll met not only Fillmore, whom she greatly admired, but William Seward and Thurlow Weed as well.[43]

Carroll used all of her political connections at this time to seek employment for both herself and her father. It was not an easy task because Anne, an unmarried woman in her midthirties, had befriended a host of married men. Rumors about her romantic connections began to circulate in Washington and some men, married ones in particular, began to keep their distance.

Carroll was forced to become more strident on her own behalf. No longer content to merely play the roles of copyist and witty and charming social ornament, she began pushing her own ideas and causes and signing her name to some of her written work. In 1849 she worked for Cornelius Garrison, a rival of Cornelius Vanderbilt, who was trying to build a railroad or canal to Nicaragua. Her duties included researching the land and the people and collecting and reproducing area maps. Garrison, though a colleague of Walker, was no match for the powerful and sometimes ruthless Vanderbilt. Records of Anne's compensation do not survive—but obviously unsuccessful lobbyists were not well paid.[44] Through his connections with Corwin and John Clayton of Delaware, Thomas King Carroll was appointed naval officer at the port of Baltimore. Now a widower, he moved into a house at 95 North Charles Street, Baltimore, with Carroll. When Corwin was appointed secretary of the treasury, Carroll joined an inner circle of the president. The Greenbies suggested that her earnings were excellent from her publications and that her father's salary added to their comfort. Carroll's correspondence at the time suggested something a little more precarious.[45] In 1852 Corwin worked hard to resurrect the candidacy of Winfield Scott. It was an uphill battle because the Whig party was losing strength and Scott was considered by many to be out of touch. But Corwin succeeded and Scott became the Whigs' standard bearer but lost the election to Franklin Pierce, a somewhat ineffective New England "intellectual" put up by the Democrats. With Scott's defeat Corwin returned to Ohio, Thomas King Carroll lost his job as naval officer, and Carroll's access to the highest political circles all but evaporated.[46]

Though still writing, Carroll also went north to raise money to pay off some of her father's debt. He continued to live incautiously by borrowing against his human collateral, and Carroll feared that scandal would attach to his excesses. In pressing for money, she wrote to many friends and acquaintances, hoping to draw sympathetic responses. On one occasion she wrote to William Seward, laying out all of her father's failures. Seward sent no money and she later apologized to him for her impertinence.[47]

By 1854 Carroll paid some of the debts and their financial situation improved. Her father found employment with the Merchant Fire and Marine Insurance Company of Baltimore and they moved to a house on Waverly Place. Carroll told friends that she worried about the vulnerability of the slaves she still owned and began a campaign to buy their freedom.[48]

Because of their friendship with her father and her connections to Walker, Democrats made overtures to both Carrolls. At this time, Jefferson Davis was promoting the Pacific railroad, and persuaded President Pierce to include a section of southern Arizona in the survey that became the Gadsden Purchase. At government expense, Davis commissioned a ten-volume report on the Southwest and hired a number of researchers including Carroll.[49]

Carroll also became vocal about what she considered undue Catholic influence in the navy. In making her case she claimed proof of a conspiracy among some of the board members Pierce appointed to investigate the navy. Their true purpose, evidenced by their Catholic backgrounds, she wrote, was "to destroy the Navy, not make it more efficient." This very public and unsubstantiated expression of anti-Catholicism set the stage for her next commission.[50]

A wing of the American Party took notice of Carroll and asked her to undertake the project of defending "native" interests by promoting candidates for office to oppose those having wealthy backers who "used immigrants to stuff the ballot boxes." It was her largest project yet, and Carroll threw herself into this cause with much enthusiasm. In 1856, she published a political tract called *The Great American Battle*, having as its premise that the Roman Catholic Church intended "to unsettle the principles of our liberty and hence to destroy them." The work was divided into three sections. The first outlined the evils of the Church. The second adopted the literary devise of a garden tea party attended by "America," his mother, and their friends, and warned of the dangers awaiting him in a world of "timid, servile serpents" of the pope. The third section presented the American Party's stance on all of the major issues of the day.[51]

There is no question that Carroll expressed her own anti-Catholic views, which were mostly compatible with those of the Know-Nothing faction of the American Party. However, she made a point of distinguishing between native Catholics, who were not evil in her view, and foreign Catholics who were—a point that others disagreed with. She did not take on this project just for the money—but the money helped. Published in March, the tract had sold 10,000 copies by May. Carroll was delighted.[52]

What was not as clear was her view on women's issues. Carroll began her work by apologizing for intruding into the masculine world of politics and protesting her innocence of intent. Having stayed there for nearly twenty years, this disclaimer was at best a sham. "I have no affiliations with any principles which place [woman] in a sphere at variance with that refined delicacy to which she is assigned by nature," she wrote. Her lapse into the popular rhetoric of Republican motherhood, "women's province was the education of children and men," and "mothers as transmitters of cultural identities and values, may be said to control the destinies of ages yet unborn!" seemed artificial. Her comment on the moral superiority of women, which she compared to the "blundering and quarrelling of men," seemed closer to her true self, but whether there was a true Anna Ella Carroll remains a subject of some debate.[53]

Harriet Tubman and the World of Work

Harriet Tubman worked all her life. She was never a lady of leisure, never, in fact, considered a lady. Her work history, like that of many black laborers on the Eastern Shore, involved not working in the fields but being "hired out," working for someone not her owner, having the ability to keep some of what she earned in the contract. Her wage labor, such as it was, began after the Civil War. It was only then that she was able to keep all the money that she earned. For all of the discussion of Tubman's strength and work outdoors before the war, there is little evidence that she did such work afterwards. Instead, she seemed able to hire herself out only as a day laborer, cooking and cleaning for someone else. Ironically, as historian Jean Humez observed, it was her influential white friends who most "deplored the tyranny of putting a woman to out door drudgery." As her first biographer, Franklin Sanborn, noted, she "drove oxen, carted, plowed, and did all the work of a man." Tubman "could lift huge barrels of produce and draw a loaded stone boat like an ox."[54]

At slavery's end few sources of paid labor were open to African American women, though their contributions to household income were critical. Those who stayed on the farm continued to work much as they had in the past, growing crops, preparing food, and tending to livestock—surviving as best they could. A relatively small percentage of them attended school and assumed revered occupations in the community, those of teaching and nursing. The rest became domestics—the despised occupation of a despised population, DuBois called it. The boundaries among these occupations were not always fixed: farm wives were often called on to do domestic service; the line between domestic service and nursing service was sometimes vague; and teachers, whose salaries were never high, supplemented their earnings however they could.[55]

In early 1865 Tubman was still in Washington, in war mode, trying to decide whether to help form a black army, a plan proposed to Lincoln by black abolitionist Martin Delaney, or continue in nursing services. Records suggest that Tubman met with Delaney in March in Charlestown, South Carolina, where he set up a recruitment office, but the exact nature of their discussions is not known.[56]

Soon after, Tubman returned to Washington en route to New York. She also stopped in Philadelphia, headquarters of the U.S. Sanitary Commission. As a result of this visit she was persuaded to go to the James River Hospital in Virginia where there was a pressing need for nursing services.[57] Tubman stayed in the area until July 1865, visiting influential friends in Washington in an attempt to get better resources for the facilities. While in Washington, she met her friend William Seward, who was recovering from an attempted assassination. Seward and David Hunter wrote letters on Tubman's behalf, and she expected that a position of "Nurse or Matron" would be offered her. When that did not happen, Tubman decided to return to Auburn and her ailing parents.[58]

Tubman's property in Auburn, purchased from Seward for $1,200, was on the outskirts of town and encompassed seven acres. "Seward gave Tubman a mortgage loan for the price of the property and charged quarterly interest." When Seward died in 1872 the purchase was not complete but his son Frederick continued to hold the mortgage. Upon her return, Tubman planted a garden and fruit trees and with her family's help lived off the land. "Rich Republican friends" and Auburn neighbors, including other members of her family who had settled there, also helped out by giving her food, money, and clothing.[59]

Whenever possible she worked as a domestic in the homes of friends. Martha Coffin Wright, sister of Lucretia Mott, lived in Auburn with her husband David, a lawyer, anti-slavery activist, and associate of William Seward. They had two married daughters: Ellen Wright Garrison, wife of William Lloyd Garrison Jr., and Eliza Wright Osborne, wife of David Munson Osborne, wealthy owner of a company that made automated farm harvesters. According to historian Jean Humez, Martha Wright's letters and diaries suggest a "web of economic exchange" between Tubman and her neighbors.[60]

> [August 31, 1868] Harriet came to see Ellen [Wright Garrison] and the babies, & brot them some fresh eggs—I engaged her late peas.

> [May 2, 1870] Harriet Tubman came to clean—Had her to help wash, & then she & Mary cleaned front parlor—Frank Round's man helped Lawrence shake carpet & Mary & Harriet got it down again in time for Mary & Lizzie to go to a wedding after tea was ready.

> [May 3, 1870] Had Harriet to clean round front door & entry steps & take nails out of front chamber carpet.

> [January 14, 1871] Saturday . . . Too muddy to go out—Harriet Tubman came & bro't hoop basket. Pd her 62 ½ c.

> [October 1872] Harriet Tubman came yesterday & got a large basket full of pears & Apples.[61]

Health problems plagued Tubman all of her life—she was said to have three or four seizures a day, seizures that made her appear to be asleep. Even if regular employment were available, she must have realized that the seizures would prevent her from taking it on.

At the same time, a number of people whom Earl Conrad called the "aged, maimed and impoverished of Harriet's color came to her door in need." Many, it may be assumed, thought the "greatest heroine of the age" had resources, or at least had more than they did. Generous of heart, Tubman did not turn them away, welcoming them and sharing whatever she had.[62]

Tubman was about fifty years old by this time and realized that she could not survive forever on the generosity of others, so she attempted to collect $1,800 from the government in back compensation owed her for war services. Sallie Holley reported to her friend Miss Putnam that "Harriet Tubman came Saturday (to Gerrit Smith's). She wants Mr. Smith to help her claim allowed against the Government. She had a letter from William H. Seward to Maj.-Gen. Hunter, dated 1865."[63] Tubman again enlisted the services of prominent military figures and politicians, but again her efforts were not successful.

Still active in political causes, she raised funds to establish and maintain freedom schools in the South. Embarrassed to ask for money for herself, she showed no compunction in begging for her causes. In fall 1867, Ellen Wright Garrison visited Auburn with her new baby. She called on Tubman but Tubman was not at home. Ellen's mother later wrote, "Harriet Tubman came on Wednesday to see you & the baby. She didn't hear of your call till the evening before, & was so disappointed that her eyes filled with tears. She never shed a tear in telling me of all her troubles."[64]

Tubman's financial situation continued to decline, so neighbor Sarah Bradford wrote a biography in 1868 and published it in 1869 to raise funds for Tubman. William Lloyd Garrison Jr. promoted the book in Boston circles, according to Martha Wright. It brought in about $1,200. Tubman used part of the money to pay some of her debt to Seward, although she continued to borrow money from him as was her practice. Seward and others then tried to get her a nurse's pension but again ran into problems with the military bureaucracy.

Tubman married for a second time in spring 1869.[65] Nelson Davis, who had served in South Carolina, was about twenty years her junior and ailing from tuberculosis. Described as tall and dark skinned, he was a brick maker by trade. While he was still healthy, Tubman and Davis attempted to start a business. Later, in testifying before Congress, Tubman said: "I never had any children nor child by the soldier nor by John Tubman."[66]

In 1873 she became involved in the "gold swindle," a scam she thought would help to fund a home and hospital for the sick and aged. (Tubman was always vocal in her outrage at the neglect of blacks and whites who fought for the country but died in poverty.) A bill for her claim for a nurse's pension was presented in Congress in 1874 by Representative Gerry Hazelton of Wisconsin, but again nothing happened. In early 1875, Tubman's periodic employer and friend Martha Wright died suddenly of what was called typhoid pneumonia.[67]

Numerous incidents recorded by locals in Auburn suggested the diminished state of Tubman's affairs. On one occasion she wandered agitatedly around a public market until tradesmen there noticed her distress and filled her baskets with food. On another occasion she borrowed $7 from an Auburn doctor, promising to pay him back. Then she borrowed $7 from Sarah Bradford to pay the doctor. Several people reported her activities as a peddler, going from house to house, selling produce that she and her visitors raised and baked.[68]

Tubman also gave talks in local churches and at organizational gatherings, speaking about her activities with the Underground Railroad and during the war. For these she was paid both in cash and in food and clothing. In the 1880s, she became involved in the women's rights movement through her friendships with Elizabeth Cady Stanton and Susan B. Anthony. These women also provided her with cash, food, and clothing.[69]

At the end of 1890 Tubman was awarded a pension of $8 per month as the widow of Nelson Davis, who died in 1888. In 1899 the amount increased to $20 per month to finally include some compensation for her nursing services. Still more active on behalf of others than herself, she bid on and received twenty-five acres of land adjoining her house in Auburn in 1896. What arrangements she made for payment and to whom are unclear. At that time Tubman was still pursuing her dream of building a home to be called the John Brown Home for the Aged and Indigent.[70]

Praise of Tubman was shared widely throughout the abolitionist community, but her bravery and sacrifices never translated into a comfortable retirement or old age. Tubman lived out her days after the war—days that actually numbered nearly half a century—in abject poverty. Perhaps at a low point, sometime in 1901 Sarah Bradford visited Tubman and reported to Franklin Sanborn, "I have been to see Harriet & found her in a deplorable condition, a pure wreck, [mind?] & body—& surrounded by a set of beggars who I fear fleece her of every thing sent her."[71]

In 1911 Tubman was interviewed by Elizabeth Smith Miller, the only daughter of Gerrit Smith, another of the second generation to look after "Aunt Harriet." Miller asked, "Do you really believe that women should vote?" Tubman replied, "I've suffered enough to believe it." She was referring to more than the right to vote.[72]

Wright family with
Lucretia Mott.
Courtesy of the Friends
Historical Library of
Swarthmore College.

Executive Committee of the Pennsylvania Anti-Slavery Society, ca. 1851.
Courtesy of the Friends Historical Library of Swarthmore College.

Mrs. Margaret Ellen Lucas and daughter Alice H. Courtesy of Conrad/Tubman Collection, Photographs and Prints Division, Schomburg Center for Research in Black Culture, The New York Public Library, Astor, Lenox and Tilden Foundations.

Left to right: Harriet Tubman; Gertie Davis (Tubman's adopted daughter); Nelson Davis (Tubman's husband); Lee Cheney; "Pop" Alexander; Walter Green; Sarah Parker ("Blind Auntie" Parker) and Dora Stewart (granddaughter of Tubman's brother, John Stewart). Courtesy of Harriet Tubman Portrait Collection, Photographs and Prints Division, Schomburg Center for Research in Black Culture, The New York Public Library, Astor, Lenox and Tilden Foundations.

Harriet Tubman. Courtesy of Harriet Tubman Portrait Collection, Photographs and Prints Division, Schomburg Center for Research in Black Culture, The New York Public Library, Astor, Lenox and Tilden Foundations.

Anna Ella Carroll. Courtesy of the Maryland Historical Society.

Frederick Douglass.
National Archives and
Records Administration,
Pictures of the Civil War,
Portraits, Abolitionists,
200-FL-22.

John Brown, ca. 1856.
National Archives and
Records Administration,
Pictures of the Civil War,
Portraits, Abolitionists,
111-SC-101021.

Millard Fillmore. Library
of Congress, Prints &
Photographs Division,
LC-DIG-cwpbh-00699.

William H. Seward,
Secretary of State.
National Archives and
Records Administration,
Pictures of the
Civil War, Portraits,
Government Officials,
111-B-4204.

Gerrit Smith. Library
of Congress Prints and
Photographs Division,
Brady-Handy Photograph
Collection, LC-DIG-
cwpbh-02632.

Franklin Benjamin
Sanborn. Courtesy of
the Concord Free Public
Library.

5 | Rules, Laws, and the Rule of Law

I should have done violence to my convictions of duty, had
I not made use of all the lawful means in my power to liberate those people, and assist them to become men and women,
rather than leave them in the condition of chattels personal.
—*Thomas Garrett, 1848*

Patty Cannon, Anna Ella Carroll, and Harriet Tubman were
all stakeholders in the ever-evolving decision-making process governing
rules, laws, and the rule of law about the institution of slavery and the
status of free blacks. Slavery, as Lawrence Friedman observed, "clearly
began as a kind of custom, a general understanding, before it was ever
formalized as 'law.'"[1]

The general understanding of slavery guided and shaped sentiment
on the Eastern Shore. As historian Philip Morgan argued, seventeenth-
century slavery in the Chesapeake Bay area was characterized by a mul-
tiracial work group, a flexible system that allowed some slaves to earn
money and even to buy their freedom, and a more pliable—though still
debased—status for blacks. By the end of the century, the ruling establishment introduced legislation with the intent, in Morgan's words, of
"fostering the contempt of whites for blacks." It included provisions such
as "no Christian white was to be whipped naked, for nakedness was appropriate only for blacks." The very need to formally specify differences
between servants and slaves, whites and blacks suggests the changing
constructions of that understanding.[2]

This incremental law was often inconsistent. At some point in their
lives, each of our Chesapeake women faced some contradictory part of that
law. Patty Cannon's fate rested on testimony of an eyewitness, who, had

he been a slave, could not have been heard in court. Anna Ella Carroll's wish to buy the freedom of her remaining slaves (rather than sell them to satisfy her father's debts) may have violated Maryland manumission law. Harriet Tubman, depending on the most logical interpretation of Athow Pattison's will, was a free woman at age forty-five and yet was sought as a fugitive because as a slave her legal rights were nonexistent.

The three Chesapeake women were hardly unusual in their confrontation with the inconsistencies of the peculiar institution. Still Cannon, Carroll, and Tubman stand out in the backstage, behind-the-scenes ways in which they challenged the rules they took issue with and dared anyone to question their right to do so.

As Antonio Gramsci has pointed out, a system of laws is a fundamental ingredient of social order and class rule. The key to ruling is the ability to contain antagonisms so that the system's legitimacy is not questioned. The great problem in the early republic was attaching some part of the system of law, a "stripped-down version" borrowed from England, to a more or less unified, functioning citizenry and nascent elite.[3]

The extent to which average citizens in the early republic followed the law may be the subject of some debate. There were federal laws, purposely few, and state laws, often contradictory, and then there was enforcement, often nonexistent. Andrew Jackson's mother's code, "Never tell a lie, nor take what is not your own, nor sue anybody for slander or assault and battery. Always settle them cases yourself," was perhaps the strongest standard.[4] Further complicating the situation was the fact that embedded in a national power system was a regional structure of southern slaveholders and a northern, nonslaveholding bourgeoisie. This produced, at best, a fragmented ruling class that struggled to come to power.

Slavery, an institution that many hoped would wither away over time, grew stronger and more entrenched in the 1790s. Since its codes predated the nation's founding, one of the first nation-building tasks was to incorporate those codes into the new government. Colonies-turned-states had a huge body of law regarding slaves, making the "institution clear, strong and permanent" even if not mentioned in the constitution.[5]

For this reason some looked upon slavery not only as a curse bequeathed to them by the British government but also as a social and political evil. Thomas Jefferson, for example, in a draft of the Declaration of Independence wrote a paragraph, later removed, indicting the king for keeping open the slave trade "against colonial efforts to close it."[6]

The former colonists worked hard at the daunting task "to create an independent republic" founded on a loose framework on which all could agree.[7] The quest for social cohesion, involving all forms of property, rights, and labor was a problem tackled not only by statesmen, politicians, and the rich, but also by ordinary citizens in the new republic. They took on the daily challenge of settling disputes and defining the public practice, ever mindful that "the yoke of law and government weighed but lightly."[8]

At a typical New England town meeting, rich and poor met to discuss and debate the minutia of public administration, but with a deep sense of individual entitlement. "Politics bulked larger to the average American," Eric Foner once wrote. Ordinary people often had strong ideas about the law and community mores. In many communities laws were viewed as a moral guide and an instrument for emergency use.[9] And entitlement did not always mean involvement—sometimes it was just the opposite. As sociologist William Cash explained, in the rural South there developed "an intense distrust of, and indeed, downright aversion to, any actual exercise of authority beyond the barest minimum essential to the existence of the social organism."[10]

The delegates to the Constitutional Convention set out for themselves the extraordinary task of building a nation and establishing a reasonable, idiosyncratic system of law and justice. This undertaking was particularly difficult given that they were newly separated from a "despotic" society whose legal code they had readily embraced. The law, they reasoned, must reflect what society thinks behavior ought to be. Their job, then, was to mold a system of law into this understanding. "The felt necessities of the time," Oliver Wendell Holmes would later explain about the life of a law, "the prevalent moral and political theories, institutions of public policy, avowed or unconscious, have a good deal more to do than the syllogism in determining the rules by which men should be governed."[11]

Slavery was the sticking point. Many of our Founding Fathers were slave owners and, as such, knew that the evil could not be eliminated by some legal sleight of hand. "People who opposed slavery were deviants," Lawrence Friedman pointed out.[12] George Washington hoped they would devise a plan "by which slavery may be abolished by slow, sure and imperceptible degrees."[13] After all, slaves were property and property was a sacred right and not to be removed by any government.[14]

At the federal level, the pro-slavery faction held enough power in Congress to impede any anti-slavery legislation. They consistently voted down anti-slavery proposals. And perhaps as consistently, though not as successfully, "abolitionists sought to impair the effectiveness of slavery through congressional action."[15]

The slavery question involved a host of interested parties: apologists, abolitionists, religious zealots, slave owners, nonowners, slaves, and free blacks. "I have seen Slavery in this Country," John Adams wrote to Thomas Jefferson in 1821, "hanging over it like a black cloud for half a century."[16]

In 1787 the framers of the Constitution articulated, with much debate and struggle, a clear mission for the new nation. By their admission it was an imperfect document. In an attached letter, George Washington, president of the convention, citing the "consolidation of our Union" as its primary purpose, wrote, "This important consideration, seriously and deeply impressed on our minds, led each State in the convention to be less rigid on points of inferior magnitude, than might have been otherwise expected."[17]

Slavery, if not to all an issue of "inferior magnitude," was an issue on which the framers could not reach "amity," and therefore, for the sake of the Union, agreed not to take on. Ending the international slave trade twenty years hence was their strongest position. It was the cost of keeping southern states in the Union. As to slavery itself, some thought it should be abolished immediately, others that it would disappear within the next twenty years, and still others that slaves were property, not the business of the Union.

The U.S. Constitution was ratified in 1788. It contained three provisions dealing with slavery, although the word itself was never used. The first involved the method of counting the population for House districts "by adding to the whole Number of free Persons, including . . . three fifths of all other Persons."[18] The second guaranteed continuing the international slave trade until twenty years hence (1808). The third mandated the return of fugitive slaves who escaped across state lines. Evidently some of the radicalism of the revolutionary period was beginning to wane as politicians and the public set about figuring out how to run a country. Elbridge Gerry of Massachusetts, both a signer of the Declaration of Independence and drafter of the Constitution, expressed a common view in stating that he "thought we had nothing to do with the conduct of states as to slaves, but ought to be careful not to give any sanction to it."[19]

The three provisions were a small arena of authority, consistent with Gerry's views, but only stopgap measures that would have to be altered over time. The Constitution did not specify "the rights of slaves, the conditions of servitude or even the responsibility of slave owners to treat their slaves humanely." All of these matters were left to the states, the courts, the local governments, and community consent.[20]

By 1789 all of the slave states enacted laws prohibiting the importation of foreign slaves, their one agreed-upon compromise. But records suggest slave importations reached an all-time high between 1790 and 1808, an indication of the effectiveness of the laws. At the same time, their passage may have reflected the belief of many slaveholders that further importations were not necessary or in their best economic interests.[21]

In May 1790 Congress passed an act governing the territory southwest of the Ohio River. The land, roughly encompassing what is now Tennessee, was to be considered one district, the inhabitants of which should enjoy all the privileges, benefits, and advantages set forth in the Ordinance of 1787 except that no regulations "made or to be made by Congress shall tend to emancipate slaves." Three years before, Congress banned slavery in that territory. So, over the span of three years, the government first banned slavery in the Northwest, then legitimized it in the Constitution, and then implied that Congress had no power at all over issue in the new territory. It was far from clear who had the right to establish or abolish slavery in the new territories. Gerry's view—that Congress should have nothing to do with the conduct of states as to slaves, but ought to be careful not to give any sanction to it—was the closest thing the nation had to a standard.[22]

When Jefferson signed the Embargo Act on March 3, 1807, which effectively ended the external slave trade, he did so with very little fanfare. Ending the international trade did not undermine the institution of slavery as some had hoped but rather reaffirmed its legitimacy. The act addressed the brutality of the slave trade, but not the inhumanity of the institution. It did not ban domestic sales of slaves between the states nor did it attempt to regulate conditions of sales.[23]

Within this legal tangle we find Patty Cannon. She ran a tavern in an isolated area of the Eastern Shore and participated in a slave-trading and free-black-kidnapping business. Cannon's thirty-plus-year career, which involved numerous instances of the illegal act of kidnapping, was protected by three things. She never knowingly stole slaves (an act potentially punishable by death); the local community had little sympathy for crimes committed against free blacks; and she provided a service (in the grand and secret Southern style) for slaveholders wanting to dispense with unwanted slaves without bringing their financial embarrassment to public attention or scrutiny.

Compared to Tubman and Carroll, Cannon's offense was relatively minor. Retrieving runaway slaves was of particular concern to slaveholders. Estimates of the cost of runaway slaves varied. States of the Deep South lost fewer slaves to the North than did the border states of Maryland, Virginia, and Kentucky. Virginia legislators placed their losses at $100,000 per year, Maryland at $80,000, and Kentucky at $30,000.[24]

Most slaveholders relied on the goodwill of those in free states to give back what had been lost. This likely occurred in many instances.

Slave owners derived support from Article IV of the U.S. Constitution, which spelled out ownership rights: "No Person held to Service or Labour in one State, under the Laws thereof, escaping into another, shall, in Consequence of any Law or Regulation therein, be discharged from such Service or Labour, but shall be delivered up on Claim of the Party to whom such Service or Labour may be due."[25]

Slave owners wanted something more definitive, something that would designate who was responsible for capturing and intervening if the property was not surrendered. In 1793 Congress enacted the Fugitive Slave Law, something less than slave owners had hoped for. The law in large part dealt with fugitives from justice and designated the reciprocities between states for the capture of criminals. The last two sections of the law laid out, somewhat by accident, the standards for fugitive slave capture. They allowed a slave owner to apply to a district circuit judge for a certificate enabling the owner to return his slave to the state from which the slave fled.[26]

The logistics of capturing and presenting a fugitive to a district judge made the exercise worthwhile only in the case of valuable slaves—healthy men and childbearing women. Pursuit of others was much less likely. Under the law, slave owners bore the costs of capture and transport. Naturally, slave owners could and did bypass the cumbersome process whenever they could.

Some states had only one district judge, making compliance all the more difficult. In communities sympathetic to slaveholders, individuals aided in recaptures, often with compensation. Slave owners complained, however, that individuals in communities unsympathetic to recapture were their biggest obstacle. "Southerners were convinced that one of the principal causes of the fugitive slave problem was the activities of abolitionists in the North."[27]

On the other hand, because of the vagueness of the statute, abolitionists feared for the safety of free Negroes living in their communities. Who would decide the value of the claim? Would the testimony of a free black be sufficient? According to Carol Wilson, "It was common in some parts of the country for kidnapping to be practiced openly, without interference from authorities or from neighbors who feared retribution if they spoke out."[28]

The criminality, then, of kidnapping free blacks was on very shaky ground and devolved as much on their status as on the act itself. There had been almost no debate about the issue of the rights of free blacks in the various constitutional conventions. Free blacks were disliked generally. Ben Wade, friend of Anna Ella Carroll, once commented that "free Negroes were despised by all, repudiated by all, outcasts upon the face of the earth, without any fault of theirs that I know of."[29]

"Kidnapping was, of course, a crime under the laws of the states generally: but in view of the seeming ease of its accomplishment and the potential value of the victims it may well be thought remarkable that so many thousands of free negroes were able to keep their liberty."[30] Most states did have laws banning the sale of free blacks. But the consequences for kidnapping and selling slaves were much harsher—upon conviction, the penalty was death. And while the conviction rate for kidnapping free blacks was miniscule, Southern jails were filled with those convicted of stealing slaves. Historian Ulrich Phillips suggested that "in the penitentiary lists of the several states the designation of slave stealers was fairly frequent, in spite of the fact that the death penalty was generally prescribed for the crime."[31]

Early on, Northern nonslaveholding states had variously introduced restrictions on free blacks voting and holding office, on marriage and inmigration from other states, and even on their right of assembly. Their jobs were at the bottom of the postrevolutionary economy and their vulnerability, due to lack of legal recourse, was very high.

In 1796, Congress debated the issue of kidnapping of free blacks by slave catchers and resolved that the issue was best left to the states to decide individually. In 1801 Congress nearly passed a law that would have required any employer in the United States to publish in two newspapers a description of black employees so that their free status could be ascertained. By 1817 there was greater concern about fugitives, so Congress passed a law directing the seizure of blacks suspected of being fugitives and ordering their removal to the state granting the warrant for their arrest.[32]

By 1820 the struggle for power between the pro-slavery South and the free-labor North expanded into the debate about the "question of imposing boundaries on the extension of slavery."[33] The legality of the anti-slavery ban of the Northwest Ordinance was in question.[34] Few cared for the Missouri Compromise—the North disliked it because of the extension of slavery into Missouri, the South because slavery was banned in much of the territory of the Louisiana Purchase. Between 1820 and 1850 debate and dissention continued over the expansion of slavery in new territories, with Southern delegations several times threatening to secede .

• • •

While the extent of Patty Cannon's crime, the kidnapping of free blacks, could be the subject of some debate, Harriet Tubman's crimes were not. She broke more laws than the average hardened criminal, stealing slaves in a guerilla operation that lasted over ten years. Penalties for such crimes were severe, and community aid in capturing fugitives and those who helped them grew over time. Even greater than the fact that Tubman ran away, or that she freed many members of her family, was that as a freed black, she was believed guilty of stirring up the slave population. For this offense, apparently, a price was placed on her head.

By 1850, unlike 1793, the South was clamoring for protection for slaveholders who went into free territory in search of their fugitives. They were convinced that abolitionists in the North—and not their happy slaves—were responsible for the fugitive slave problem and wanted an effective, stringent, and enforceable law. In all of the measures agreed upon in the Compromise, the fugitive slave provisions were the only bone given to the South. It was a large bone that gave powers to slave owners, support from federal marshals, and penalties for those caught aiding and abetting fugitives. The law permitted slaveholders to pursue fugitives into free states and capture and return them without due process of law.[35]

Some debate about the law centered on the question of free blacks and that hearings before a fugitive slave commission were summary in nature and evidence of ownership was ex parte. Thus, it was argued, free blacks could be remanded into slavery. This provision bothered President Millard Fillmore who, upon signing the law, asked Attorney General John Crittenden whether it was constitutional. Crittenden opined that it was because states had the right to protect the personal liberty of free persons within their jurisdictions. With this assurance, Fillmore instructed his administration to uphold the law.[36]

The 1850 Fugitive Slave Law had a particular effect on Harriet Tubman. It made her and any people she rescued unsafe in the United States; anyone in the Underground Railroad network who was not a fugitive was also likely subject to penalty. Thomas Garrett, her longtime friend and supporter, was convicted in 1848 of aiding in a slave rescue and initially fined $5,400, a sum that would have forced him to sell all his possessions.[37] He was forced out of his business as a result. But at his second sentencing when the judge asked whether he had learned not to interfere with the cause of justice, Garrett replied that any fugitive needing help should come to him.[38] After the passage of the law, penalties became even more severe.

It is difficult to know how much Tubman knew about current events. Obviously some of her stories, all recorded by amanuenses, were embellished. But slaves also participated in a complex communication network that made them better informed in some cases than their owners. Tubman, for example, told Sara Bradford that they discussed the Nat Turner rebellion on the Eastern Shore shortly after it occurred. In an interview in 1865 she appeared to be making a joke about the Dred Scott decision. "They say the Negro has no rights a white man is bound to respect," she said, "but it seems to me they send men to Congress, and pay them eight dollars a day, for nothing else but to talk about the Negro."[39]

In her later edition of Tubman's biography, Bradford interviewed Oliver Johnson of the New York Anti-Slavery Society, who recalled meeting Tubman and Josiah Bailey. "'Well, Joe,' he said, 'I am glad to see the man who is worth $2,000 to his master.'" Panicked, Joe asked how Johnson knew him. "'Here is the advertisement in our office and the description is so close that no one could mistake it.'" This referred to a provision of the 1850 law with which both men were familiar. "After that," she told Bradford, "I wouldn't trust Uncle Sam wid my people no longer, but I brought 'em all clar off to Canada."[40]

Still, whether out of litigiousness or spite or some combination of the two, enforcement was not easy. To legally recover a runaway slave, the owner had to go to a court of record in his own state and establish that his slave had escaped and that the slave owed service or labor to the claimant. The owner also had to provide a general description of the fugitive. This part was relatively simple though time consuming. If the judge of the local court was satisfied with the evidence, a record was made of the proceedings, and an official transcript was given to the claimant. The claimant or his agent had to take the transcript to a fugitive slave commissioner in the district where the fugitive slave could be found. The commissioner, after verifying the documentation, would then issue a warrant to a federal marshal for the arrest of the fugitive. Once arrested, the fugitive was brought before the commissioner who had only to ascertain whether the prisoner was the person described in the transcript. If convinced, the commissioner was required to issue a certificate authorizing the removal of the fugitive back to the state from which he had escaped. If the slave owner believed there would be trouble, he was given protection at federal expense.[41]

The protracted nature of these proceedings was a problem. Slave owners could incur expenses at each level, making the return of slaves possibly more expensive than their original cost. Much of the burden of the process fell on slave owners and, although they complained about weak federal enforcement, the sparse records suggest that the real problem was not enforcement but that most slave owners chose not to pursue it. Rough estimates indicate that some 8,000 to 15,000 slaves escaped between 1850 (when the law was established) and 1860. During this time approximately 191 fugitive slave cases were heard before federal tribunals. Most of these (157 out of 191) were successful, that is, the fugitives were returned to their owners; only 11 involved mistaken arrests.[42]

Compared to the number of slaves who fled, the number returned was very small. The law was not very effective. It seems probable that

owners, unwilling to go through the expense and the delay of the formal proceedings, retrieved fugitives outside the law. And border communities filled with Southern migrants would be more likely to allow
the owners to retrieve their property informally. Numbers of informally
returned slaves were not counted but they were assumed to be fewer
than those who fled. The failure of the Fugitive Slave Law was one of
the grievances sited by the Confederacy in 1861.[43] Some Northern states
did adopt personal liberty laws to protect their free black populations,
as Crittenden indicated they could. Connecticut, Massachusetts, Rhode
Island, Vermont, Ohio, Michigan, and Wisconsin all had such laws hoping to discourage slave owners from entering their states and kidnapping
free blacks. These laws, while in some cases providing legal counsel for
those seized, did not challenge the federal authority in these matters and
over time there was little resistance to actual seizures. Public opinion in
the North seemed to distinguish between the institution of slavery, an
evil, and obedience to enforcement of the law. Better enforcement than
disunion, it was said.[44]

• • •

Anna Ella Carroll paid off her father's debts not by selling his remaining slaves but by freeing them. She also took it upon herself to advise
President Lincoln on matters of emancipation, compensation, and colonization of former slaves and free blacks. At the time, women were
supposed to guide husbands, sons, and daughters—not make policy—as
historian Linda Kerber pointed out.[45] Yet Carroll attempted to explain
constitutional law to the Republican Party and the president. And still
later she tried to be publicly recognized and paid for it.

Like those in the rest of the Chesapeake, Maryland's manumission
laws changed over time. In 1790 slaveholders were free to manumit by
will any adult slave over age forty-five. Manumission by deed was legal
even before that. Egalitarian ideals in the years following the Revolution
offer one explanation for the change. Thousands were released from bondage during that time. "Whole families," recalled a Maryland abolitionist,
"were often liberated by a single verdict, the fate of one relative deciding
the fate of many."[46]

But after 1800 manumissions declined sharply. By 1806, in both Maryland and Virginia all blacks were required to leave the state a year after
being freed or face reenslavement. By 1850 Maryland and all Southern
states prohibited manumission altogether. Hostile judges rejected liberal
interpretations of manumission law from earlier eras and essentially made
manumission a judicial prerogative. Lawyers, sensitive to public hostility,
declined participation even where slave clients had good cases.[47]

As historian Ira Berlin pointed out, "Harsh laws, judicial obstructions, and hostile public opinion slowed the rate of manumission," but they could not stop a master intent on freeing his slaves. "With all the restrictions which legislation has imposed on manumission," a Baltimore politician observed, "it may be taken for certain that they will go on." Though not alone in her actions, Carroll was clearly circumventing the law.[48]

In addition to manumission, Carroll devoted herself to related areas of legal wrangling—that of compensated emancipation and colonization—subjects about which women typically did not claim expertise. "Delicacy and propriety," historian Drew Faust wrote, "enjoined ladies from speaking in public, from signing their names in print, and even permitting their names to be mentioned in the public press."[49] Once again, Anna Ella Carroll broke the rules.

The colonization movement developed in the midst of early-nineteenth-century debates about slavery, fugitives, and the incorporation of free blacks into society. The American Colonization Society was founded in 1816 with the object of sending freed people to Africa. Ironically, one of its major centers was Philadelphia, home of many abolitionists and free blacks and a city called the "cradle of liberty."

But the society had an ethical stance. Henry Clay would later observe, "There is a moral fitness in the idea of returning to Africa her children, whose ancestors have been torn from her by the ruthless hand of fraud and violence."[50] The colony of Liberia, on the west coast of Africa, was chosen as a favorable site. Favorable to whom was one of those questions answered by feet. By 1830 only 1,162 Negroes had been sent to Liberia.[51]

One premise, perhaps the major premise of the colonization movement, was that free blacks could never advance in American society. As James Madison observed, "The repugnance of the whites to their continuance among them is founded on prejudices, themselves founded on physical distinctions, which are not likely soon, if ever, to be eradicated."[52]

The early colonization movement focused on repatriation to Africa with the goal of not only solving the race problem but "fulfilling a great religious end. American Negroes would serve as Christian missionaries bringing the gospel to the Dark Continent."[53] A small group of African Americans established the colony in Liberia. But larger numbers of both free blacks and black and white abolitionists opposed the colonization plans, viewing them as a cynical attempt to strengthen slavery by removing free blacks.

The unwillingness of free and freed blacks to voluntarily go to Africa in large numbers put a damper on the movement but not on belief in the soundness of the principles of colonization. The movement was revitalized in the 1850s by the location of new territory in Central America. It was hardly accidental. Central America was "a hot bed of international conflict, with the United States and Britain vying for dominance."[54] Francis Blair, one of the leaders of the new movement, declared at one point, "Central America would in fact, become our India."[55]

The pro-slavery wing of Congress, not to be left out of the debate, saw Central America as a new site for the expansion of slavery. This position was scorned by many who favored colonization. The idea of Blair and his group was to create a free black power, a colony that would trade freely with the United States, "but subject to our influence."[56] Emancipation with compensation was a central part of the plan, thereby removing from the South the fear that "abolition meant Negro equality." Frank Blair (Francis's son) said, "The idea of liberating the slaves and allowing them to remain in the country, is one that never will be tolerated."[57]

The year 1862 became pivotal in these debates as many of the separate parts converged into a chaotic storm cloud. Beginning in August 1861 a certain number of slaves were liberated by the Confiscation Act, and President Lincoln in December called attention to the problems this act created. The ex-slaves, he said, depended on the government and had to be provided for in some way. He proposed removing them to "some place, or places in climate congenial to them." "To carry out the plan of colonization may involve the acquiring of territory, and also the appropriation of money beyond that to be expended in the territorial acquisition. Having practiced the acquisition of territory for nearly sixty years, the question of constitutional power to do so is no longer open to us."[58]

The proposal to acquire territory advanced the matter into a diplomatic arena and called for the involvement of Secretary of State William Seward. Seward sought international approval and instructed his "ministers to ascertain the views of the governments near which they served, and to inform him of the results."[59] Great Britain, France, Holland, and Denmark, all of whom had interests in Central America, expressed no interest, fearing they would be drawn into the war. Central American republics, hearing of the proposals, raised concerns about accepting waves of black immigrants. Colonization plans, barely formed, were already being squashed.

And the issue of colonization did not head Lincoln's list of priorities. The Army of the Potomac, headed by General George McClellan, experienced several humiliating defeats at the hands of a smaller, less-well-armed Confederacy. Lincoln constantly sent notes to McClellan complaining of his "over-cautiousness."[60] At each battle, streams of contraband (slaves) attempted to surrender to the Union troops. Without an official policy some generals emancipated them, some sent them back.

Lincoln spent much time in 1861 and 1862 rescinding the more radical of these orders. But the contraband kept coming. Some cabinet members began demanding more concerted efforts, including McClellan's removal; radical members of Congress demanded the emancipation of slaves. Colonization schemes arose as a kind of magic cure-all. But true to American political tradition, there was not one plan but many; not a single set of proponents but many.

Newspaper campaigns (a favorite strategy of Anna Ella Carroll) began championing the cause of colonization and promoting, in some cases, the idea of Negro superiority. The *Albany Evening Journal* wrote, for example, "The American Negro was a race vastly superior, physically and in intellect, to the dwarfed and imbecile natives of Latin America." Some believed that black ability attached to climate. Senator James R. Doolittle of Wisconsin believed that "only the blacks could establish American influence in the tropics, because in that climate, the white race is doomed."[61]

Such puffery did not mask the fact that money could be made in "Negro Colonization." Lincoln authorized Seward to ascertain which foreign powers having territory within the tropics would welcome immigration. The administration received a number of propositions with varying levels of state approval; Lincoln seriously considered three of them.

The first would establish a colony in the harbor of Chiriqui in the northeastern part of Panama. The plan appeared favorable not only because of soil, climate, and location but because of a report of rich coal fields. Senator Samuel Pomeroy, a close friend of Salmon P. Chase, was a major backer of the plan.

The second would establish a colony on the island of Île à Vache in Haiti. The site was described as beautiful, healthy, fertile, and encompassing about one hundred square miles. Sugar, coffee, cotton, and indigo were indigenous. The plan called for the colonization of 5,000 blacks who would be furnished with comfortable homes, churches, schools, and jobs for the fee of $50 per head.

Anna Ella Carroll supported the third plan, which called for gradual emancipation, federal compensation to slaveholders, and voluntary colonization. She wrote in the *New York Times* on March 6, 1862, "Hundreds of thousands of this unfortunate people, and among them many of the most advanced intelligence, can now be colonized and made free and independent, without any settlement beyond the limit of our own territory. This can be done now." On April 15 she received a note from Attorney General Edward Bates suggesting that Lincoln was impressed with her ideas, having mentioned them in a cabinet meeting. Carroll, who had been working as a lobbyist for Aaron Columbus Burr, a New York merchant and agent of a British Honduran landowner, was pressing for the purchase of land there. She said the land was close to the United States, and had direct trading tracks by the sea, fertile soil, a tropical climate, and a friendly government. British Honduras wanted colonists, she claimed. It represented "a way for the United States to remove the colored race and make them useful to themselves."[62]

Learning that other sites were under consideration, Carroll wrote to Lincoln on May 19 to press her claim and disparage the others. Transportation costs to Liberia were too costly to be borne by our government, she said. Also, "experience has demonstrated the opposition of the negroes to leave this country for Africa; and this is so strong, that it is not probable, a large number could ever be induced to go there, without, compulsion. Haiti was just as objectionable. The island was too small to accommodate a black population now numbering over four million. A few would succeed but not enough to be worth the cost and effort. British Honduras was the answer."[63]

Although records of their meetings are few, it is likely that Lincoln and Carroll had face-to-face interactions as well as correspondence. Carroll expressed strong objections to the president about his proposal to abolish slavery in the District of Columbia. Lincoln signed the bill in July 1862. Carroll also expressed strong warnings about the Second Confiscation bill, raising concerns about the taking of property and emancipation. Lincoln, too, worried about the taking of property but not about emancipation. Again he signed it. In late July he circulated a draft of the Emancipation Proclamation to his cabinet but put off any further action.[64]

At that time, the Army of Northern Virginia was moving toward Washington, a city in chaos, and Carroll worked feverishly to have a plan in place should the Union be victorious. Lincoln favored, she thought, the coupling of emancipation with colonization. In late August Carroll was still convinced her plan held the edge.

In August Lincoln also met with a delegation of African American leaders, expressing his support for the concept of colonization and of a site in Central America. "There is an unwillingness on the part of our people, harsh as it may be, for you free colored people to remain with us. It is better for us both, therefore, to be separated."[65] "The place I am thinking about for a colony is in Central America. It is nearer to us than Liberia—not much more than one fourth as far as Liberia, and within seven days' run by steamers. Unlike Liberia, it is a great line of travel—it is a highway."[66] It is thought that Lincoln was referring to the Chiriqui plan.

But the colonization movement also had important political detractors. Charles Sumner of Massachusetts wrote that "the deportation of three million slaves will deprive the country of what it needs, most, which is labor."[67] Salmon Chase had always been cool to the idea because, he said, "no man, native or naturalized may be driven forth from his country." And William Seward, while promoting the administration's efforts, said, "I am always for bringing men and States into this Union, never for taking any out."[68]

It was Seward's staff who first raised questions about the existence of valuable beds of coal in the Central American region and pressed for geological surveys. They also indicated that Panama, New Granada, and Costa Rica might have a land dispute there. The cabinet eventually decided against Chiriqui.

Lincoln then moved to examine other plans. There is no evidence of how deeply he investigated the British Honduran plan. In September, when Carroll thought that Chiriqui had been chosen, she wrote to Burr, "Chiriqui property will be bought & fortunes made for the white speculators through the poor Africans who will hew the wood & draw the water."[69] When Chiriqui was not selected she arranged to meet with Lincoln on October 21 "as a sincere friend of the colored to argue for the British Honduras site." But she failed to convince him and a contract for the Île à Vache site was signed in December 1862.

Lincoln often argued that the movement had to be voluntary but struggled with how to get "the colored race interested." Even plans that made emancipation contingent upon emigration were poorly received, and as it turned out Île à Vache was a disaster.[70]

• • •

The point of this chapter has not been to render Patty Cannon or Anna Ella Carroll sympathetic or Harriet Tubman a monster but rather to examine their positions in terms of the then-existing social order. While many of Cannon's activities were legal, Carroll's manumission actions were borderline and her attempts to devise a plan to compensate those whose property had been taken away were unsuccessful but not illegal. At the same time, most of Tubman's actions were illegal. A moral conundrum was created. Power sharing between the Northern bourgeoisie and the Southern "slaveocracy" began to unravel.

By the 1830s, "the South was declining in its share of national population and wealth," while the North was in its ascendancy.[71] New leaders in the North made claims about laws having higher authority than the Constitution: "the laws of nature, the laws of God, the moral law, the spirit of the age, and the law of majority rule," according to historian Charles Sydnor. Some, less radical, insisted at the least that the changing times produced a change in interpretation of significant parts of the Constitution.[72]

As late as March 1861, Lincoln in his first inaugural address stated, "I have no purpose, directly or indirectly, to interfere with the institution of slavery in the States where it exists. I believe I have no lawful right to do so, and I have no inclination to do so."[73] But the exigencies of war forced him to issue a preliminary emancipation proclamation in September 1862. In December of that year he wrote in his annual address, "A nation may be said to consist of its territory, its people, and its laws. The territory is the only part which is of certain durability."[74] Lincoln's acceptance of the durability of law seemed to refer to the Constitution itself. To save the Union, he explained, he had the power and the responsibility to free the slaves. "In giving freedom to the slave, we assure freedom to the free—honorable alike in what we give and what we preserve. We shall nobly save or meanly lose the last, best hope of earth. Other means may succeed; this could not fail. The way is plain, peaceful, generous, just—a way which, if followed, the world will forever applaud, and God must forever bless."[75] He called upon those higher laws—of God, moral law, and the spirit of the age. And so it was perhaps both fitting and understandable that of our three subject women it was Cannon alone who died in jail.

6 | The Mantle of Domesticity
Living within a Woman's Place and Space

I doubt if history affords a parallel to the deep and bitter enmity of the women of the South . . . begging with one breath for the soldiers' rations and in another praying that the almighty or Joe Johnson will come and kill us, the despoilers of their homes and all that is sacred.
—*William Tecumseh Sherman*

Historians have variously defined the accepted roles for middle-class white women of the nineteenth century. Deputy wives, republican mothers, and Southern ladies often head the lists. It was assumed that "inferior" women—slaves, poor whites, and women who never married—would stand at a distance and in silence, trying as best they could to mirror the accepted ways of their betters. However, partly by circumstance, partly by choice, the reality of the other women's lives varied in a complex mosaic that often differed from the expected niche. Most probably believed that "love leading to marriage was the highest gift which life can offer to a woman," and wanted to preserve as much of that traditional role as possible. "All were cognizant," in the words of historian Brenda Stevenson, "that marriage and family wove together the disparate threads of their individual and communal existence."[1]

Moses, the Monster, and Miss Anne each created their own codes of personal and community life—in their attitudes toward marriage and the household, in their relations with men and authority, and in their heightened political activity. They each had a worldview that ignored significant parts of accepted mores and values, and that expressed more of a consistency with one another than would have been predicted, given their differences in race and class. All three seemed inclined to follow a path of their own making. The ancient soul of the Chesapeake, isolated and independent, was in their blood. Historian Darlene Clark Hine who, disquieted about how little we really know of women's lives, urged "Black women historians (and sociologists) to begin to research and write histories of white women" to develop and refine "our methodologies for comparative and intersectional analysis," of a world perhaps inhabited by "lower class" whites and unmarried ladies who have escaped our gaze.[2]

Particularly in isolated places like the Eastern Shore, the households of the nonelite—those owning little land and few slaves (as Carroll's household came to be) were often ruled by a male head but relied greatly on the labor of women. In her work, *Masters of Small Worlds*, historian Stephanie McCurry provides us with a glimpse of yeomen households in antebellum South Carolina Low Country that, although she claims their uniqueness, may help us understand parts of the lives of all three Chesapeake women. McCurry argues that while all family members were subordinated to the male head, "the work done by wives, sons and daughters was, by definition, crucial to the calculus of production." Though women were excluded from direct political participation, male heads in South Carolina realized "that almost everything they ate, grew, raised, preserved or cooked was done by women."[3]

Yet, as she points out, "gender ideology in the South occluded the centrality of white women's work." To acknowledge white women's work in the fields was to create a separation between them and white women on plantations, a dangerous challenge to stated notions of white superiority. The unstated reality was that because they did not own slaves, white wives and daughters did work in the fields. It is likely that their actual contributions gave these women a source of power their more privileged sisters missed.[4] In a similar way, Tubman's rescues, Cannon's contributions in the tavern, and Carroll in her paid labor may also have empowered them.

All three led rather than followed, "unruly women" who were not afraid to challenge male authority. Perhaps like their foremothers on the Eastern Shore, who lived in families truncated, anomalous, and unstable, their lives were independent of church and state—what historian Mary Beth Norton called "a practical laboratory for the dichotomous theory of authority."[5] Patty Cannon was said to arrange bribes with local authorities and to have the strength to take down grown men, a "disorderly woman presuming upon the privileges of her sex."[6] According to the *Denton* (Maryland) *Journal*, "When pursued by the Delaware authorities, Patty Cannon would take refuge in the part of the tavern that stood over the Maryland line." Harriet Tubman, a woman in charge of all her rescues, carried a gun and threatened to shoot any man or woman who disobeyed her. "Dead niggers tell no tales," she said.[7]

Women could not vote at this time and were strongly discouraged from political involvement. Politics was a man's world. Anna Ella Carroll was often in the company of men—participating in their discussions, lobbying for their support, and attempting to influence their actions. Lemuel Evans wrote that the Tennessee Plan was Carroll's idea. She did the research, drew the maps, and presented them to the Lincoln administration. In 1869, Senate President Benjamin Wade wrote to Carroll, "I cannot take leave of public life without expressing my deep sense of your services to the country during the whole period of our national troubles."[8] While direct political involvement outside of auxiliaries and campaigns against drinking and prostitution was frowned upon, speaking out was the most objectionable act. "Public speaking," historian Shirley Yee pointed out, "was an activity in which an individual assumed a role of authority long the domain of political leaders and a male clergy and forbidden to women by social and religious custom." Censures crossed race lines as black minister Samuel Cornish in 1839 warned female readers of the *Colored American* to beware of Fanny Wright, a British abolitionist lecturer, for her "male assumptions, male speculations and male experiments which had addled her brain and male achievements had engrossed her soul."[9] Harriet Tubman frequently ventured into public speaking, at times having to be nudged on stage because she had fallen into one of her sleeps. All three women imposed themselves in significant ways on these traditionally male domains.

• • •

It is unfortunate that we know so little about the life of Patty Cannon. At the time she lived her occupation was unusual, thought to be the preserve of an underclass but not generally frowned upon. We also know that some of the "best" families in her area owned slaves, and when the slaves escaped they hired people like Cannon and her husband to get them back. She was married perhaps as long as thirty years to Jesse Cannon, but had only two children, apparently eschewing the typical pattern of childbirth every other year. She could not read or write, owned no land for most of her life, and had few marketable skills. To that extent she lived a rather ordinary life.

Yet the Patty Cannon that emerged was a kind of "Haiduk," as Eric Hobsbawm described this bandit group, a flunkey of nobility—in this case slaveholders—in league with them for the money but also in rebellion against authority.[10] Whenever authorities arrived at the tavern to serve warrants or question inhabitants, they were resisted, sometimes at gun point. Patty Cannon ran the tavern with an iron fist, stored human cargo in chains for future sale and transport, and did her own bouncing. Believing in property rights and the right to privacy, her code, like that of Andrew Jackson's mother, was to settle most things "on your own." This was not a woman who feared authority.

Patty Cannon, outlaw and kidnapper, was out of step with societal expectation of class and gender. She had a traditional marriage that detractors had to alter to fit their perceptions of a female criminal mind. Little is known about her private life, and we can only guess at her true feelings about life, love, and work, representing as she did a group of "wives of farmers and slave women who lived, bore children, worked hard and died, leaving little trace for the historian coming after."[11] Prior to her arrest public information about "Mrs. Cannon" was sparse. The tavern, when mentioned, was said to be owned by Jesse Cannon or son-in-law Joe Johnson and the gang headed by one of them as well. Patty Cannon was rarely discussed. Later detractors, bothered by her early invisibility, explained her absence in published reports as a result of her sexual privilege.

Three newspaper articles were written about her at the time of her arrest. One unsigned and undated document, found in state archives, may have been written at that same time. The first article appeared in Wilmington's *Delaware Gazette* on April 10, 1829. It reported the discovery of bones, the arrest of Patty Cannon and her servant Cyrus James, and their conviction for murder. A second article appeared a week later, reporting that the trial had not occurred and therefore there had been no conviction. It did, however, provide further evidence of the crime, stating, "Some circumstances respecting a most diabolical course of conduct which, for some years past, has been carried on in Sussex County, in this state, the evidences of which have just been brought to light." The article identified Patty Cannon as living on a farm with her son-in-law, the "celebrated" Joseph Johnson, "negro trader." It gave no further details and did not identify Patty Cannon as the head of the business.[12]

Hezekial Niles, of *Niles Weekly,* picked up the story from the *Delaware Gazette* and on May 23 wrote the third article. "The Delaware Journal says, 'at the Court of Quarterly Sessions recently in Sussex County, the grand jury found three indictments against Patty Cannon for murder.'" The *Niles Weekly* article also mentioned the Johnson brothers, Joseph and Ebenezer, who "reside out of state," and concluded, "We take it for granted that the proper steps will be taken to discover and bring them to justice."[13]

The origins of the final document are less certain. H. C. Conrad, a Delaware historian who published a three-volume history of the state, discovered it in 1927. Its tone suggested that someone on the scene wrote it. "Much excitement now prevails in this county in consequence of the discovery of the bodies of several persons, interred upon the premises of the celebrated Patty Cannon, who lives upon the line of the state and whose house has been for a long time the resort of all the kidnapping and negro traders in this part of the peninsula."

It is interesting that the word "celebrated" was applied to Patty Cannon, suggesting at least local knowledge of her part in the "negro trading business." Further on she was referred to as "Mrs. Cannon," a conference of some status. "A man by the name of Cyrus James," it continued, "who was raised by Mrs. Cannon and who has been an inmate of her family ever since, is likewise imprisoned. He was present at the disinterring of the bodies and directed the persons engaged in it where to find them."[14] This account confirmed the report that James cooperated with authorities.

But doubt was also expressed in the final line. "How the truth is, or who was the actual perpetrator of these horrible deeds, it may be difficult to ascertain, but there is no doubt that these persons have been murdered and the suspicion at present rests upon this degraded woman." Use of the phrase "degraded woman" to describe Patty Cannon may have reflected her local reputation or may have applied more generally to any woman taken to jail.

Conrad found the document in state archives. "The handwriting of the document," he stated, "I do not know." It contained an attached note, however, that he claimed was in the handwriting of Henry M. Ridgely, a Delaware lawyer and member of a prominent family. He was elected to Congress in 1811 and 1813 as a Federalist; served as Delaware secretary of state in 1817 and 1824; and in 1827 was elected to the U.S. Senate, two years before his friend John Clayton. The pursuit, capture, and demise of the Cannon-Johnson gang helped to further advance his career. Exposure of the wrongdoing brought both the activities and the candidates to the public's attention.[15] Public accounts rarely mention that she was indicted only once previously and not prosecuted; at the time of her arrest was somewhere between the ages of sixty and seventy; and until then a member of good standing in the community. The Patty Cannon story did not promise a career-making set of circumstances.

Reconstruction of her story was crucial. John Middleton Clayton began the process in 1837 by detailing his version of the 1821 arrest and further exposing details of the crimes. "Johnson himself made a fortune at the business (of kidnapping) and easily escaped justice by removing from one county or state to another when pursued by an officer with a posse. . . . He was arrested at last in 1822 (sic) by the Sheriff of Sussex with a posse at the house of the notorious Patty Cannon." Hal Roth pointed out numerous discrepancies between the 1821 news reports and this letter. He found it particularly interesting that Clayton referred to "the house of the notorious Patty Cannon," though she was not mentioned in the news reports, and that at least one report stated it was the house of Jesse Cannon.[16]

It was not known whether Ridgley or Clayton provided information for the 1841 narrative, but readers were assured "they may rely upon accounts as being correct, as they have been gathered from the most authentic sources." No sources and no author were cited although the names Clinton Jackson and Erastus E. Barclay, probably fictitious, were listed in the copyright. The account did include events described in local news accounts.[17]

The *Narrative and Confessions of Lucretia P. Cannon* was published in New York. The complete title was actually a paragraph long and ended "An account of Some of the Most Horrible and Shocking Murders and Daring Robberies ever committed by One of the Female Sex." This work represented the birth of the Patty Cannon legend and the transformation of her marital situation into one more fitting a "monster." The first thing the authors did was to kill off her spouse. They said that Jesse died mysteriously after discovering the real character of the woman he married and that she probably poisoned him. And at the end of the book, the authors included her confession to his murder. While there was no death certificate for the real Jesse Cannon, his indictment in 1821 and failure to be indicted in 1826 suggested that he died sometime between 1822 and 1826. The real Patty Cannon had a marriage of some thirty years, one based on a partnership in crime but obviously a lived experience inconvenient for the legend.

The authors' intent to "shock" the audience was clear from the start. "It has probably never fallen to the lot of man to record a list of more cruel, heart-rending, atrocious, cold-blooded and horrible crimes and murders, than have been perpetrated by the subject of this narrative." They found it "doubly shocking and atrocious" that the crimes were "committed by one of the female sex." Women behaving in this manner were particularly depraved because, "females are known for having a higher regard for virtue and a far greater aversion to acts of barbarity."[18]

To underscore the "barbarity," the authors changed Patty's first name to Lucretia, a reference no doubt to the infamous poisoner Lucrezia Borgia. Her husband's name was changed to Alonzo. The narrative also claimed that her father was a clever but dissolute and disinherited son of Yorkshire nobility who married a gypsy and was forced to flee to Canada. There he ran a smuggling business until he was convicted of murder and hung. Lucretia was the youngest child of this couple. Again, without evidence, the authors fabricated a disreputable woman, part gypsy, with "genes" from clever but tainted nobility—evil mixed with ability—a dangerous combination.[19]

After her husband's death at her hand, the authors wrote, "She became one of the most abandoned and notorious of women, giving loose to every species of licentiousness and extravagance." The Lucretia of the narrative, a woman alone, also has supernatural powers, "the master spirit and deviser of ways and means," the authors said.

Lucretia's wickedness included such acts as enticing men "by exciting and gratifying their feelings by her wit and fascinating conversation"; leading her gang to unlawful acts "dressed in men's attire"; beating the head of an unsuspecting money-carrying traveler while asleep, "until his brains strewed the floor"; and tossing a crying infant into a fire and watching him burn to death.

When finally caught and taken to jail, Lucretia "obtained poison to avoid the disgrace of exposure and public execution." While dying, "she raved like a maniac, tearing her clothes from off her body and tore her hair from her head by the handfuls, attempting to lay hold and bite everything in her reach, cursing God and the hour that give her birth." After these fits of insanity, "a measure of reason was restored and she had pangs of guilty conscience, and remorse, feeling the torments of hell and reproaching herself for her awful crimes."[20]

In their work the authors devoted far more space to Lucretia's wicked character than to the crimes themselves. Kidnapping and selling free people into slavery was nothing compared to her dressing in men's attire or her beating of men in the business or her licentious extravagance. The authors were uncomfortable that her reputed feminine lapses—her strength, her combativeness, her trade—could be linked to a long and enduring marriage, so they eliminated the marriage. Joe Johnson, her son-in-law, thought to have committed far more crimes than Patty, never was depicted as a maniac. Some claimed that after leaving Maryland he became a judge in Arkansas. As historian Anne Firor Scott pointed out, "Men were encouraged, applauded, and rewarded for diligent self-improvement. A woman who followed the same pattern ran the risk of being seen as a deviant, labeled 'strong-minded,' caricatured, scorned."[21] Patty Cannon, strong-willed and married to a criminal for over thirty years, became a villain.

• • •

Anna Ella Carroll, in contrast to Cannon, left a visible record of letters, notes, books, articles, and memorials. A lobbyist and publicist by trade, she constructed several versions of herself, none of which managed to reveal the "true woman," a phrase she used to capture her sense of a woman's place in antebellum society. Carroll's agency, a more activist view of self, challenged the public perception of a Southern lady of her race and class, a lady trained to be at least outwardly subordinate and obedient.[22]

She attempted to influence national affairs by constantly offering advice to governors, senators, members of the cabinet, former presidents, and President Lincoln himself. She worked on political campaigns, attended party conventions, and wrote pamphlets and articles attacking the positions of key candidates and political parties. She also planned a military campaign, complete with maps and charts, a campaign that many prominent politicians believed she alone designed. It changed the course of the war.

An unmarried Southern lady, Carroll, by contrast, maintained long-term relations with three different married men. Harriet Tubman, a slave "who grew up like a neglected weed," married her second husband only after her first had died (though they were estranged for many years).

Carroll's life would certainly have been easier had she married. Marriage to some political figure she promoted would have provided an easier reception to her ideas. Her notions of relationships were far from the accepted norm and probably fueled some of the vicious gossip that she had been charged with embezzlement, raped by a black man, and lived, without benefit of clergy, with Lemuel Evans.

Rarely seen alone in public, Carroll was deeply attached, "like brothers" her sisters said, to three different married men. This was not for the want of beaus, as she and they were fond of mentioning. Several unattached men were associated romantically with her—some by rumor and gossip, and some by her own admissions. Her biographers have developed scenarios about her failure to marry. Marjorie Greenbie, attributing Carroll's situation to the role of devoted daughter, wrote, "She received early in life much attention and offers of marriage from many distinguished parties but she never seemed inclined to change her condition or to give up the beloved companionship of her father." Others commented on what appeared to be her platonic attraction to married men. "Except in the single case of Breckenridge, Anne had a happy way of placing the wife of the man she liked in the mental category of her sister," the Greenbies wrote in the later volume, "and then was free and frank in her affections as she was in relation to her several brothers-in-law."[23]

The most prominent of her special friends were Robert Breckenridge, of the Kentucky Breckenridge family; John Causin of Maryland; and Lemuel Dale Evans, a Know-Nothing congressman from Texas. Carroll's relationships with these men were all shrouded in some mystery. All were lawyers, and at least two of the three were married. Piecing together what was known and may be surmised, we discover a woman "unhappy in love," as Victorian novelists would say—but also one who refused to settle for another if her first choice was unavailable.

Marjorie Greenbie reported that when the Carroll family moved north to Dorchester, Carroll and her sisters entered a whirl of social activities that included "every young man within range of a day's sailing or riding." In the midst of this Carroll, age twenty-five in 1840, "rose up and said she was going to Baltimore to support herself and her servants." While shocking her family with such a declaration, she assured them that she "wouldn't dream of emerging from the sphere to which Providence had assigned her female delicacy." There was little explanation for Carroll's departure beyond the noted attributes of her personality and that she knew of her father's financial difficulties.[24]

In their revised biography, the Greenbies added details to Carroll's acquaintance with Robert Breckenridge. A friend of her father's and twenty years older than Carroll, he took her "under his wing" in her early days in Baltimore. Breckenridge was brought up as a landed gentleman with a strong sense of duty to state and country. His father was attorney general under Jefferson and his nephew John would later be vice president. Breckenridge knew horses, could talk of crop rotation with Thomas Carroll, and deplored the evils of slavery although not as an abolitionist. Attractive, intelligent, and trained in the law, he married young, lost two children while still in his twenties, and was "thrown into ill-health" as a result. To heal himself he turned to religion and was appointed pastor of the Second Presbyterian Church in Baltimore. From there Breckenridge visited the Carrolls at Kingston Hall when Carroll was in her teens. When she declared her intention to move to Baltimore, her father asked Breckenridge to serve as Anne's guardian. The Greenbies added somewhat coyly, "Perhaps it was he (Breckenridge) who persuaded her to come to the city."[25]

Once she arrived in Baltimore, Carroll and Breckenridge were often in each other's company. He introduced her to prominent Whigs of his acquaintance, including Henry Clay, and they were seen together "amidst the social circles to which they both belonged." Carroll attended and later joined his church, creating "an ever-warmer friendship." Throughout this time Breckenridge's wife had been ailing and was rarely seen in public. In 1845 Anne's father "unexpectedly arrived in Baltimore," having been appointed commissioner of lotteries. One writer suggested that his appearance may have been in response to rumors about his daughter. Carroll immediately moved out of the boardinghouse Breckenridge found for her. Their friendship seemed to end abruptly. Breckenridge's wife died later that year and he left Baltimore to become the president of Jefferson College in Kentucky. Neither he nor Anne corresponded for the next twenty years, leaving the distinct impression that a disapproving father ended their relationship.[26]

John M. S. Causin was also a close acquaintance of Carroll's. Born in St. Mary's County in western Maryland in 1811, he studied law and was admitted to the bar in Prince George's County about 1836. He was elected to the state house of representatives in 1837 and 1843. In 1843, he was also elected as a Whig to the Twenty-eighth Congress and served until 1845.[27]

Whether or not Carroll knew Causin before this time, it is likely that their friendship began at this point. In 1845, the year that Breckenridge left the state, Causin moved to Annapolis, not far from Baltimore where he practiced law and served as a delegate to the state constitutional convention. In 1848 he was a presidential elector on the Whig ticket of Taylor and Fillmore. In 1858, Causin moved to Chicago, Illinois, and resumed the practice of law. He died of apoplexy in 1861.[28] We know little of his activities in the years between 1848 and 1858. Carroll was busy in Maryland and national politics, trying to piece together a coalition of Whig and American Party elements. Although Causin was rarely mentioned in her surviving correspondence, other documentation suggested that their association must have been intimate.

After Causin's death, his brother-in-law L. E. Barber wrote three letters to Carroll. The first gave notice of Causin's death and of the death of his mother "as she waited for her son's body to come home." Barber added that he was "aware that Causin had regarded you with affectionate esteem" and promised to return the letters she had written to Causin. Carroll quickly replied, requesting as well a copy of Causin's last speech. Barber wrote again, suggesting that in settling his brother-in-law's affairs, he found that there were "many—very many" letters from Carroll and proposed burning them. He added in obvious embarrassment that he had accidentally read one "at a part which gave full expression to the feelings of the writer—the whole heart was bare before me." Barber worried about returning the letters through the mail, suggesting, "It would be mortifying if by any accident your letters should fall into other hands."[29]

Carroll agreed that Barber should burn the letters and asked him to "suspend judgment" until he "knew the facts" regarding her relationship with Causin. Barber wrote a third time, assuring her he could conceive that their relationship, whatever it might have been, "could not depreciate you in our estimation. Can it be that I would estimate less one whom he loved for returning that love?" Barber said he could not "altogether acquit Causin of imprudence and of weakness in this regard," but added, "I know nothing, believe nothing, suspect nothing other than the simple fact that there existed a mutual affection." He enclosed locks of hair both from Causin and his mother, thanked Carroll for allowing (Causin's) sister to keep Carroll's daguerreotype, and "sent her violets from the graves of the dead."

Historian Janet Coryell thought that Carroll and Causin were lovers, a fact that would explain the tone of Barber's letter and his mild censure of his brother-in-law. He did not wish to drag either family into scandal. At the same time, he could not resist chastising his brother-in-law for imprudence and weakness. Whether it was because Causin was a married man or because Carroll was a woman of "good standing" or simply because it violated a moral code is not known.[30]

Carroll's third beau was Lemuel Dale Evans, born in Tennessee in 1810. Like Breckenridge and Causin, he studied law and was admitted to the bar. In 1843 he moved to Marshall, Texas, and served as a member of the state convention that annexed Texas in 1845. State records listed him as married. He was elected to the U.S. House of Representatives in 1855 as a candidate of the American Party but was not reelected.

Evans was a railroad man and promoted the building of a railroad to the Pacific in the 1855 election campaign. He said it was vital to maintaining the Union. "We must build the southern route, and add California to the southern interest, and raise the South to such a degree of importance, as to enable it to command the respect of the North," he stated in campaign speeches.[31]

He also argued that "when Jefferson and the great founders of our institutions spoke of the equality of men, they were referring to the American people, the Anglo-Saxon race. They were not constructing a form of government for the negro race, or the Irish, the German or any other race in Europe." He felt that "the Anglo-American race was the only one capable of self-government." The rest, he said, "poor ignorant creatures care nothing for the country, so they get employment and pay and from their ignorance and dependence, become the tools of political demagogues."[32]

Carroll's relationship with Evans began in the late 1850s. Coryell hinted that Carroll got involved with Evans because Causin left town. For whatever reason, once begun, they were constantly seen together. "Give my greeting to Miss Carroll, if you dare," Connecticut Senator Truman Smith wrote to Evans on one occasion. Historian Charles Snyder observed that Lemuel Evans was "a frequent companion and a source of perennial gossip regarding their relationship." Carroll visited him often in Texas, where he returned after the war. She was with him at the constitutional convention of 1868–69. In 1870 he was appointed to the position of chief justice of the Texas Supreme Court, the "Semicolon Court," by Major-General Philip Sheridan, commander of the Texas and Louisiana District during the Reconstruction era, and served until 1871. Evans often returned to Washington to be with Carroll, sitting beside her at her Congressional appearances; when apart they wrote long letters filled with politics and reconstruction. On several occasions during this time, Carroll nursed him back to health. She was with him at his death in 1877.[33]

The attachment of an unmarried woman to a married man was certainly frowned upon in nineteenth-century Maryland. Carroll's attachment to three different married men made her something of a novelty though not, for reasons unknown, an outcast.

• • •

Harriet Tubman, like other slaves before her, was "much of a woman."[34] Though illiterate like Cannon, she challenged the right of slaveholders to own human beings. "I have heard their groans and sighs, and seen their tears, and I would give every drop of blood in my veins to free them," she told her biographer Sarah Bradford. She had more than a passing knowledge of national politics, assuming her scribes were faithful recorders. She told Ednah Cheney, "They say the Negro has no rights a white man is bound to respect; but it seems to me they send men to Congress, and pay them eight dollars a day, for nothing else but to talk about the Negro."[35] On another occasion she said that she didn't like Lincoln. "You see we colored people didn't understand then [that] he was our friend. All we knew was that the first colored troops sent south from Massachusetts only got seven dollars a month, while the white regiment got fifteen."[36] And on many occasions she rose in public to speak out and make her feelings known.

Drawing on a host of private and public models, she believed the sanctity of marriage was a gift from God. She married John Tubman, a free man, in 1844 and—I suspect and many others agree—loved him all her life. Twice she attempted to persuade him to join her in an escape. His refusal brought great sadness. One observer noted, "At first her grief and anger were excessive. She did not care what master did to her, she thought she would go right in and make all the trouble she could, she was determined to see her old man once more." Though interviewed about her life on numerous occasions, beyond the humorous asides her marriage to John Tubman was one subject she refused to share with others.[37] Harriet Tubman obviously believed in the sanctity of marriage and, as argued, had deep love for first husband, John Tubman. But Harriet's ideas of marriage were her own. She waited two years after escaping to rescue him, and though filled with pain at his refusal, moved on. She was also childless.

The accepted wisdom of much of the early republic was that everyone should marry and bear children. Unmarried women were viewed as a curiosity. Sallie Holley complained to a friend about the incessant questions she received on her lecture tours. "Is thee married? How old is thee? Does thee reside with relations?"[38] The marriage sacrament was

"God-ordained" and carried prescribed and complementary roles. A wife was expected, according to historian Anne Firor Scott, "to love, honor, obey, and occasionally amuse her husband, to bring up his children and manage his household."

Recognition of their proper and subordinate place was women's first responsibility, a practice that varied little by social class. "There is no slave, after all, like a wife," Mary Chestnut complained in her diary.[39] Yeomen and artisans readily emulated or at least mimicked the marital structures of the upper classes. Slave wife Minnie Faulkes reported on her marriage,

> I slept in bed he on his side and I on mine for three months an' dis aint no lie. He never got close to me 'cause mama had sed, "Don't let no body bother yo'
> Principle, 'caus dat waz all yo' had." I 'bey my mama, an toll him so, and I Said to go an' ask mama an' ef she sed he could get close to me hit alright. An' he an' I went together to see and ask mama. Den mama said, "Come here Chillum," and she began telling me to please my husband, an it was my duty as a wife, dat he had married a pu'fect lady."[40]

Tubman's childlessness probably weighed on her. Women were to aspire to be wives and mothers. "One of the most persistent threads in the romantication [sic] of woman was the glorification of motherhood."[41] Mary Chestnut recalled: "Mrs. Chestnut was bragging to me one day, with exquisite taste—to me, a childless wretch—of her twenty-seven grandchildren; and Colonel Chestnut, a man who rarely wounds me, said to her: 'You have not been a useless woman in this world.' But what of me!"[42] To have babies every other year and to be constantly consumed with their care, feeding, and instruction was the highest calling. A childless wife was the subject of scorn and pity.

It was also the case that infertility haunted many slavewomen. Heavy work loads, poor diet, and inadequate medical care hampered reproduction. Even though slavewomen had children earlier than white women, they had fewer of them and the space between births was longer and more erratic.[43] Slavemen attached to childless women sometimes moved on.

One cannot overstate the importance of children in slave families. "Slave children were potentially important resources for family members and their masters. Slaves viewed their young as extensions of themselves and kinship lines, often naming them for favorite family members. Slave children also were providers of future security for their parents and kin, persons whom they could depend on for love, comfort, and service once they became old and infirm."[44]

This is the backdrop for one of the strangest rescues recorded for Harriet Tubman—that of "a niece named Margaret Stewart." Earl Conrad first mentioned it, suggesting the event occurred in the mid-1850s, after Tubman was acquainted with William Seward but before she moved to Auburn. Conrad got his information from Alice Brickler of Wilberforce, Ohio, who was the daughter of Margaret Stewart.[45]

Brickler told Conrad that "Aunt Harriet," as she called her, "kidnapped my mother from her home on Eastern Shore, Maryland, when she was a little girl eight or nine years old."[46] Brickler suggested that her mother's life began then because Stewart had few memories of her life before the kidnapping. This seems a curious admission as children eight or nine usually have at least some memories. In any case, Stewart did remember "that neither she, her brothers or her mother had ever been slaves. Her grandfather," Stewart said, "on her mother's side had bought his wife and children's time which made them free." Stewart's mother married one of Tubman's brothers, an ex-slave who "owned a pair of slick chestnut horses and a shiny carriage in which they rode to church."[47]

The problem with this tale is that there is no record of such a brother nor any mention of him by Harriet, John, or Harriet's parents. Where he lived and what he did, assuming he existed, is a mystery. It is possible that he was a brother of John Tubman rather than Harriet. This is more plausible as many in John Tubman's family were free or freed, as was John himself. Further, Harriet stayed at least once after her escape with John's brother Tom, who lived in Baltimore and worked on the docks. Kate Larson found, moreover, that a child named Margaret Stewart was born in Baltimore in 1850.[48]

Margaret Stewart told her daughter that sometime in the mid-fifties Harriet Tubman came to visit her family, fell in love with her, and as daughter Alice Brickler wrote, "without so much as a by-your-leave, took the little girl with her to her Northern home."[49]

Brickler provided several explanations for the abduction, all passed on, no doubt, by her mother. The first was, in her words, "maybe in mother she saw the child she herself might have been if slavery had been less cruel." The second was "because she knew the joys of motherhood would never be hers and she longed for some little creature who would love her for her own self's sake." Brickler only hints at a third explanation, "Strange to say, mother looked very much like Aunt Harriet," an explanation Larson suggested may point to the fact the child was actually Tubman's own.[50]

If true, Tubman never admitted to this last explanation. In fact, she testified before a federal commission that she had never given birth. Nor would it be something either the Ohio family or the New York family would permit to be said publicly about Tubman. The New York family, in fact, admitted the resemblance but dismissed much of the tale as a hoax. And much of Brickler's story seems far-fetched. For example, "They made the trip by water as that was what impressed mother so greatly that she forgot to weep over her separation from her twin brother, her mother and the shiny carriage she liked so much."[51] Some of Tubman's rescues involved water trips, but few if any were conducted in what could be called pleasant circumstances; most, in fact, in terror and with great discomfort. If true, how was this one managed differently?

Brickler also suggested that Tubman realized "she had violated her brother's home and sorrow and anger were there." This is meant to acknowledge that Tubman realized the guilt of her action but only adds more questions. Why did she disrupt this child's life? Why did the child's family not respond? Brickler provided no explanation but instead concluded that Tubman, in contrition, "decided to place her dearest possession in the hands of friends in the North. She gave the little girl to Mrs. William H. Seward, not as a servant but as a guest within her home."[52]

This, too, represented something of an exaggeration. Tubman's friend Martha Coffin Wright gave a very different account. She wrote to her sister, "Mrs. Worden was just here. She has taken a contraband 10 yrs. old to live with her, a niece of Harriet Tubman. This arrangement appears to have been made just before Tubman left for the South earlier in May." (Lazette Miller Worden was the widowed sister of Frances Seward, William Seward's wife.) Wright's use of the term "contraband" rather than a given name makes it unlikely the child was thought of as a guest. Wright provided no details of the arrangement but Brickler did state that her mother was "taught to cook and clean and read and write and speak like a lady," not uncommon for faithful household servants.[53]

Stewart's embellishment of her circumstances and spotty memory may suggest that Tubman did rescue her from some terrible situation that she, Margaret Stewart, chose not to reveal or could not remember. Tubman preferred not to take children on her escapes because of the dangers, but she did so on occasion. Rescuing Stewart was a special circumstance. Saving one who resembled her, knowing, as Brickler suggested, "she would never experience the joys of motherhood," makes the most sense given what we know of Tubman. Her relatives all agree that the kidnapped child remained a favorite throughout Tubman's life.[54]

Interpretations of this event expose views of slave families in this era that are more fractured, matrifocal, and fictive than many popular explanations. As Brenda Stevenson noted about slave families in colonial and antebellum Virginia, "Across time and space, the frequent and indiscriminate separation of slave spouses, temporarily and permanently denied them the opportunity to live together, to share the responsibilities of their households and children, and to provide each other with socio-sexual outlets." In her work Stevenson depicts a woman's role as head of a matrifocal family that well describes Harriet Tubman. The family head, Stevenson wrote, "had to act protectively and aggressively for the sake of her dependents" and did not hesitate to "rebel against the poor material support owners provided." Such acts were greeted by other black women and men with pride and esteem, seen as they were as portraits of "self-protection, self-reliance, and self-determination." It is this Harriet Tubman who journeyed to freedom; returned to rescue as many others as she could; organized and participated in military campaigns; nursed the war sick; and started, later in life, an old age home for the indigent. Extraordinary feats measured against the duties of privileged women, but understandable as well in terms of William Still's comment on Tubman's "ordinariness."[55]

. . .

The willingness of our three Chesapeake women to travel roads not approved by society was a major part of the danger they represented. It was not that they each publicly flaunted a rebellious spirit or, as Frederick Douglass offered, "enjoyed the applause of the crowd," but that they privately sowed seeds of discontent in a manner unfamiliar to their contemporaries. While not having the same intent—to undermine the institution of slavery—they all played significant supporting roles in the epic drama. Abolitionist Lydia Maria Child, writing in an autograph book of young Franky Garrison outlined the drama's plot: "How a very small mouse helped to gnaw open a net that held a great lion." William Still's use of the term "ordinariness" in connection with Tubman underscores this point.[56]

The case is easily made with Carroll and Tubman. Anna Ella Carroll was not strong-minded in the way feared by her family, but did take it upon herself to use her education, a thing denied to Southern women, to influence public policy. Charles Snyder produced the clearest understanding of her contribution. "During her declining years," he wrote, "Miss Carroll lived her self-ascribed role as 'A Military Genius,' and 'The Great Unrecognized Member of Lincoln's Cabinet.' Obscured by this not altogether convincing characterization was a woman at war with Victorian conventions and fighting for the freedoms of the twentieth century as a pamphleteer, propagandist and politician."[57]

Harriet Tubman was not a modern-day Joan of Arc, a single woman sacrificing her life to challenge the Church. Tubman was a heroic figure who, by saving her family, helped enlarge the cracks in the institution of slavery. On one occasion, then an old lady living in Auburn, New York, she said, "When I made it to freedom, I could not believe how good it was. But I was still sad, because I missed my family. I tried to get my husband to come and join me but he was afraid to come, so I had to leave him there. I was not going to be a slave anymore!" Perhaps she was another of the little ladies who with a small act made a great war.[58]

Patty Cannon's case is more difficult to understand in this context. Much of her contribution to the dismantling of the institution of slavery was not of her own making. She engaged in a grotesque business that brought misery and suffering to the lives of many but that was legal or only quasi-legal. To confirm her villainy, anti-slavery forces transformed her into a degraded murderer of husband and children. But there were two Patty Cannons: the gang member who we can at best only get a faint glimpse of, and the legend. As such, she becomes a kind of two-headed Janus—demon to the anti-slavery community and tenacious symbol to the slaveholders, a woman alone traveling to jail, an omen of the war and ruin that would be their fate.

In these disparate ways all three women engaged rather dramatically in the destruction of a "proper" woman's sphere. They did so not as outsiders banging on the door of opportunity or as pleaders for social justice but as insiders who knew the rules but chose another way. When caught, Patty Cannon walked quietly to the jail in Georgetown. Anna Ella Carroll, despite the rumors that swirled about her, stood by the married men she loved. And Harriet Tubman, courageous, armed, and dangerous, both in reality and historical memory, outlived them all.

7 | Beginnings at the End

Religions boil up from the basic, magic rim of *myth* . . .
the secret opening through which the inexhaustible energies
of the cosmos pour into human cultural manifestation.
  —*Joseph Campbell*

Superstition is religion out of fashion, and religion is
superstition in fashion.
  —*Ernestine L. Rose*

In August 1929, one hundred years after Patty Cannon died, Langston Hughes wrote his friend Wallace Thurman of a planned visit to the Eastern Shore of Maryland. Hughes was fascinated by the area. "It is not far away," he wrote. "All one does is go to Baltimore and take a Jim Crow boat to the land of miscegenation where every colored lady has at least six little half-breeds for practice before she gets married to a Negro. And where the word Mammy is still taken seriously, and the race is so far back that it has an illimitable potential—like me!" The source of Hughes's information is unknown, but his thoughts echo those of observers like Frederick Douglass who commented on the area's peculiarity.[1]

The Eastern Shore, perched between the Atlantic Ocean and the Chesapeake and Delaware bays, lies east of most roads on the Atlantic Coast. Much of its land is so close to sea level ("bears the aspect of a great shoal risen from the sea") that locals claimed on four occasions it sank below the sea and predicted that it could disappear again with even minor climate change. Travel through many parts was difficult. As one observer boasted, "Until the railroad was built in modern times, nobody ever passed through the Eastern Shore. . . . Few strangers came among them. They nourished and ripened and handed down their own notions undisturbed."[2]

Even today, the marshy terrain and mosquito infestations have kept much of its coast pristine. The low population density and "loamy, sometimes sandy soil varied by long aisles of pond and brackish sound" have always contributed to its isolation. Delaware, wrote Harlem Renaissance writer Alice Dunbar Nelson, "has three counties, two in high tide."[3]

Shoremen, isolated and uncontrolled, both male and female, black and white, developed minds of their own. Those who lived south of the Choptank were known particularly for their quaint eating and drinking habits; their love of sport and leisure; and their hospitality, at times lavish. Shoremen, meaning women as well as men, always spoke their mind "in company without fear or favor." Anna Ella Carroll's "unconventional career," historian Janet Coryell observed, "no doubt owes much to her birthplace."[4]

Given the area's hundreds of rivers and inlets, it was not surprising that the populace had always been strongly influenced by the water. The Cannon-Johnson gang used watercraft to haul their captured prey into the heart of darkness. Anna Ella Carroll claimed her Eastern Shore childhood was her major source of inspiration about the advantages of the Tennessee River over the Mississippi. And Harriet Tubman used these same waterways as an avenue of escape, her knowledge of them part of common lore. On one occasion she recalled that, in the month of March, a group came to a small stream of tidewater with no boat or bridge. "The water came up to . . . [my] arm-pits," she said, "and the men refused to follow til they saw . . . [me] safe on the opposite side."[5]

But more than lore, lifestyle, and the water, the Eastern Shore was filled with an array of religious beliefs, as was Maryland itself. Its isolation reinforced the common threads of nonconformity and dissent. Early settlers were represented by many clusters of people who followed no one's view of God or man but their own. The region was filled with deeply religious Methodists, Quakers, Presbyterians, and transplanted Puritans, as well as those who professed no religion at all.

Harriet Tubman said she spoke to God every day and was, as a result, fearless in her rescues. "I have never met with any person of any color" wrote Quaker Thomas Garrett in 1868, "who had more confidence in the voice of God, spoken direct to her soul." Anna Ella Carroll, raised on weekly tirades against the Church in Rome by her childhood ministers, stated in her first published book that it was the dangerous aim of that institution "to unsettle the principles of our liberties and hence destroy them." Hal Roth, in researching the life of Patty Cannon, came upon a group of elderly African American women who were familiar with her name. "What did you hear about her?" Roth asked. "She was a conjure," they replied.[6]

All of the early dissenters, foreparents to our three "dangerous" women, were loosely connected to warring evangelical Protestant sects at odds with the Church of England; or with the original Catholic colonists who, through charter, intermittently ran the Maryland government; or with the Church of Rome itself. Though all other religions were viewed with suspicion, Catholicism held a special place of enmity, here and in other parts of the colonies.[7]

It was not uncommon to critique the religious beliefs and practices of others. Frederick Douglass spoke harshly of religion on the Eastern Shore and took pains to distinguish that "corrupt, women-whipping, cradle plundering, hypocritical slaveholding religion" with "Christianity proper." He raged, "He who sells my sister, for purposes of prostitution, stands forth as the pious advocate of purity. He who proclaims it a religious duty to read the Bible denies me the right of learning to read the name of the God who made me. He who is the religious advocate of marriage robs whole millions of its sacred influence, and leaves them to the ravages of wholesale pollution."[8]

But Douglass also revealed something of his own faith. "I love the pure, peaceable, and impartial Christianity of Christ," he said.[9] In *My Bondage, My Freedom*, he explained that his "religious nature was awakened by the preaching of a white Methodist minister, named Hanson," who thought that all men, bond and free, were sinners in the sight of God and must repent their sins. Hanson's teachings gave Douglass "love of all mankind, slaveholders not excepted," a desire to convert the world to this wondrous knowledge and, most of all, to read the Bible. Through contact with Hanson and an old colored man named Lawson, who taught him "to trust in the Lord, have faith and the Lord can make you free," young Douglass left the Eastern Shore steeped in a deep religious spirit infused by others but one mainly of his own construction.[10]

Historian Nell Painter described somewhat different religious influences for the Northern-born Isabella Van Wagenen (Sojourner Truth) but suggested a similarly self-constructed inner spirit. Painter wrote,

> As a vulnerable young woman—deprived of her parents, over-worked, neglected, beaten, and sexually abused—she had approached the world with a vivid sense of her worthlessness, convinced that insuperable barriers separated her from the prominent people she worked for. Now she had a friend in Jesus, whom she sometimes likened to "a soul-protecting fortress," sometimes to a power that raised her "above the battlements of fear." The assurance of her sanctification and God's constant support released Isabella from the crippling conviction that

she was nothing. She discovered a new means of power, what pente-
costals call the power of the Spirit, that redressed the balance between
someone poor and black and female and her rich white masters.[11]

Moses, the Monster, and Miss Anne by no means shared the same
faith. Tubman, always spiritual, joined an African Methodist Episcopal
church later in her life; Cannon's religious preference was unknown; and
Carroll was a devoted Presbyterian. But they shared a set of values that
put great stock in the concepts of individual responsibility and direct
communication with God, concepts embedded in most of the evangelical
Protestant sects. Tubman talked often of "conscience," a concept used
by both Quakers and Methodists; Cannon, though silent on her beliefs,
nonetheless made a familiar statement of individual responsibility in
marching alone to the Georgetown jail when indicted in 1829; and Carroll spoke of the importance of religious edification and reflection. These
were their shared roots.

These dangerous women had in common the values and knowledge
of the sociological collective of the Eastern Shore. All were familiar with
the adages and wise sayings, linguistic traditions, institutional frames of
influence, and symbolic universe of their experience. All were part of a
social construction of reality, intensified by isolation and longevity, an
ancient part of the new world.[12]

By the time of the American Revolution, three-quarters of the entire
population could be said to be members of some dissenting Protestant
sect; but this did not suggest uniformity of belief, and misunderstandings
between sects were common. Harriet Beecher Stowe once asked Quaker
William Lloyd Garrison if he was a Christian. Garrison replied that her
question was too indefinite and he could not answer it. Stowe then asked
him if he believed in atonement. He replied that he did not, nor did he
believe that Jesus could atone for one's sins. "Only a loving spirit like his
could redeem us, our character must be like his or we die in our sins," he
said. To which Mrs. Stowe responded, "I used to think you were a wolf
in sheep's clothing, but now I think you a sheep in wolf's clothing."[13]

Maryland, and the Eastern Shore in particular, filled as it was with
anti-slavery reformers, abolitionist infidels, and Bible-thumping preach-
ers, was unique in both the variety of sects and the clash of perspectives.
"Lacking the religious unity that characterized Virginia and much of New
England," Mary Beth Norton pointed out, "Maryland became a de facto
secular state even before the adoption of its famous Act for Religious
Toleration in 1649." In the Chesapeake, she added, "the family could not
serve as a model for the state—or vice versa—because families were too
truncated, anomalous, and unstable. . . . The peculiar nature of the fam-

ily and the absence of strong church structures turned the region into a practical laboratory for the dichotomous theory of authority (separation of church and state) years before Locke systematically formulated his ideas."[14] All lived side by side in uneasy proximity.

In 1634 the Calvert family, Roman Catholics, established Maryland's first colony at St. Mary's in the southern part of the Western Shore. By 1646 the settlement had dwindled to less than one hundred people when Cecil Calvert, second Lord Baltimore and family head, appointed William Stone, a Protestant, as governor. Probably at Lord Baltimore's suggestion, Stone persuaded a group of Puritans to come to Maryland from New England to settle there. Puritans believed they were a chosen people, charged with bringing God's message to a heathen land previously ruled by the devil. Many also had negative, sometimes violent reactions to the Catholic Church.[15]

As their population grew, Maryland Puritans attacked and plundered Catholic plantations and forced Lord Baltimore's brother to flee. They took power in 1654, abolished the religious toleration act enacted by the Calverts and denied Catholics the right to vote. With the restoration of the monarchy in England, four years later, Maryland was returned to the Calverts four years later, but with an uneasy rule.[16]

In 1715, moreover, the then-current Lord Baltimore converted from the Church of Rome to the Church of England and gained, as a result, more control. The Church of England became the established church in Maryland, though its numbers were small compared to other Protestant groups. While this regime was more tolerant than previous governments, many Catholics were forced to practice their faith behind closed doors.[17] Most prominent among the Catholic families were the Carrolls, rumored to have purchased land in Louisiana in preparation for possible flight. They did not have to flee—instead, they became wealthy and more open in their religious practice. Some sixty years later, Charles Carroll, a distant relative of Anna Ella, gained ultimate legitimacy as a signer of the Declaration of Independence.

The Protestant dissenters established themselves in many forms on colonial soil in Maryland—not only as Puritans, but also as Quakers, Methodists, Presbyterians, and many smaller sects—each locally centered and following a single leader. Religious belief, even among the Protestants, was far from homogeneous and groups were often at odds with each other. In 1689 Quakers, always bothersome in their opposition to authority, were also denied the right to vote.[18]

Sects varied greatly in the extent of their proselytizing. At one end, the Church of England tried by edict to become the only religious group of the area in the 1700s. At the other, Quakers distinguished "birthright

Quakers" and discouraged others from joining for fear of contamination. Sects varied in their beliefs. Quakers and Methodists preached against the evils of slavery and ownership of slaves. Presbyterians also feared the moral decay of slavery, though some perhaps were less convinced of the perils of ownership. Presbyterians like Sir Thomas Carroll also believed Catholicism was an evil associated with the doctrine of divine right and arbitrary rules. His granddaughter Anna Ella saw foreign Catholics as a threat to "Americanism . . . with their allegiance to a foreign potentate, the Pope, who . . . had evinced a great desire to control the spiritual and temporal interests of this young world." The Roman Catholic Church, she feared, had the dangerous aim to "unsettle the principles of our liberties and hence to destroy them."[19]

All sides had champions and detractors on the Eastern Shore. This was in sharp contrast to the religious climate of those farther south who were critical of the lack of moral cohesion in the North (which was defined by numerous and conflicting sects) and saw themselves as "the major bastion of resistance against Yankee enterprise and Yankee morals." The South would later find both justification and consolation for the war in their religion.[20]

Friends, as Quakers called themselves, were dissenters who believed in a functional rather than a symbolic form of worship. In particular, they rejected the "outward ceremonial," seeking instead plain dress and secular meeting rooms of worship. Implied in many of the dissenting sects, but particularly noteworthy among Quakers, was a rejection of state authority. Friends believed that individuals did not have to rely on priests, the church, or even the Bible as a final authority. "Truth," they believed, could only be found in an inward quest of "personal experience and direct communion with God."[21]

They believed there was an inner light within each individual (that of God in every man) that was a spirit and a grace by which "all might know salvation." For this reason Friends believed that violence against another human was violence against God. They held meetings for worship in silence so that members could achieve "insight heightened by group devotion" and wait for the Lord. The inner light, they thought, was not the same as *conscience*, which was a human faculty and subject to corruption. Still they did not reject conscience, believing it to be the highest ethical development humans were capable of before receiving the light. Also important to Friends was "concern," a term used by them to mean an obligation "to do something, or to demonstrate sympathetic interest in some individual or group, as a result of what is felt to be direct intimation of God's will."[22]

Over time, some members rebelled at what was considered the "stern discipline" of the group. A case in point was William Stevens, a Friend living in Compton, Maryland, who in the 1680s doffed his hat to Lady Baltimore when she arrived at Oxford. He was rebuked at his meeting for showing undue respect for authority, whereupon he and all his connections, resenting the interference, left the meeting and sought another faith.[23]

Friends became ardent abolitionists by the mid-1700s when John Woolman, a New Jersey Friend, out of concern, toured nearby slave settlements in Maryland, Virginia, and North Carolina. Upon his return, Woolman declared "slave keeping inconsistent with the Christian religion" and began a campaign to rid Quaker families of slaves. Many were persuaded by his reasoning and freed their slaves. "I believe," he concluded, "that liberty was the natural right of all men equally." As Friends who owned slaves began freeing them, meetings pressured others to follow and expelled members for purchasing chattel. According to historian Kate Larson, by 1790, Eastern Shore meetings had no known slave owners.[24] John Wesley, a founder of Methodism, came to the American colonies in the late 1760s. He wrote a pamphlet on slavery in 1774, stating "I absolutely deny all slave holding to be consistent with any degree of natural justice, mercy, and truth," and concluded, "Have you, has any man living, a right to use another as a slave? It cannot be."[25]

By the 1770s the Church of England was in decline on the shore, partly through the neglect of poorer whites by Anglican ministers and partly as a reaction to "evil" King George and Parliament. Methodists were gaining in number. Unlike the Church of England, which preached "obedience to the social order," Methodists assumed "everyone was a sinner in some way" and stressed forgiveness and redemption. Methodism spread rapidly in Dorchester County. It appealed to the very community—poorer whites and also blacks—that the Church of England had ignored.[26]

In 1785, a religious revival, the Second Great Awakening, emerged in the James River area of Virginia and spread north. Like the first Great Awakening of the 1730s and 1740s, it was a movement of redemption, of seeking forgiveness for great wickedness, and included condemning the evil of slavery and counseling emancipation as penance. Some Revivalists went so far as to combine anti-slavery religious notions with the new revolutionary ideology of equality and used the two in combination to promote abolition.[27] These were dangerous ideas.

Thomas Coke, an Anglican priest and Methodist minister, experienced the shore's religious disobedience to authority. Arriving from England in 1784, he and a group of ministers toured the middle states on horseback and preached about "the brotherhood of man." Coke visited Cambridge in early December and, though an ordained Anglican priest, was locked out of the local church. He said the ladies in general favored allowing him to speak, "but the gentlemen prevailed." The church door, which had been left open for "cows, and dogs, and pigs," was closed to him. Coke instead read prayers and preached at a nearby cottage and "had one of the largest congregations I have had in America."[28]

In the beginning Coke urged Methodists to, like the Quakers, "emancipate their slaves, declaring slavery contrary to the laws of God, of men, and of nature." He said that slavery was "hurtful to society and contrary to the dictates of conscience and pure religion."[29] So powerful was his message that many free blacks joined his religion—in some cases black Methodists outnumbered white parishioners in the churches of Maryland and South Carolina. But the message of emancipation began to change. By 1796 Methodists were allowed to purchase slaves, though only for a limited and specified time. But this revised practice also met with resistance, and church records suggest that many members were expelled for refusing to free slaves at the appointed time.[30]

Slaveholder Robert Gould Shaw of Vienna, Maryland, provided insight into how Methodism was viewed by his community. Publishing an ad in the *Maryland Herald and Eastern Shore Intelligencer*, the first newspaper printed on the Eastern Shore, Shaw provided a description of his fugitive slave George. "George is a well-set, yellowish kind of negro," he said "from 28 to 30 years of age, five feet six or seven inches high." As to his character, Shaw wrote, ". . . he is artful, and no doubt will attempt to pass for a free man; he has a great share of Methodism." This phrase—"having a share of Methodism"—was often repeated in ads, suggesting "those Methodist anti-slavery ideas influenced running away," historian Kay McElvey observed.[31]

The Eastern Shore also participated in the development of an independent black church. Richard Allen, a slave born in Delaware, had converted to Methodism in 1777 and convinced his owner to allow him to buy his freedom over time. He broke away from the church in 1786 out of unhappiness with his treatment by white parishioners (a further indication of the shifting attitudes of Methodists), and organized the Bethel African Methodist Episcopal Church. By 1816 an independent church organization of black leaders from Delaware, Maryland, Pennsylvania, and New Jersey had been formed.[32]

Also founded in Philadelphia in 1816 was the American Colonization Society, an organization that advocated purchasing slaves to allow their emigration rather than emancipation. Early on, the colonization movement had black supporters—but not among the masses. It was, commented abolitionist Benjamin Lundy, "an outrage, having no other object in view than the benefit of the slaveholding interests of the country."[33] Feeling that the society was moving too slowly, white Eastern Shoremen formed an organization of their own with the expressed intent to send free blacks to Africa. The first step, they said, "in ameliorating the condition of the negro lay in removing him from the white man's society to one of his own." Richard Allen believed that "the new wave of anti-negro feeling was caused by the American Colonization Society pretending to be concerned about free blacks having a better life." Increasing unhappiness with established white churches and anti-slavery societies fueled the search for alternatives.[34]

Eight AME (African Methodist Episcopal) churches were established by 1824 with over five hundred members. "Worship for blacks in the region," historian Catherine Clinton observed, "was strictly supervised. Slaves could congregate for religious services only with white approval and under white surveillance."[35] Since blacks were prohibited from owning church property, all churches had to have white trustees, a significant part of the supervision. Dorchester did not have an AME church until 1826. The organizers included two free men—the Drivers, father and son—and Benjamin Jennifer, a slave of Cambridge lawyer Josiah Bayly (the lawyer for Patty Cannon and perhaps the lawyer that Harriet Tubman consulted about her mother's status).[36]

In 1830 two black Bethel ministers came to Dorchester to establish a church totally independent of white control. As the ministers explained the concept, which included affiliation with an all-black conference in Baltimore and the potential for top decision-making positions, a group of armed white protesters marched in front of the building where the blacks were meeting. A fight ensued, several blacks were arrested, and two homes in Cambridge were burned. It was unclear whether there were fatalities. This rebellion reflected not only the long-denied desire for black control of worship and white fear of black self-determination but also the entrenched oppositional consciousness (i.e., awareness that ideas like "inalienable rights" were more likely to apply to the status quo then the disenfranchised) within the Eastern Shore black community.[37]

• • •

Harriet Tubman's religious views, like those of many slaves, evolved in stages. She sang Methodist hymns like "Bound for the Promised Land," and spirituals like "Sweet Chariot" and "Steal Away" as both revelation and revolt. Thomas Garrett reported to his friend Eliza Wigham that "Harriet has a good deal of the old fashion Quaker about her."[38] When Tubman made her first successful flight, she confided her plans to a white woman who lived in the area, as she later told her friend Helen Tatlock. Tatlock thought that the woman was a Quaker because "it was Quakers who then gave escaping slaves the most aid." For her help, Tubman gave this woman a prized bed quilt that she had sewn. Kate Larson suggested that Tubman was living in Poplar Neck in Caroline County at that time, not far from the Marshy Creek Friends Meeting, one of the oldest Quaker settlements in the area.[39]

Tubman heard lines of scripture from other slaves and committed them to memory, but she remained cautious about the slaveholders' religion. As a child she was forced to pad herself against her pious mistress's beatings, she told Edna Cheney. "When invited into family prayers, she preferred to stay on the landing, and pray for herself: 'and I prayed to God,' she says, 'to make me strong and able to fight, and that's what I've always prayed for ever since.'" It was in vain, Cheney said, that she tried to persuade Tubman that her prayer was a wrong one. "She always maintains it to be sincere and right, and it has certainly been fully answered," Cheney wrote.[40]

After the injury to her head, Tubman devoted more time to reflection, telling Cheney of a religious epiphany on one occasion. "'We had been carting manure all day, and the other girl and I were going home on the sides of the cart, and another boy was driving, when suddenly I heard such music as filled all the air'" and she saw "a vision which she described in language which sounded like the old prophets in its grand flow."[41] As historian Jean Humez observed, "There is plenty of informal evidence that a vital, distinctly African American form of evangelical Christianity flourished in the part of the slave's cultural world that was beyond the direct control of the slaveholders' churches."[42]

On another occasion, when telling a group in Boston of her last journey from Maryland, Tubman was asked, "'Didn't you almost feel when you were lying alone, as if there was no God?' 'Oh, no Missus,' said Harriet looking up in her child-like, simple way. 'I just asked Jesus to take care of me, and He never let me get frost-bitten one bit.'"[43] She had great confidence that "God will preserve her from harm in all her perilous journeys, as she says she never goes on her mission of mercy without his consent, or approbation," Thomas Garrett told a friend.[44]

Tubman displayed a deep faith, telling Cheney, "When I think of the prayers and groans I've heard on dem plantations, an' 'member dat God's a prayer-hearing God, I feel dat His time is near." Yet it was not a vengeful faith. "I tink dar's many a slaveholder'll git to Heaven. Dey don't know no better. Dey acts up to de light dey hab. You take that sweet little child (pointing to a lonely baby)—'pears more like an angel dan anyting else—take her down dere, let her nebber know nothing 'bout niggers but they was made to be whipped, an' she'll grow up to use the whip on 'em jus' like de rest. No, Misses, it's because dey don't know no better."[45]

She was said to be the most shrewd and practical person in the world, and yet Tubman was a firm believer in omens, dreams, and warnings. Garrett called them spiritual manifestations. She always knew when there was danger near her, Franklin Sanborn noted.[46] At the same time, she was said to not be superstitious, surprising friends by telling them she would walk through cemeteries at night. "They're all quiet there," she said. "All peaceful."[47]

Some religious practices were blended. "All the other Fridays of the year except Good Friday, Tubman's father 'nebber ate till the sun goes down; den he takes a little tea and a piece of bread.' 'But is he a Roman Catholic?' her interviewer asked. 'Oh no, Misses; he does it for conscience; we was taught to do so down South. He says if he denies himself for the sufferings of his lord an' Master, Jesus will sustain him.'"[48]

Tubman trusted few strangers and typically proceeded with great caution. There was probably no white person Tubman respected more than John Brown, and yet here too she had doubts about his motives, Sanford claimed. "That a white man should so take upon himself the burden of a despised race, she could not understand and she took refuge from her perplexity in the mysteries of her fervid religion." Sanborn surmised. Over time, she became a believer. On hearing of his death she said, "It's clear to me that it wasn't John Brown that was hung on that gallows—it was God in him."[49]

· · ·

Anna Ella Carroll's views about religion and society were also pronounced. Her critiques of Catholicism, more than anything, reveal the Eastern Shore antipathy toward the established church, be it in London or in Rome. Unlike Friends, Presbyterians believed that the Bible was the literal word of God, inspired by the Holy Spirit. It was God's truth. Sinners were not able to save themselves. Unlike Methodists, who believed that all were sinners and could be saved, Presbyterians thought only the elect, chosen by God, could be saved from their sins. Visible signs, they believed, were evidence of God's grace. They appeared to worship a somewhat unforgiving God, who left lonely sinners to their own devices rather than allowing them to rely on an intermediary bishop or congregation to provide some absolution.[50]

Presbyterians observed prescribed forms of worship, more elaborate than the Friends but still Spartan compared to the Catholics. They held revivals on a regular basis and periodically sent missionaries out to save Native Americans and slaves. As to the institution of slavery itself, they held a middle ground. Friends, after 1750, forbade members from owning slaves. Presbyterians condemned the evil of slavery but not necessarily the evil of slaveholding. The uncertainty in this position caused even further division within the Presbyterian community.[51]

Robert Breckenridge, Carroll's first religious instructor, wrote an article about the slavery debate in Kentucky just prior to the Civil War, providing insight into Presbyterianism in general and expressing perhaps some of the foundations of Carroll's religious views. Presbyterians, he said "have taken the lead in the struggle for emancipation." They were, however, against the doctrine that immediate and universal emancipation was the imperative duty of all slaveholders. Rather, he suggested, holding slaves is right or wrong according to circumstances but the slave owner "had no right to use his power to prevent the intellectual, moral, and social improvement of his subjects, in order that his authority may be undisturbed and perpetuated." This view, rejected in much of the South, tore at the very foundation of slavery. It advocated importance of individual religious instruction for all at a time most thought any education of slaves would undermine the system.[52]

He was aware of the dissenting view of the equality of man, a position he supported with reservations. The heart of the problem, he thought, was that "while we joyfully admit the negro race to be bone of our bone and flesh of our flesh, to be brethren of the same great family to which we ourselves belong, it would be folly to deny that the blacks are as a race inferior to the whites. This is a fact which the history of the world places beyond dispute." Breckenridge was not sure whether at some future point "they might rise to an equality with their more favored brethren," but that was not his interest.[53]

Breckenridge's emancipation plan, a gradual one, had three parts. First, he proposed appointing a public officer who would set a value on the services of the slave that the master would be bound to accept. When the slave had accumulated one-sixth of his value, and paid it to his master, he would have Mondays free. This arrangement would continue "until his whole time was his own." Along the way, Breckenridge argued, "The slave would be trained to the habits of industry and self-control, and prepared to provide for himself."[54]

The second part of his plan would compensate the owners of slaves. This was justified because "slavery was the work not of the individual but the community" and "would not exist without positive enactments," such as property laws. The state had condoned the holding of slaves, therefore the state "must bear the expense of rectifying its mistake."[55]

The final feature of Breckenridge's plan would expatriate the liberated blacks. He thought it very likely that blacks would "prove the stronger race in the West India Islands, and in some other places still nearer the equator." The basic principle, he felt, was that whether white or black, the weaker race sinks and perishes in the presence of the stronger.[56] "With a plan of expatriation," he concluded, "the state, freed from its black population, would soon find itself filled with intelligent and prosperous farmers and mechanics from other portions of the Union and from the Old World."[57] God would smile upon this plan, he indicated. The American character, formed in the cradle of the first colonists, would see it through.

Breckenridge's ardent anti-Catholicism was based in part on the idea of discouraging independent thinking among believers. In *The Great American Battle*, his pupil Carroll wrote, "The Pope, who sitting and trembling upon the great shield of the Vatican at Rome, evinced a great desire to control the spiritual and temporal interests of his young world."[58] Breckenridge saw it as a great advantage that early settlers were spared the "thousands of Romanists who now pour in on us."[59]

Breckenridge did not recommend ending immigration, as many Know-Nothings did. Immigrants, he thought, could be improved, and he recommended a limited immigration policy where "the new colonists should not be so numerous as to oppress the resources, and choak [*sic*] the avenues of life in these recent settlements, and they should be sufficiently enlightened to fall in the spirit of the community of which they become members."[60] Anna Ella Carroll's views on all of these issues had the same Breckenridgian, religious base. She learned her lessons well.

• • •

It is unfortunate that we know nothing of Patty Cannon's religious views or indeed whether she had any. Some members of the Cannon family, to whom she was attached by marriage, were prominent Methodists, believers in what Max Weber called "a fulfillment of duty in worldly affairs as the highest form which the moral activity of the individual could assume."[61] For example, William Cannon, born in Sussex County, Delaware, though a slaveholder, "was a bitter opponent of slavery and a staunch supporter of the Union." Elected governor of Delaware in 1863, his efforts to keep Delaware from seceding were often heralded by the president and members of Congress.[62] Bishop James Cannon (a distant relation to Jesse), a Methodist minister, was considered one of the strongest church proponents of Prohibition and sometimes called the "Dry Messiah." Such acts suggest the strong commitment to conscience characteristic of early Methodism. By contrast to these Cannons, Jesse was called a "black sheep."[63]

Historian Mary Beth Norton, in *Liberty's Daughters*, argued that the revolution left a positive imprint on women's lives by disrupting old lines of authority and work habits in the family, thus creating a strong sense of self-esteem. They became, Norton suggested, active members of society. And so it may be said of Patty Cannon.

But the reality was that Patty Cannon's misdeeds, revealed only after her death, got her labeled conjurer, an appellation reserved for witches, older women who were thought to practice harmful magic. In a pre- and early-Enlightenment world, to alter slightly a phrase from Norton, witches provided a plausible explanation for the origins of misfortunes.[64] For religious groups in particular, witches served as a foil against doubts and contradictions. Possessed by an evil spirit, they corrupted innocents and tested the faith of all. Such labels were not unusual for active women, women who took charge, regardless of the act. As historian Dickson Preston observed, "Dorchester-born Harriet Tubman whose mysterious comings and goings and miraculous feats made her a saint among blacks, made her a devil among slaveholding whites."[65]

In nineteenth-century Chesapeake, as in seventeenth-century New England, hunting witches was not so much about the belief of the individuals as it was about the etiology of belief. The presence of witches in a community explained illness, untimely deaths, plagues, and disasters. They were not only the source of evil, but dwelling as they did within the community they could also symbolize individual, internal conflict— the enemy within. Witch-hunting, casting out the demons, was an act of personal salvation.

Historian John Demos, in an examination of witchcraft, outlined what he considered a typical profile. Predominately women, they were also of middle age, married—though often childless—and actively engaged in some manner in the local community. Many were knowledgeable about medicines and cures. Some, like Anne Hutchinson of the Massachusetts Bay Colony, were midwives. Interestingly, by Demos's account, they had a higher than normal record as litigants in court and as defendants in minor criminal cases, even before discovery of their so-called witchery. Most had a reputation for abrasiveness and assertiveness. Their alleged victims were usually young and defenseless. Witches not only harmed people, but were also accused of sickening animals, influencing weather patterns, causing crops to fail and infestations to occur. Blaming events on witches, Demos argued, was a simple way of making sense of the insensible world.[66]

Witch hunts occurred not only in seventeenth-century New England but in England and much of Europe as well. It was only in 1736 that witchery ceased to be a crime in England. But crime or not, popular attacks on supposed witches continued into the nineteenth century in both England and America. It was in preindustrial towns and villages, where village folk had frequent interaction, observation, and interpersonal conflict with each other, that accusations of witchcraft were most likely to emerge. Demos suggested that hostility and suspicion against an assertive and aggressive woman may have festered for years, only to suddenly erupt into criminal action. Identifying a witch was a way of both personifying evil and sharpening moral boundaries.[67]

When hostility exploded into accusation and trial, the community exercised its right to hear the evidence, weigh the crimes and, by conviction, affirm its righteousness. It was thought that at the least the threat of expulsion would serve to dissuade others from similar deviant behaviors. Take Grace White, born about 1660 in Princess Anne County, Maryland, who later married James Steward. She commonly dressed in men's clothing and was considered by her neighbors a strong-willed woman unafraid to speak her mind and therefore a witch. Between 1697 and 1707 she was in and out of court on charges brought by her for defamation and by her neighbors who claimed she cast spells, killed animals, and destroyed crops. Finally, a test of trial by water ("ducking") was devised where her right thumb was tied to her left big toe and her left thumb was tied to her right big toe and she was thrown into water "above man's depth." If she sank, she was not a witch. With great difficulty Grace Steward remained afloat, failed the test, and was sentenced to jail for perhaps as long as seven years. In any case, she was forever believed to be a witch, even after her death in 1740.[68]

There are obvious parallels to the case of Patty Cannon, a middle-aged widow known for her aggression and assertiveness. Contemporary observers noted on many occasions that community hostility toward the Cannon-Johnson gang was long standing, but locals feared intervening. The chance discovery of bones on property she once lived on was sufficient evidence to start the criminal process.

Edmund Morgan in his review of Demos's book pointed out that witchcraft had a lot to do with a devout public grappling with notions of sin and evil and an imperfect world. It was not, one could surmise, the alleged perpetrator's beliefs that were at issue but doubts about the validity of their own. In commenting on the sentence of Anne Hutchinson, a midwife found guilty of "rank familism" (but not witchcraft) and a woman who had miscarried, Reverend Thomas Weld wrote, "See how the wisdom of God fitted this judgement to her sinne in every way, for looke as she had vented misshapen opinions, so she must bring forth deformed monsters. . . ."[69] Weld believed that God punished wrongdoers in dramatic ways as a sign and lesson to those of little or slipping faith.

Transforming Patty Cannon into a conjurer and source of evil also had the effect of casting much of slaveholding society—the ordinary slaveholders—as victims and not transgressors. The institution was safe, the wrongdoers the exception. Nineteenth-century slaveholders, historian

Walter Johnson remarked, "broke the system of slavery into hundreds of thousands of isolated sets of human relations between individual masters and individual slaves and argued that the violence of slavery was a matter of generally benevolent human relations gone awry, of personal failings of particular owners, of bad masters who gave slavery a bad name, not an inevitable feature of the system itself."[70]

In 1909, Quaker poet John Greenleaf Whittier was asked to write an introduction to the *Journal of John Woolman*. Whittier played an important cameo role in the abolitionist movement, helping to pay the $50 Baltimore jail fine of William Lloyd Garrison, a gesture that enabled Garrison to return to Boston and start his own paper. John Woolman, called by Whittier an "unlearned workingman of New Jersey," had, through his Quaker ministry, precipitated the dismantling of slavery in the region. In explaining Woolman's extraordinary contribution, Whittier observed, "Some great reform which lifts the world to a higher level, some mighty change for which the ages have waited in anxious expectancy, takes place before your eyes, and, in seeking to trace it back to its origin, we are often surprised to find the initial link in the chain of causes to be some comparatively obscure individual, the divine commission and significance of whose life were scarcely understood by his contemporaries, and perhaps not even by himself."[71]

• • •

This seems a fitting closing tribute to Moses, the Monster, and Miss Anne. Tubman's lonely journeys in the dead of night helped to topple a system of labor and a way of life. And in some mysterious and inverted way, Cannon's notoriety served to expose the wicked practice of trafficking in human flesh, while Carroll's persistent intervention, whatever its actual form, helped to save the holy experiment that was the Union. Perhaps a "divine commission" in the case of Tubman and "significances" in the case of Cannon and Carroll were "scarcely understood by contemporaries, and perhaps not even by themselves."[72]

More than most, Frederick Douglass understood the contribution that Marylanders, in all their combinations and permutations, made to such "significances." When he first returned to Baltimore in 1864, twenty-six years after his escape, he told a gathered crowd, "I rejoice that we are able to meet here on the soil of our birth—to meet not only as men, but as Marylanders—children of Maryland—the land at whose sparkling foundations we first quenched our thirst—the land whose fields, when we were hungry first gave us bread, to meet here upon our own dear native soil."[73] Maryland, he continued, "is now a glorious free state, here the revolution is genuine, full and complete." Douglass had always proclaimed his love for the state. "Its geography, climate, fertility, and products, are such as to make it a very desirable abode for any man. It is not that I love Maryland less," he said, "but freedom more."[74] On this point, Moses and the Monster and Miss Anne could all agree.

Notes

Introduction

1. Barbara J. Fields, *Slavery and Freedom on the Middle Ground: Maryland during the Nineteenth Century* (New Haven, Conn.: Yale University Press, 1985), xi, 17.

2. Sarah H. Bradford, *Scenes in the Life of Harriet Tubman* (Auburn, N.Y.: W.J. Moses, 1869; repr. North Stratford, N.H.: Ayer, 1971), 7; Sallie Holley, "Letter to Mr. Powell." In *National Anti-Slavery Standard* (November 1867). Holley said that $10,000 was not too much, making her statement more speculation than fact.

3. Sarah E. Blackwell, *A Military Genius: A Life of Anna Ella Carroll of Maryland* (Washington, D.C.: Judd & Detweiler, 1891).

4. Historian Larry Gara quoted in James McGowan, *Station Master on the Underground Railroad: The Life and Letters of Thomas Garrett* (Moylan, Pa.: Whimsie Press, 1977), 15.

5. John Greenleaf Whittier, in Introduction, in John Wollman, *Journal of John Woolman* (London: Andrew Melrose, 1871), i.

6. Three historians, Kate Clifford Larson, *Bound for the Promised Land: Harriet Tubman, Portrait of an American Hero* (New York: Ballantine, 2004); Jean McMahon Humez, *Harriet Tubman: The Life and Life Stories* (Madison, Wis: University of Wisconsin Press, 2003); and Catherine Clinton, *Harriet Tubman: The Road to Freedom* (Boston, Mass: Little, Brown, 2004) have recently published significant biographies and research on Tubman. After an unexplained drought of nearly sixty-five years, their careful scholarship has finally given Harriet Tubman the attention and scrutiny she so richly deserves. We are all in their debt. Their insights and discoveries infuse this book.

7. Anne Firor Scott, *Making the Invisible Woman Visible* (Urbana: University of Illinois Press, 1984), 31, 39.

8. "Dangerousness," according to Michael Foucault, "meant that the individual must be considered by society at the level of his potentialities and not at the level

of his acts. Not as someone who had actually violated a law, but as someone whose potential behavior had to be subject to control and correction." *Abnormal: Lectures at the College De France, 1974–1975* (New York: Picador, 1999), xxiii.

9. Catherine Clinton, *Harriet Tubman: The Road to Freedom* (New York: Little Brown, 2004), 17.

10. Larson, *Bound for the Promised Land,* 17.

11. Hal Roth, *The Monster's Handsome Face: Patty Cannon in Fiction and Fact* (Vienna, Md: Nanticoke Books, 1998), 129. Roth identifies Josiah Bayly as Cannon's lawyer. His office was opposite the courthouse in Cambridge, a familiar site for Tubman. The speculation that he was Tubman's lawyer is my own.

12. Dickson J. Preston, *Young Frederick Douglass: The Maryland Years* (Baltimore: The Johns Hopkins University Press, 1980), 3.

13. Earl Conrad, *Harriet Tubman* (Washington, D.C.: Associated Publishers, 1943), 6.

14. Hulbert Footner, *Rivers of the Eastern Shore* (Cambridge, Md.: Tidewater Publishers, 1944), 170.

15. Two other states comprise the area also known as the Delmarva Peninsula—all of tiny Delaware and an even smaller part of eastern Virginia. About two hundred miles long and from five to eighty miles wide (depending on the shoreline), it has deep waterways and many islands. Wilmington, the largest city in Delaware, with a population just over 10,000 in 1845, was the home of Thomas Garrett. Sallie Holley visited Garrett in 1852and highlighted some of the contradictions of the place. "The fact that I am in a slave state," she wrote, "constantly presses upon my mind. It seems very strange and awful. I am told the pillory is in use in this city. Persons who steal are publicly whipped, both men and women." She also added, "I gave my first lecture in Wilmington Saturday, October 30th. A crowded town hall listened with great respect; some slaveholders present; collection $7.06! Quite a surprise to the anti-slavery folks here." (Sallie Holley and John White Chadwick, *A Life for Liberty: Anti-Slavery and Other Letters of Sallie Holley* [New York: G.P. Putnam's Sons, 1899], 98.)

16. Footner, *Rivers of the Eastern Shore,* 170.

17. H. L. Mencken, quoted in Jane Maneely, "The Great Divide," in *Chesapeake Bay Magazine* 30 (October 2000), 2.

18. Fields, *Slavery and Freedom on the Middle Ground,* 5.

19. Walter Johnson, *Soul by Soul: Life Inside the Antebellum Slave Market* (Cambridge, Mass.: Harvard University Press, 1999), 5.

20. Fields, *Slavery and Freedom on the Middle Ground,* 5.

21. Ibid., 6.

22. Ibid., 32.

23. Ted Giles, *Patty Cannon, Woman of Mystery* (Eastern, Md.: Easton Publishing, 1965), 20.

24. Carroll would later make this claim before Congress with support from Abraham Lincoln's appointees. Like Tubman, her first biographers were sympathetic nonhistorians. The recent work of Janet Coryell provides a more balanced examination with a well-documented account of her life. Coryell, *Neither Heroine nor Fool: Anna Ella Carroll of Maryland* (Kent, Ohio: Kent State University Press, 1990), 70–89.

25. Philip Morgan, *Slave Counterpoint: Black Culture in the Eighteenth-Cen-*

tury Chesapeake & Lowcountry (Chapel Hill: University of North Carolina Press, 1998), 9.

26. Kay McElvey, "Early Black Dorchester, 1776–1870: A History of the Struggle of African Americans in Dorchester County, Maryland, to Be Free to Make Their Own Choices" (Ph.D. dissertation, University of Maryland, 1991), 247.

27. W. E. B. DuBois, *John Brown* (New York: Modern Library, 2001), 41.

28. Eugene D. Genovese, *Roll, Jordan, Roll: The World the Slaves Made* (New York: Pantheon Books, 1974), 35.

29. Clinton, *Harriet Tubman: The Road to Freedom*, 7.

30. Frederick Douglass, *My Bondage and My Freedom* (New York: Arno/New York Times, [1855] 1969), 412.

31. Fields, *Slavery and Freedom on the Middle Ground*, 24.

32. Peter Kolchin, *American Slavery: 1619–1877* (New York: Hill and Wang, 1993), 49.

33. Ira Berlin, *Slaves without Masters: The Free Negro in the Antebellum South* (New York: Pantheon Books, 1974).

34. Fields, *Slavery and Freedom on the Middle Ground*, 3.

35. David Brion Davies, *Challenging the Boundaries of Slavery* (Cambridge: Harvard University Press, 2003), 31.

36. Kolchin, *American Slavery*, 39.

37. Ibid., 96.

38. William Faulkner, *Absalom, Absalom!* (New York: Modern Library, 1964).

39. Johnson, *Soul by Soul*, 5.

40. Holley and Chadwick, *A Life for Liberty*, 75.

41. Eric Foner, *Free Soil, Free Labor, Free Men: The Ideology of the Republican Party before the Civil War* (New York: Oxford University Press, 1970), 7.

42. Genovese, *Roll, Jordan, Roll*, 50.

43. Charles S. Sydnor, "The Southerner and the Law," *Journal of Southern History* 6 (February 1940), 7.

44. Ibid., 8.

45. Ibid., 10.

46. Ibid., 12.

47. Carol Wilson, *Freedom at Risk: The Kidnapping of Free Blacks in America, 1780–1865* (Lexington: University of Kentucky Press, 1994), 12.

48. Walter Johnson stated that "the boom years of the 1830s were followed by the depression in the 1840s and then another decade of massive volume in the 1850s," *Soul by Soul*, 6. Ulrich B. Phillips, *American Negro Slavery: A Survey of the Supply, Employment and Control of Negro Labor as determined by the Plantation Regime* (Baton Rouge: Louisiana State University Press, [1918] 1966), 190.

49. Johnson, *Soul by Soul*, 54.

50. James Madison, *The Federalist Papers*, no. 42 (New York: Signet Classic, 1966), 263. Walter Johnson pointed out that "a portion of slaveholders, mostly Virginians, feared that the continued importation of slaves would dilute the social power that their own slaves supported." *Soul by Soul*, 5.

51. *Constitution of the United States*, Article IV, Section 2.

52. Anne Boylan, *The Origins of Women's Activism: New York and Boston, 1797–1840* (Chapel Hill: University of North Carolina Press, 2002), 6.

53. Bayard Taylor, "Down the Eastern Shore," in *Rediscovery of the Eastern Shore*, ed. Harold Jopp (Wye Mills, Md.: Chesapeake College Press, 1986), 32.

54. Jeanne Boydston writes of "large numbers of women in paid labor by 1830's and that industrialization transformed much of women's work into wage labor." "The Woman Who Wasn't There: Women's Market Labor and the Transition to Capitalism in the United States," in Paul A. Gilje, *Wages of Independence: Capitalism in the EarlyAmerican Republic* (Madison: Madison House, 1997), 23.

55. Drew Gilpin Faust, *Mothers of Invention: Women of the Slaveholding South in the American Civil War* (New York: Vintage, 1997), 64.

56. Brenda Stevenson, *Life in Black and White: Family and Community in the Slave South* (New York: Oxford University Press, 1996), 6.

57. Faust, *Mothers of Invention*, 8.

58. Marjorie B. Greenbie, *My Dear Lady: The Story of Anna Ella Carroll, the "Great Unrecognized Member of Lincoln's Cabinet"* (New York: Arno Press/New York Times, 1974), 71.; Richard C. Rohrs, "Public Attention for . . . Essentially Private Matters," *Journal of the Early Republic* 24 (Spring 2004), 107.

59. Nell Irvin Painter, *Sojourner Truth: A Life, A Symbol* (New York: Norton, 1996), 134.

60. Giles, *Woman of Mystery*, 23.

61. Ibid.

62. Bradford, *Scenes in the Life*, 79.

63. Greenbie, *My Dear Lady*, 27.

64. C. Kay Larson, *Great Necessities: The Life, Times, and Writings of Anna Ella Carroll, 1815–1894* (Philadelphia: Xlibris, 2004), 17.

65. *Narrative and Confessions of Lucretia P. Cannon* (printed for the publishers, 1841), 14.

66. Shirley Yee, *Black Women Abolitionists: A Study in Activism, 1828–1860* (Knoxville: University of Tennessee Press, 1992), 41.

67. Earl Conrad, *Harriet Tubman* (Washington, D.C.: Associated Publishers, 1943), 32.

68. Mary Chestnut, *A Diary from Dixie* (Cambridge: Harvard University Press, 1980), 21.

69. Blackwell, *A Military Genius*, 83, provides evidence of a paper Carroll wrote on November 30, 1861, recommending the Tennessee over the Mississippi. And a letter from Edward Bates to Carroll dated April 15, 1862, stated that "the President paid you a very handsome compliment in the Cabinet meeting yesterday, in reference to your usefulness to the country" (47). These are Carroll's strongest documents.

70. Scott, *Making the Invisible Woman Visible*, 103.

Chapter 1: The Monster's Handsome Face

1. Thomas Jefferson and William Harwood Peden, *Notes on the State of Virginia*, (Chapel Hill: University of North Carolina Press, 1955), 164–65. Quoted in Drew R. McCoy, *The Elusive Republic: Political Economy in Jeffersonian America* (Chapel Hill: University of North Carolina Press, 1980), 15.

2. Walter Johnson, *Soul by Soul: Life Inside the Antebellum Slave Market* (Cambridge, Mass.: Harvard University Press, 1999), 24.

3. Winfield H. Collins, *The Domestic Slave Trade of the Southern States* (New York: Broadway Publishing, 1904), 15.

4. Ibid.

5. Johnson, *Soul by Soul*, 27.

6. Hal Roth, *The Monster's Handsome Face* (Vienna, Md.: Nanticoke Books, 1998), 1.

7. Jerry Shields, *The Infamous Patty Cannon in History and Legend* (Dover, Del.: Bibliotheca Literaria Press, 1990), 8.

8. Roth, *The Monster's Handsome Face*, 34.

9. *Narrative and Confessions of Lucretia P. Cannon, The Female Murderer*, twenty-three-page booklet (New York: 1841).

10. Roth, *The Monster's Handsome Face*, 123.

11. Sallie Holley and John White Chadwick, *A Life for Liberty; Anti-Slavery and Other Letters of Sallie Holley* (New York: G.P. Putnam's Sons, 1899), 91; Ted Giles, *Patty Cannon, Woman of Mystery* (Eastern, Md.: Easton Publishing, 1965), 19.

12. James A. McGowan, *Station Master on the Underground Railroad: The Life and Letters of Thomas Garrett* (Moylan, Pa.: Whimsie Press, 1977), 50; Marjorie B. Greenbie, *My Dear Lady: The Story of Anna Ella Carroll, the "Great Unrecognized Member of Lincoln's Cabinet"* (New York: Arno Press/New York Times, 1974), 24.

13. Quoted in Giles, *Woman of Mystery*, 29.

14. J. H. K. Shannahan, *Tales of Old Maryland* (Baltimore: Meyer & Thalheimer, 1907), 65.

15. Ibid., 66.

16. Sydney Greenbie and Marjorie B. Greenbie, *Anna Ella Carroll and Abraham Lincoln* (Manchester, Maine: Falmouth Publishing, 1952), 28.

17. George Massey, quoted in Roth, *The Monster's Handsome Face*, 197–99.

18. Hal Roth, *Now This Is the Truth . . . and Other Lies: Tales from the Eastern Shore . . . and More* (Vienna, Md.: Nanticoke Books, 2005), 127; Roth, *The Monster's Handsome Face*, 226.

19. Brenda Stevenson, *Life in Black and White: Family and Community in the Slave South* (New York: Oxford University Press, 1996), 5.

20. Roth, *Now This Is the Truth*, 47–50.; Roth, *The Monster's Handsome Face*, 49.

21. Roth, *Now This Is the Truth*, 51.

22. Shields, *The Infamous Patty Cannon*, 9.

23. Giles, *Woman of Mystery*, 18.

24. John Blassingame, *Slave Testimony: Two Centuries of Letters, Speeches, Interviews, and Autobiographies* (Baton Rouge: Louisiana State University Press, 1977), 183–84.

25. Roth, *Now This Is the Truth*, 52.

26. Stevenson, *Life in Black and White*, 8.

27. Susan Branson, "Women and the Family Economy in the Early Republic: The Case of Elizabeth Meredith," *Journal of the Early Republic* 16 (Spring 1996), 49.

28. Anne Firor Scott, *Making the Invisible Woman Visible* (Urbana: University of Illinois Press, 1984), 176.

29. Sherry H. Penny and James D. Livingston, *A Very Dangerous Woman: Martha Wright and Women's Rights* (Amherst: University of Massachusetts Press, 2004), 7–10.

30. Jean Humez, *Harriet Tubman: The Life and Life Stories* (Madison: University of Wisconsin Press, 2003), 20.

31. Penny and Livingston, *A Very Dangerous Woman*, 10.

32. Giles, *Woman of Mystery*, 19, 23, 19, 14.

33. Ibid., 14, 20.

34. Ibid., 20.

35. Fletcher Pratt, *The Heroic Years: Fourteen Years of the Republic, 1801–1815* (New York: H. Smith and R. Haas, 1934).

36. Carol Wilson, *Freedom at Risk: The Kidnapping of Free Blacks in America, 1780–1865* (Lexington: University of Kentucky Press, 1994), 7.

37. Collins, *The Domestic Slave Trade of the Southern States*, 22.

38. Herman Freudenberger and Jonathan B. Prichett, "The Domestic United States Slave Trade: New Evidence," *Journal of Interdisciplinary History* (Winter, 1991), 461, 462.

39. Collins, *The Domestic Slave Trade of the Southern States*, 27, 28, 22; Johnson, *Soul by Soul*, 5; Ulrich B. Phillips, *American Negro Slavery* (Baton Rouge: Louisiana State University Press, [1918] 1969), 188.

40. Frederic Bancroft, *Slave Trading in the Old South* (Columbia: University of South Carolina Press, 1996), 22.

41. Phillips, *American Negro Slavery*, 189–90.

42. David B. Davies, *Challenging the Boundaries of Slavery* (Cambridge: Harvard University Press, 2003),

43. Collins, *The Domestic Slave Trade of the Southern States*, 38.

44. Phillips, *American Negro Slavery*, 174, 189, 191.

45. Johnson, *Soul by Soul*, 36.

46. Freudenberger and Prichett, "Domestic United States Slave Trade," 452.

47. Phillips, *American Negro Slavery*, 192.

48. Bancroft, *Slave Trading in the Old South*, 58, 61, 62.

49. Kay McElvey, "Early Black Dorchester, 1776–1870: A History of the Struggle of African Americans in Dorchester County, Maryland, to Be Free to Make Their Own Choices" (Ph.D. dissertation, University of Maryland, 1991), 244.

50. Johnson, *Soul by Soul*, 74.

51. Ibid, 49–50.

52. E. A. Andrews, *Slavery and the Domestic Slave-Trade* (Boston: Light & Stearns, 1836), 143; Collins, *The Domestic Slave Trade of the Southern States*, 22.

53. Bancroft, *Slave Trading in the Old South*, 62.

54. Roth, *The Monster's Handsome Face*, 2.

55. Johnson, *Soul by Soul*, 48.

56. McElvey, "Early Black Dorchester," 241.

57. Carol Wilson, *Freedom at Risk: The Kidnapping of Free Blacks in America, 1780–1865* (Lexington: University of Kentucky Press, 1994), 41; Don E. Fehrenbacher, *Slavery, Law, and Politics: The Dred Scott Case in Historical Perspective* (New York: Oxford University Press, 1981), 21.

58. Fehrenbacher, *Slavery, Law, and Politics*, 21.

59. Roth, *Now This Is the Truth*, 71.

60. Andrews, *Slavery and the Domestic Slave-Trade*, 59.

61. Wilson, *Freedom at Risk*, 41.

62. Ibid., 26.

63. Giles, *Woman of Mystery*, 21.

64. 2 Del. 622 (1821).

65. Wilson, *Freedom at Risk*, 21

66. Blassingame, *Slave Testimony*, 179.

67. Wilson, *Freedom at Risk*, 22.

68. Ibid., 27, 29.

69. In 1821, Joe Johnson, Jesse Cannon, James Jones, and a man named William Goslin, according to the *Eastern Gazette*, were issued writs to "recover the possession of" three blacks. The July 23, 1821, article stated, "on the 14th inst. three writs were issued in Sussex County in the state against James Jones, Jesse Cannon, Joseph Johnson, and William Goslin, to replevy Thomas Carlisle, negro, another to replevy Nochre Griffith, negro, and a third to replevy Isaac Griffith, negro." According to the article Nochre and Isaac Griffith were slave children aged nine and four belonging to Nancy Griffith, who sold them to James Jones who, in turn, sold them to Joseph Johnson. They and several others were chained in the attic "awaiting the arrival of a vessel for transporting them to the South." The article also states that two sheriffs and three constables went to the house of Jesse Cannon to execute their writs. Johnson resisted, threatening at first to shoot them, but later surrendered. He was not charged.

70. Blassingame, *Slave Testimony*, 179.

71. Ibid., 180.

72. Wilson, *Freedom at Risk*, 28.

73. Ibid., 30.

74. Roth, *The Monster's Handsome Face*, 61.

75. Wilson, *Freedom at Risk*, 128.

76. Roth, *The Monster's Handsome Face*, 226.

77. John M. Clayton to W. W. Boardman, July 7, 1830 (Special Collections, University of Delaware).

78. Joseph P. Comegys, *Memoir of John M. Clayton* (Wilmington: Historical Society of Delaware, 1882), 18.

79. Ibid., 32.

80. Ibid.

81. Ibid.

82. Roth, *The Monster's Handsome Face*, 49.

83. Ibid., 33.

84. Jerry Shields, *The Infamous Patty Cannon in History and Legend* (Dover, Del.: Bibliotheca Literaria Press, 1990), 10.

85. Ibid.

86. Giles, *Woman of Mystery*, 39.

87. Roth, *The Monster's Handsome Face*, 73.

88. Giles, Woman of Mystery, 6.

89. Ibid., 84.

90. Shields, *The Infamous Patty Cannon*, 12. In 1829, the Delaware State Legislature appointed Clayton to the U.S. Senate, the youngest member of that august body.

91. George Alfred Townsend and Hal Roth, *The Entailed Hat, or Patty Cannon's Times* (Vienna, Md: Nanticoke Books, 2000), 415.

92. Ibid., 419, 426.

93. Roth, *The Monster's Handsome Face*, 224.

94. Ibid., 134–35. As noted in the introduction, Bayly's office was on High Street in Cambridge. Bayly "owned" Benjamin Jenifer, a slave and recognized commu-

nity religious leader. This connection would make Bayly an obvious choice for Tubman, although there is no record of who she hired. For details on Jenifer see McElvey, *Early Black Dorchester*, 345–46.

95. Shields, *The Infamous Patty Cannon*, 7.

96. Roth, *The Monster's Handsome Face*, 124.

97. Ibid., 153; Giles, *Woman of Mystery*, 9.

98. Roth, *The Monster's Handsome Face*, 77.

99. Davies, *Challenging the Boundaries of Slavery*, 32.

Chapter 2: Maryland, My Maryland

1. Janet L. Coryell, *Neither Heroine nor Fool: Anna Ella Carroll of Maryland* (Kent, Ohio: Kent State University Press, 1990), 1.

2. Charles McCool Snyder, "Anna Ella Carroll, Political Strategist and Gadfly of President Fillmore," *Maryland Historical Magazine* 68 (Spring 1973): 36–62, 38.

3. Sarah Blackwell, *A Military Genius: Life of Anna Ella Carroll of Maryland* (Washington: Judd & Detweiler, 1891), 44.

4. Coryell, *Neither Heroine nor Fool*, 6.

5. Ibid., 5.

6. C. Kay Larson, *Great Necessities: The Life, Times, and Writings of Anna Ella Carroll, 1815–1894* (Philadelphia: Xlibris, 2004), 77.

7. Sallie Holley and John White Chadwick, *A Life for Liberty; Anti-Slavery and Other Letters of Sallie Holley* (New York: G.P. Putnam's Sons, 1899) 38.

8. Anna Ella Carroll, *The Great American Battle; or, the Contest between Christianity and Political Romanism* (New York: Miller, Orton, and Mulligan, 1856), 13.

9. Coryell, *Neither Heroine nor Fool*, 6.

10. Anne Firor Scott, *Making the Invisible Woman Visible* (Urbana: University of Illinois Press, 1984), 92.

11. Coryell, *Neither Heroine nor Fool*, 10.

12. Snyder, "Anna Ella Carroll, Political Strategist," 38.

13. Ibid.

14. Holley and Chadwick, *A Life for Liberty*, 60.

15. Snyder, "Anna Ella Carroll, Political Strategist," 38.

16. Coryell, *Neither Heroine nor Fool*, 8.

17. Ibid.

18. The Know-Nothing, or American, party, formed in the 1850s, was very popular in Maryland. Indifferent to slavery, but representing a white majority with no stake in the system, they proposed reforms to reduce the disproportionate representation of slaveholders in the legislature. Barbara Fields, *Slavery and Freedom on the Middle Ground* (New Haven, Conn.: Yale University Press, 1985), 58–59.

19. Snyder, "Anna Ella Carroll, Political Strategist," 40.

20. Carroll, *The Great American Battle*, v.

21. C. Kate Larson, *Great Necessities*, 146.

22. Marjorie B. Greenbie, *My Dear Lady: The Story of Anna Ella Carroll, the "Great Unrecognized Member of Lincoln's Cabinet"* (New York: Arno Press/ New York Times, 1974), 73.

23. Coryell, *Neither Heroine nor Fool*, 20.

24. C. Kate Larson, *Great Necessities*, 115.

25. Sidney Greenbie and Marjorie B. Greenbie, *Anna Ella Carroll and Abraham Lincoln* (Manchester, Maine: Falmouth Publishing Co. 1952), 368.

26. Coryell, *Neither Heroine nor Fool*, 12; C. Kate Larson, *Great Necessities*, 126.

27. James A. McGowan, *Station Master on the Underground Railroad: The Life and Letters of Thomas Garrett* (Moylan, Pa.: Whimsie Press, 1977), 127–28; Holley and Chadwick, *A Life for Liberty*, 163.

28. Anna Ella Carroll, *Which? Fillmore or Buchanan!* (Boston: James French, 1856), 17.

29. Snyder, "Anna Ella Carroll, Political Strategist," 39.

30. Coryell, *Neither Heroine nor Fool*, 41.

31. Ibid.

32. M. B. Greenbie, *My Dear Lady*, 107.

33. Carroll's relationship with Lincoln is unclear. While biographers call her the unacknowledged member of his cabinet, their correspondence is thin and often caustic.

34. M. B. Greenbie, *My Dear Lady*, 107.

35. Anna Ella Carroll, *The War Powers of the General Government* (Washington, D.C.: Henry Polkinhorn, 1861), 69.

36. Coryell, *Neither Heroine nor Fool*, 53.

37. Ibid., 14.

38. Carl Sandburg, *Abraham Lincoln: The War Years*, 4 vols. (New York: Harcourt Brace, 1939), 275.

39. Ibid., 228.

40. C. Kate Larson, *Great Necessities*, 306.

41. Blackwell, *A Military Genius*, 39.

42. M. B. Greenbie, *My Dear Lady*, 129.

43. Greenbie and Greenbie, *Anna Ella Carroll and Abraham Lincoln*, 10.

44. Sandburg, *Abraham Lincoln*, 228.

45. Greenbie and Greenbie, *Anna Ella Carroll and Abraham Lincoln*, 348; quoted in C. Kay Larson, *Great Necessities*, 611.

46. Lemuel Evans, quoted in Greenbie and Greenbie, *Anna Ella Carroll and Abraham Lincoln*, 450; C. Kay Larson, *Great Necessities*, 326.

47. Cooling B. Franklin, *Forts Henry and Donelson: The Key to the Confederate Heartland* (Knoxville: University of Tennessee Press, 1987), 14.

48. Ulysses S. Grant, *Personal Memoirs of U. S. Grant* (New York: Penguin Books, 1999), 136.

49. Paper presented to Thomas Scott, Assistant Secretary of War, November 30, 1861. Quoted in Blackwell, *A Military Genius*, 2.

50. Grant, *Personal Memoirs*, 149.

51. Greenbie and Greenbie, *Anna Ella Carroll and Abraham Lincoln*, 294.

52. Ibid.

53. Ibid., 326.

54. Sandburg, *Abraham Lincoln*, 462.

55. Ibid., 474.

56. Coryell, *Neither Heroine nor Fool*, 77.

57. Grant, *Personal Memoirs*, 320.

58. Ibid.

59. William T. Sherman, *Memoirs by Himself*, vol. 1 (New York: Appleton & Co., 1877), 277.

60. Carroll, *The War Powers*, 64.

61. Greenbie and Greenbie, *Anna Ella Carroll and Abraham Lincoln*, 326.

62. Ibid., 327; Coryell, *Neither Heroine nor Fool*, 60.

63. Sandburg, *Abraham Lincoln*, 564.

64. Coryell, *Neither Heroine nor Fool*, 62.

65. Anna Ella Carroll, *The Relation of the National Government to the Revolted Citizens Defined* (Washington, D.C.: Henry Polkinhorn, 1882), 111, 63. The first Confiscation Act, passed on Aug. 6, 1861, authorized Union seizure of rebel property, and stated that all slaves who fought with or worked for the Confederate military services were freed of further obligations to their masters. Lincoln objected to the act on the basis that it might push border states, especially Kentucky and Missouri, into secession in order to protect slavery within their boundaries. The second Confiscation Act, passed on July 17, 1862, was virtually an emancipation proclamation. It said that slaves of civilian and military Confederate officials "shall be forever free," but was enforceable only in areas of the South occupied by the Union Army. Lincoln was again concerned about the effect of an anti-slavery measure on the border states and again urged these states to begin gradual compensated emancipation.

66. Coryell, *Neither Heroine nor Fool*, 62.

67. Ibid., 61.

68. Ibid., 66–67.

69. Ibid., 91–92, 377.

70. Ibid., 80; Greenbie and Greenbie, *Anna Ella Carroll and Abraham Lincoln*, 351–54.

71. Coryell, *Neither Heroine nor Fool*, 69.

72. Greenbie and Greenbie, *Anna Ella Carroll and Abraham Lincoln*, 397.

73. J. M. Winchell, "Pomeroy Circular," Letter to the *New York Times*, September 14, 1874.

74. Ibid.

75. Grant, *Personal Memoirs*, 413.

76. Eric Foner, *Reconstruction: America's Unfinished Revolution 1863–1877* (New York: Harper and Row, 1988), 129.

77. Ibid.,178.

78. Greenbie and Greenbie, *Anna Ella Carroll and Abraham Lincoln*, 414.

79. Ibid., 441.

80. Carroll wrote to Lemuel Evans, who was back in Texas in 1867, to get his views on the Johnson administration. His reply begins with the suggestion that Johnson wanted to form a new party of moderate Republicans and resolved that he can not live with the "radical parties." He also indicated that the radicals had no one to turn to but Grant and that Johnson hoped a split in the Republican Party would aid his nomination by the Democrats. Anna Ella Carroll to Lemuel Evans, 1867, Carroll Papers, Carroll, Cradock and Jensen Collection, Maryland Historical Society.

81. Greenbie and Greenbie, *Anna Ella Carroll and Abraham Lincoln*, 440; Coryell, *Neither Heroine nor Fool*, 97.

82. Coryell, *Neither Heroine nor Fool*, 98.

83. Ibid., 99; Greenbie and Greenbie, *Anna Ella Carroll and Abraham Lincoln*, 456.

84. M. B. Greenbie, *My Dear Lady*, 240; Grant, *Personal Memoirs*, 152. Military historians are divided on the issue of Halleck.

85. Coryell, *Neither Heroine nor Fool*, 86–87; Greenbie and Greenbie, *Anna Ella Carroll and Abraham Lincoln*, 444, 445, 450.

86. Coryell, *Neither Heroine nor Fool*, 84–86.

87. Ibid., 103.

88. Ibid., 104; Samuel T. Williams, quoted in the *Congressional Record*, "You should have had your substantial reward long ago but for the very absurd opinion that by some fixed mysterious law of nature, the labor done by women is worth less than precisely similar labor done by men." Greenbie and Greenbie, *Anna Ella Carroll and Abraham Lincoln*, 458–59.

89. Foner, *Reconstruction*, 520.

90. Coryell, *Neither Heroine nor Fool*, 104.

91. Coryell thought there was logic in Carroll's selection of the National Woman Suffrage Association because of its constituency but also mentions the bad timing with Victoria Woodhull (ibid.). See also Greenbie and Greenbie, *Anna Ella Carroll and Abraham Lincoln*, 474.

92. Victoria Woodhull's crusade was another of women's causes that burned brightly for a few moments and disappeared. See Elizabeth Cady Stanton, Susan B. Anthony, and Ellen Carol DuBois, *Elizabeth Cady Stanton, Susan B. Anthony, Correspondence, Writings, Speeches*, (New York: Schocken Books, 1981).

93. Foner, *Reconstruction*, 521.

94. Blackwell, *A Military Genius*, 187.

95. Coryell, *Neither Heroine nor Fool*, 109.

Chapter 3: Harriet Tubman, Called Moses of Her People

1. Sarah H. Bradford, *Scenes in the Life of Harriet Tubman* (Auburn, N.Y.: W.J. Moses, 1869; repr. North Stratford, N.H.: Ayer, 1971), 21. I am indebted in this chapter to the members of the Harriet Tubman Discussion Group who met in 2001 and 2002 to discuss and debate this remarkable woman and her life. John Creighton, local historian, who has researched and gathered documents on Tubman for many years, led the group, which also included Mrs. Evelyn Townsend, head of the Harriet Tubman organization in Cambridge; Vernetter Pender, society secretary; Kate Larson, author, *Bound for the Promised Land*; and Pat Lewis, Wilmington researcher.

2. Helen Tatlock, 1939, as quoted in Jean M. Humez, *Harriet Tubman: The Life and the Life Stories* (Madison: University of Wisconsin Press, 2003), 216.

3. Bradford, *Scenes in the Life*, 19; Humez, *Harriet Tubman*, 217; Frederick Douglass, *My Bondage and My Freedom* (New York: Arno/New York Times, 1969), 281.

4. Frederick Douglass, *Narrative of the Life of Frederick Douglass, An American Slave, Written by Himself* (New York: W.W. Norton, 1997), 12. Frederick Douglass, William L. Andrews, and William S. McFeely, *Narrative of the Life of Frederick Douglass, an American Slave, Written by Himself: Authoritative Text, Contexts, Criticism* (New York: Norton, 1997), 12.

5. Kate Clifford Larson, *Bound for the Promised Land: Harriet Tubman, Portrait of an American Hero* (New York: Ballantine, 2004), 10.

6. Franklin Sanborn, 1863, in Bradford, *Scenes in the Life*, 53–55; Humez, *Harriet Tubman*, 264, 265.

7. Ednah Dow Littlehale Cheney, *Reminiscences of Ednah Dow Cheney (Born Littlehale)* (Boston: Lee and Sheppard, 1902), 82.

8. Sarah H. Bradford, *Harriet Tubman: The Moses of her People* [1886] (reprt. Bedford, Mass.: Applewood Books, 1993); Bradford, *Scenes in the Life,* 19; see Humez, *Harriet Tubman,* 197–98, and Kate Larson, *Bound for the Promised Land,* 305

9. Franklin Sanborn, "Harriet Tubman," *Boston Commonwealth* (July 17, 1863); Cheney, *Reminiscences;* and Sallie Holley, "Letter to Mr. Powell," in *National Anti-Slavery Standard* (November 30, 1867).

10. Bradford, *Scenes in the Life,* 15; Bradford, *The Moses of Her People,* 15.

11. Emma Telford interview quoted in Humez, *Harriet Tubman,* 174.

12. James McGowan, *Station Master on the Underground Railroad: The Life and Letters of Thomas Garrett* (Moylan, Pa.: Whimsie Press, 1977), 36.

13. Humez, *Harriet Tubman,* 174.

14. Douglass, *Narrative of the Life of Frederick Douglass.* According to historian Anne Boylan, "Recent historical work has refuted Douglass's claim—recognizing that owners had an economic interest in keeping families together." Private correspondence, Anne Boylan, professor of history, University of Delaware.

15. Marjorie B. Greenbie, *My Dear Lady: The Story of Anna Ella Carroll, the "Great Unrecognized Member of Lincoln's Cabinet"* (New York: Arno Press/ New York Times, 1974), 31.

16. John Hope Franklin and Alfred A. Moss, *From Slavery to Freedom: A History of African Americans* (New York: McGraw-Hill, 1998).

17. There is some disagreement among researchers about the actual dates in the absence of records. See Kate Larson, *Bound for the Promised Land,* 298–99; Telford interview quoted in ibid., 20, 312n22.

18. Priscilla Thompson, "Harriet Tubman, Thomas Garrett and the Underground Railroad," *Delaware History* 22 (1986), 4; Kate Larson, *Bound for the Promised Land,* 20, 326n87.

19. Telford quoted in Humez, *Harriet Tubman,* 205.

20. Kate Larson, *Bound for the Promised Land,* 18, 20.

21. Barbara J. Fields, *Slavery and Freedom on the Middle Ground: Maryland during the Nineteenth Century* (New Haven, Conn.: Yale University Press, 1985); Sanborn, "Harriet Tubman."

22. Sanborn quoted in Bradford, *Scenes in the Life,* 75.

23. Ednah Cheney, in *Freedmen's Record* 1 (1865), reprinted in Blassingame, *Slave Testimony,* 457.

24. Telford quoted in Humez, *Harriet Tubman,* 205; see Kate Larson, *Bound for the Promised Land,* 310n13.

25. McGowan, *Station Master on the Underground Railroad,* 89; Bradford, *Scenes in the Life,* 135–37; Humez, *Harriet Tubman,* 208.

26. Bradford, *Scenes in the Life,* 13.

27. Benjamin Drew, "Harriet Tubman," in A *North-Side View of Slavery: The Refuge: Or The Narrative of Fugitive Slaves in Canada* (Boston: J.P. Jewett, 1856), 30.

28. Bradford, *The Moses of Her People,* 15.

29. Kate Larson, *Bound for the Promised Land,* 15.

30. Bradford, *Scenes in the Life,* 74.

31. Earl Conrad, *Harriet Tubman* (Washington, D.C.: Associated Publishers, 1943), 16.

32. Bradford, *Scenes in the Life*, 14.

33. Frederick Douglass, *My Bondage and My Freedom* (New York: Arno/New York Times, [1855] 1969), 81.

34. Deborah Gray White, *Ar'n't I a Woman? Female Slaves in the Plantation South* (New York: Norton, 1987), 77.

35. Bureau of the Census, 1850 Federal Census.

36. Kate Larson, *Bound for the Promised Land*, 19.

37. Bradford, *Scenes in the Life*, 9–10.

38. Will of Anthony Thompson, 1836 (Dorchester County Courthouse, Maryland Registrar of Wills).

39. Fields, *Slavery and Freedom*, 27.

40. Ibid.

41. While more complicated, the basic facts are these: Absalom, much younger than Anthony, lived on a farm in adjoining Talbot County, not far from the Covey farm where Frederick Douglass lived. Absalom was about fifteen at that time and was "given several slaves in exchange for a one-third interest in their earnings." See Kate Larson, *Bound for the Promised Land*, 70–71.

42. Ibid., 68, 71.

43. Ibid., 198.

44. Ibid., 60–61.

45. Ibid., 63.

46. Fields, *Slavery and Freedom*, 31.

47. Conrad, *Harriet Tubman*, 32.

48. Humez, *Harriet Tubman*, 256.

49. Catherine Clinton, *Harriet Tubman: The Road to Freedom* (Boston: Little, Brown, 2004), 27.

50. Kate Larson, *Bound for the Promised Land*, 62.

51. Conrad, *Harriet Tubman*, 19.

52. Kate Larson, *Bound for the Promised Land*, 64.

53. Ibid., 74; Bradford, *Scenes in the Life*, 107.

54. Conrad, *Harriet Tubman*, 32–33. Conrad gives no source for this information. It may be simply his speculation; Clinton, *The Road to Freedom*, 28.

55. Bradford, *Scenes in the Life*, 16.

56. William Still, *The Underground Rail Road*, (Philadelphia: Porter and Coates, 1872), 411; as Sanborn noted, "For the last two years of slavery (1848 and 1849) she lived with Dr. Thompson." Quoted in Bradford, *Scenes in the Life*, 75; Conrad, *Harriet Tubman*, 35.

57. When Brodess died, his estate by law would have fallen to his oldest son—assuming the first lived—who would have been twenty-two at his father's death. He was not listed in the 1850 census. Conrad suggested that the young heir may have died shortly after his father. The census lists the eldest child as Richard, aged nineteen. Sanborn indicated that the eldest was too young to take charge of the estate (which was correct if John was dead), and so a guardian was appointed. The guardian was identified as Dr. Anthony Thompson Jr. Conrad confirmed Sanborn's identification of a guardian but no other sources did so.

58. Kate Larson, *Bound for the Promised Land*, 77.

59. On June 17, 1850, Brodess and Mills sold niece Harriet and her child locally to Thomas Willis for $375. Ibid.

60. Pattison's lawyer was James Stewart, ambitious and strongly pro-slavery, who later launched a political career as a spokesman for the rights of slavehold-

ers. Losing in lower court, he then took his case to a higher court, where he also lost. See ibid., 74–75.

61. Anthony Thompson, 1853 Thompson Deposition, Equity Papers 249, Maryland State Archives.

62. Clinton, *Harriet Tubman*, 10.

63. Ibid., 75.

64. Douglass, *Narrative of the Life of Frederick Douglass*, 176.

65. Ednah Cheney, "Moses," *Freedmen's Record* 1 (1865): 35.

66. Humez, *Harriet Tubman*, 150.

67. Clinton, *Harriet Tubman*, 26.

68. Quoted in Walter Johnson, *Soul by Soul: Life Inside the Antebellum Slave Market* (Cambridge, Mass.: Harvard University Press, 1999), 73.

69. Bradford, *Scenes in the Life*, 16.

70. In 1849, Anthony C. Thompson, the son of Dr. Anthony, married Mary E. Leverton, the daughter of Hannah and Jacob Leverton of Caroline County. Hannah Leverton was an "active abolitionist," according to historical records. The Levertons lived close to the Thompson property at Poplar Neck, where Rit and Ben then lived. Jacob Leverton died in 1847. In 1849 when Harriet escaped, she told Helen Tatlock that "she found a friend in a white lady, who knew her story and helped her on her way." The widow Leverton was a likely prospect. Quoted in Humez, *Harriet Tubman*, 216.

71. Ibid.

72. Still, *The Underground Rail Road*. The Pennsylvania Anti-Slavery Society, begun in 1837, is often confused with the Pennsylvania Abolition Society, founded in 1775.

73. Kate Larson, *Bound for the Promised Land*, xvii; Priscilla Thompson also mentions William Brinkly. Priscilla Thompson, "Harriet Tubman, Thomas Garrett, and the Underground Railroad," *Delaware History* (Spring/Summer 1986): 4.

74. Kate Larson, *Bound for the Promised Land*, 88.

75. Clinton, *Harriet Tubman*, 52.

76. Kate Larson, *Bound for the Promised Land*, 240.

77. McGowan, *Station Master on the Underground Railroad*, 63.

78. Bradford, *Scenes in the Life*, 24, 76–77; Charles L. Blockson, *The Underground Railroad: First Person Narratives of Escapes to Freedom in the North* (New York: Prentice Hall, 1987), 167, 175. Garrett and John Hunn helped Samuel Hawkins, a free black, his wife, and their six children escape from the Eastern Shore in 1846. In 1848, they were tried and Garrett was assessed damages of $5,000.

79. Reports often listed Kessiah as Tubman's sister. Historian Kate Larson's careful research concludes that she was actually a niece, a relationship more fitting to what we know of Tubman's family. Kate Larson, *Bound for the Promised Land*, 89–90, 93.

80. Douglass gave a brief description of the group as "not very fastidious in either direction, and were well content with very plain food, and a strip of carpet on the floor for a bed, or a place on the straw in the barn loft." Frederick Douglass, *The Life and Times of Frederick Douglass: From 1817–1882*, ed. John Lobb, F.R.G.S. (London: Christian Age Office, 1882), 231–32.

81. Kate Larson, *Bound for the Promised Land*, 104.

82. Sanborn quoted in Bradford, *Scenes in the Life*, 77.

83. Interview of Henry Stewart, 1863, Canada, in Blassingame, *Slave Testimony,* 414–16.

84. Bradford, *Scenes in the Life,* 57–58.

85. Ibid., 62.

86. Kate Larson, *Bound for the Promised Land,* 76–78.

87. Ibid., 114.

88. Conrad, *Harriet Tubman,* 73.

89. Kate Larson, *Bound for the Promised Land,* 225.

90. Conrad, *Harriet Tubman,* 95–96; Kate Larson, *Bound for the Promised Land,* 141–42.

91. Ibid.

92. Conrad, *Harriet Tubman,* 102.

93. Tubman helped thirty-nine slaves escape in the fall, and two weeks later, fifteen more left. One contingent was fully armed with "revolvers, pistols, sword canes and butcher knives." Kate Larson, *Bound for the Promised Land,* 144–45.

94. Conrad, *Harriet Tubman,* 92, 93; Kate Larson, *Bound for the Promised Land,* 138–39. Garrett quoted in Conrad, *Harriet Tubman,* 98.

95. Seward's abolitionist sympathies, even without knowledge of his support of Tubman, were said to be instrumental in his failed presidential bid in 1860. Foner, *Free Soil,* 40, 97.

96. Humez, *Harriet Tubman,* 294.

97. Ibid., 231; Cheney suggested two children; Garrett, three.

98. Still, *The Underground Rail Road,* 531; Kate Larson, *Bound for the Promised Land,* 184; Sherry Penney and James D. Livingston, *A Very Dangerous Woman: Martha Wright and Women's Rights* (Amherst: University of Massachusetts Press, 2004) 132.

99. W. E. B. DuBois, *John Brown* (Philadelphia: George W. Jacobs, 1909), 63.

100. Foner, *Free Soil,* 94.

101. Conrad, *Harriet Tubman,* 114–15; DuBois, *John Brown,* 124–38.

102. Conrad, Harriet Tubman, 116; Kate Larson, *Bound for the Promised Land,* 157.

103. Conrad, Harriet Tubman, 116; Kate Larson, *Bound for the Promised Land,* 161.

104. Conrad, *Harriet Tubman,* 120, 121, Kate Larson, *Bound for the Promised Land,* 162–63, 174–77.

105. Conrad, *Harriet Tubman,* 122. DuBois, *John Brown,* 178.

106. Ibid., 183, 182.

107. Clinton, *Harriet Tubman,* 133, 219.

108. DuBois, *John Brown,* 178, 211.

109. Ibid., 63; Foner, 69.

110. Humez, *Harriet Tubman,* 365. Tubman was not the only one to go to Canada. Douglass fled there and later to Europe. Secret Six members Sanborn and Stearns went there briefly. Gerrit Smith did not leave but had a breakdown and went into an asylum in Utica, New York, until after Brown's hanging. Howe at first denied any knowledge of involvement with John Brown but later testified before Congress on his involvement. Higginson also stayed and refused to testify about Brown. Parker died in spring 1860. Conrad, *Harriet Tubman,* 147.

111. Clinton, *Harriet Tubman,* 142, 147.

112. Ibid., 149.

113. Willie Rose, *Rehearsal for Reconstruction: The Port Royal Experiment* (New York: Oxford University Press, 1964), 30.

114. Ibid., 18–23.

115. Humez, *Harriet Tubman*, 51.

116. Rose, *Rehearsal for Reconstruction*, 16.

117. Charles Wood, "Manuscript History Concerning the Pension Claim of *Harriet Tubman*," HR 55A-D1, Papers Accompanying the Claim of Harriet Tubman, Record group 233, National Archives, Washington, D.C.

118. Foner, *Free Soil*, 52.

119. Kate Larson, *Bound for the Promised Land*, 205.

120. Conrad, *Harriet Tubman*, 161.

121. Kate Larson, *Bound for the Promised Land*, 368n8.

122. Clinton, *Harriet Tubman*, 142.

123. Conrad, *Harriet Tubman*, 163.

124. Ibid., 165.

125. Rose, *Rehearsal for Reconstruction*, 171.

126. Ibid.

127. Ibid., 167, 174.

128. Rose, *Rehearsal for Reconstruction*, 252.

129. Conrad, *Harriet Tubman*, 177.

130. Rose, *Rehearsal for Reconstruction*, 247.

131. Ibid., 255.

132. Ibid., 206.

133. Ibid., 257; Clinton, *Harriet Tubman*, 178; Kate Larson, *Bound for the Promised Land*, 220.

134. Conrad, *Harriet Tubman*, 181; Clinton, *Harriet Tubman*, 178.

135. Tatlock quoted in Humez, *Harriet Tubman*, 219.

136. Conrad, *Harriet Tubman*, 177. Kate Larson suggested this may have been earlier, although Tubman would have been in Auburn in November, South Carolina in February, and back in Auburn in June. Kate Larson, *Bound for the Promised Land*, 221, 222.

137. Wood, an Auburn acquaintance and ex-military man, agreed to compile the military information for Bradford's book, though in the end it was not included. Like Bradford, Wood relied on official documents to verify Tubman's accounts. Charles P. Wood, "Manuscript History Concerning the Pension Claim of *Harriet Tubman*," National Archives, Washington, D.C., 10.

138. Conrad, *Harriet Tubman*, 187.

139. Wood, "Pension Claim of *Harriet Tubman*," 10; Bradford, *Scenes in the Life*, 46.

140. Conrad, *Harriet Tubman*, 193.

141. Ibid., 196; Kate Larson, *Bound for the Promised Land*, 241.

142. Kate Larson, *Bound for the Promised Land*, 240–42.

143. Conrad, *Harriet Tubman*, 206.

144. Kate Larson, *Bound for the Promised Land*, 272, 274.

145. Sallie Holley and John White Chadwick, *A Life for Liberty; Anti-Slavery and Other Letters of Sallie Holley* (New York: G.P. Putnam's Sons, 1899), 205; Conrad, *Harriet Tubman*, 201.

146. Kate Larson, *Bound for the Promised Land*, 257; Conrad, *Harriet Tubman*, 209.

147. Conrad, *Harriet Tubman*, 217.

148. Humez, *Harriet Tubman*, 315.

149. Ibid., 319.

150. Ibid., 323.

151. Ibid.

152. Conrad, *Harriet Tubman*, 220.

153. Humez, *Harriet Tubman*, 327.

154. Ibid., 328; Conrad, *Harriet Tubman*, 191.

Chapter 4: Political Economy and Marginalization

1. Ulrich Phillips, *American Negro Slavery: A Survey of the Supply, Employment and Control of Negro Labor as Determined by the Plantation Regime* (Baton Rouge: Louisiana State University Press, [1918] 1966), 356.

2. Ibid., 355.

3. Ibid.

4. Drew Gilpin Faust, *Mothers of Invention: Women of the Slaveholding South in the American Civil War* (New York; Vintage, 1997), 5–6, 10.

5. Jeanne Boydston, "The Woman Who Wasn't There: Women's Market Labor and the Transition to Capitalism in the United States," in Paul A. Gilje, *Wages of Independence: Capitalism in the Early American Republic* (Madison: Madison House, 1997), 39; Alice Kessler Harris, *Out to Work: A History of Wage-Earning Women in the United States* (New York: Oxford University Press, 1982), viii; Faust, *Mothers of Invention*, 6, 12.

6. Faust, *Mothers of Invention*, 6.

7. Eric Foner, *Free Soil, Free Labor, Free Men: The Ideology of the Republican Party before the Civil War* (New York: Oxford University Press, 1970), 13.

8. Ibid., 47.

9. Ibid., 15.

10. Ibid., 41.

11. George A. Townsend, "The Chesapeake Peninsula," in Harold D. Jopp, *Rediscovery of the Eastern Shore: Delmarva Travelogues of the 1870s* (Wye Mills, Md.: Chesapeake College Press, 1986), 52; Walter Johnson, *Soul by Soul: Life Inside the Antebellum Slave Market* (Cambridge, Mass.: Harvard University Press, 1999), 6.

12. Barbara Fields, *Slavery and Freedom on the Middle Ground: Maryland during the Nineteenth Century*, (New Haven, Conn.: Yale University Press, 1985), xii, 1, 3–4.

13. Ibid., 4.

14. Brenda Stevenson, *Life in Black and White: Family and Community in the Slave South* (New York: Oxford University Press, 1996), 3.

15. Quoted in Drew R. McCoy, *Elusive Republic: Political Economy in Jeffersonian America* (Chapel Hill: University of North Carolina Press, 1980), 7.

16. Ibid., 137–46.

17. Ibid., 146–62.

18. Ira Berlin, *Slaves without Masters: The Free Negro in the Antebellum South* (New York: Pantheon, 1974), 26.

19. Ibid., 49.

20. Phillips, *American Negro Slavery*, 200.

21. Frederick Bancroft, *Slave Trading in the Old South* (Columbia: University of South Carolina Press, 1996), 28–31, 40–43.

22. Townsend, "The Chesapeake Peninsula," 46; Jeanne Boydston, "The Woman Who Wasn't There: Women's Market Labor and the Transition to Capitalism in the United States" in Paul A. Gilje, *Wages of Independence: Capitalism in the Early American Republic* (Madison: Madison House, 1997), 23.

23. J. H. K. Shannahan, *Tales of Old Maryland* (Baltimore: Meyer & Thalheimer, 1907), 69.

24. Ted Giles, *Patty Cannon, Woman of Mystery* (Eastern, Md.: Easton Publishing, 1965), 24.

25. Shannahan, *Tales of Old Maryland,* 69.

26. Bancroft, *Slave Trading in the Old South,* 30; William McFeely, *Frederick Douglass* (New York: Norton, 1991), 30–31.

27. Carol Wilson, *Freedom at Risk: The Kidnapping of Free Blacks in America, 1780–1865* (Lexington: University of Kentucky Press, 1994), 13.

28. Dorothy Sterling, *We Are Your Sisters: Black Women in the Nineteenth Century* (New York: Norton, 1997), 228.

29. Johnson, *Soul by Soul,* 116.

30. Faust, *Mothers of Invention,* 10.

31. Sidney Greenbie and Marjorie B. Greenbie, *Anna Ella Carroll and Abraham Lincoln* (Manchester, Maine: Falmouth Publishing, 1952), 52; Janet Coryell, *Neither Heroine nor Fool: Anna Ella Carroll of Maryland* (Kent, Ohio: Kent State University Press, 1990), 5–6. Carroll wrote to William Seward on one occasion: "by education & association my interest is more than that of ladies ordinarily. I read, think & write." Ibid., 9.

32. Greenbie and Greenbie, *Anna Ella Carroll and Abraham Lincoln,* 48; Coryell, *Neither Heroine nor Fool,* 5–6. Coryell dates the closing of the school to 1843 and urges caution in accepting interpretations from the Greenbies because of some of their "extravagant and unsupported claims" (118). The Greenbies were both upset and defensive because, in 1950, historian Kenneth P. Williams disputed much of Carroll's claim. As Coryell pointed out, he convinced much of the academic community that Carroll's claim was not valid. Coryell also cited his later, rather specious suggestion (regarding Carroll's choice of the Tennessee River) that it was "unnecessary to give her credit even if she thought of it, it was so obvious" (119). Coryell further suggested that interviews with family members brought forth additional details. In the case of the school, the family remembered the founding occurring at an earlier date (118).

33. Ibid., 5; Greenbie and Greenbie, *Anna Ella Carroll and Abraham Lincoln,* 56.

34. Coryell, *Neither Heroine nor Fool,* 10; Greenbie and Greenbie, *Anna Ella Carroll and Abraham Lincoln,* 61.

35. Greenbie and Greenbie, *Anna Ella Carroll and Abraham Lincoln,* 71, 79.

36. Ibid., 88; C. Kay Larson, *Great Necessities: The Life, Times, and Writings of Anna Ella Carroll, 1815–1894* (Philadelphia: Xlibris, 2004), 73.

37. Daniel Webster said of the election, "I believe it to be an unquestionable fact that the masters of vessels having brought over immigrants from Europe have, within thirty days of their arrival, seen those very persons carried up to the polls, and give their votes for the highest offices in the state and national governments. . . ." Quoted in Greenbie and Greenbie, *Anna Ella Carroll and Abraham Lincoln,* 90.

38. Ibid., 81–83. Carroll often claimed friendships (Fillmore, Seward, and Weed) that in surviving correspondence appeared more one-sided. In the case of Corwin, however, a more personal acquaintance is evident. As Coryell observed on one occasion, "He sadly recounted to her that he was a failure in life, unable to accept happiness in his own life or manifest joy at the happiness of others." Coryell, *Neither Heroine nor Fool*, 127.

39. Greenbie and Greenbie, *Anna Ella Carroll and Abraham Lincoln*, 77; a letter from Breckenridge to Carroll suggested the twenty-year gap (C. Kay Larson, *Great Necessities*, 471).

40. Greenbie and Greenbie, *Anna Ella Carroll and Abraham Lincoln*, 88.

41. Ibid., 88–89. Walker wanted to open a southern route for the railroad to the Pacific. He expected Jefferson Davis to push the proposal through Congress and expected Anne to write about it and lobby members of Congress. Anne's rooms at the boardinghouse were said to be filled with railroad maps and surveys. Sarah Blackwell, *A Military Genius: Life of Anna Ella Carroll of Maryland* (Washington: Judd & Detweiler, 1891), xiv.

42. Greenbie and Greenbie, *Anna Ella Carroll and Abraham Lincoln*, 82.

43. Ibid., 90.

44. Greenbie and Greenbie, *Anna Ella Carroll and Abraham Lincoln*, 100–101; Coryell, *Neither Heroine nor Fool*, 7.

45. Coryell, *Neither Heroine nor Fool*, 5.

46. Greenbie and Greenbie, *Anna Ella Carroll and Abraham Lincoln*, 125.

47. Coryell, *Neither Heroine nor Fool*, 8.

48. Greenbie and Greenbie, *Anna Ella Carroll and Abraham Lincoln*, 123. She eventually raised over $4,000. Contributors included Gerrit Smith, the wealthy abolitionist and member of the Secret Six, who had briefly served in Congress. Smith's second wife was Anne Carroll Smith of the western Maryland Carroll family. Gerrit was a close friend of Harriet Tubman and a cousin to Elizabeth Cady Stanton. Sallie Holley pointed out that Gerrit "is constantly receiving letters from a great variety of people" and "says he does not comply with one in a hundred." Carroll's success in getting money from Gerrit was noteworthy. R. J. Walker, Gerald Halleck, Frances Wayland, and E. B. Hall of Rhode Island also made contributions.

49. Ibid., 9.

50. Ibid., 169–70.

51. Coryell, *Neither Heroine nor Fool*, 15–16; Larson, *Great Necessities*, 147.

52. Coryell, *Neither Heroine nor Fool*, 19–20.

53. Coryell, *Neither Heroine nor Fool*, 124.

54. Jean Humez, *Harriet Tubman: The Life and Life Stories* (Madison: University of Wisconsin Press, 2003), 178–79.

55. Ibid., 113.

56. Earl Conrad, *Harriet Tubman* (Washington, D.C.: Associated Publishers, 1943), 184–85; Kate Clifford Larson, *Bound for the Promised Land: Harriet Tubman, Portrait of an American Hero* (New York: Ballantine, 2004), 229–30; Jean McMahon Humez, *Harriet Tubman: The Life and Life Stories* (Madison, Wis: University of Wisconsin Press, 2003), 65.

57. Conrad, *Harriet Tubman*, 186.

58. It is on this journey that Tubman was assaulted by a conductor of a train who refused to honor her nurse's pass. Tubman was thrown into the baggage car and suffered injuries. Hearing of the incident, friends in Auburn suggested that Tubman sue the railroad—but that too did not happen. Kate Larson, *Bound for the Promised Land*, 232.

59. Ibid., 232; Conrad, *Harriet Tubman*, 213; Humez, *Harriet Tubman*, 87.

60. Humez, *Harriet Tubman*, 323.

61. Sherry H. Penney and James D. Livingston, *A Very Dangerous Woman: Martha Wright and Women's Rights* (Amherst: University of Massachusetts Press, 2004), 175–76.

62. Conrad, *Harriet Tubman*, 192.

63. Sallie Holley and John White Chadwick, *A Life for Liberty; Anti-Slavery and Other Letters of Sallie Holley* (New York: G.P. Putnam's Sons, 1899), 205.

64. Penney and Livingston, *A Very Dangerous Woman*, 176.

65. Kate Larson, *Bound for the Promised Land*, 248. John Tubman, her first husband, was murdered in October 1867. Some claim that Harriet made her one and only visit to the Eastern Shore after the war to attend the trial of his "alleged" murderer, who was found not guilty for lack of evidence. Ibid., 239–41; Conrad, *Harriet Tubman*, 218–20.

66. Humez, *Harriet Tubman*, 86.

67. Kate Larson, *Bound for the Promised Land*, 256–57; Humez, *Harriet Tubman*, 88.

68. Penney and Livingston, *A Very Dangerous Woman*, 176; Conrad, *Harriet Tubman*, 32; Kate Larson, *Bound for the Promised Land*, 249–50.

69. Kate Larson, *Bound for the Promised Land*, 272–74.

70. Ibid., 277–79; Humez, *Harriet Tubman*, 287.

71. Humez, *Harriet Tubman*, 110.

72. Ibid., 109.

Chapter 5: Rules, Laws, and the Rule of Law

1. Lawrence Meir Friedman, *Law in America: A Short History* (New York: Modern Library, 2004), 26.

2. Philip D. Morgan, *Slave Counterpoint: Black Culture in the Eighteenth-Century Chesapeake & Lowcountry* (Chapel Hill: University of North Carolina Press, 1998), 5–23.

3. Friedman, *Law in America*, 26, 29–30.

4. Charles S. Sydnor, "The Southerner and the Laws," *Journal of Southern History* 6 (February 1940): 12.

5. Friedman, *Law in America*, 29.

6. Ulrich B. Phillips, *American Negro Slavery; A Survey of the Supply, Employment and Control of Negro Labor as determined by the Plantation Regime* (Baton Rouge: Louisiana State University Press, [1918] 1966), 116.

7. Friedman, *Law in America*, 29–30.

8. Ibid., 32–33.

9. Eric Foner, *Free Soil, Free Labor, Free Men: The Ideology of the Republican Party before the Civil War* (New York: Oxford University Press, 1970), 6–7.

10. W. J. Cash, *The Mind of the South* (New York: Vintage, 1941), 35.

11. Oliver Wendell Holmes, quoted in Friedman, *Law in America*, 29.

12. Friedman, *Law in America*, 29.

13. Phillips, *American Negro Slavery*, 123.

14. Friedman, *Law in America*, 150.

15. Stanley W. Campbell, *The Slave Catchers: Enforcement of the Fugitive Slave Law, 1850–1860* (Chapel Hill: University of North Carolina Press, 1970), 7–9.

16. John Adams, Abigail Adams, Thomas Jefferson, and Lester Jesse Cappon, *The Adams-Jefferson Letters: The Complete Correspondence between Thomas Jefferson and Abigail and John Adams* (Chapel Hill: University of North Carolina Press, 1959), 571.

17. Letter from George Washington, "In Convention, September 17, 1787," in *The Constitution of the United States, with the Declaration of Independence* (Boston: Pathmark Books, 1973), 24.

18. U.S. Constitution, Art. I, Sec. 2, cl. 3.

19. Phillips, *American Negro Slavery*, 129.

20. Robert William Fogel, *Without Consent or Contract: The Rise and Fall of American Slavery* (New York: Norton, 1989), 238.

21. Peter Kolchin, *American Slavery: 1619–1877* (New York: Hill and Wang, 1993), 94.

22. Fogel, *Without Consent*, 288–89.

23. Ibid., 32.

24. Campbell, *The Slave Catchers*, 6.

25. U.S. Constitution, Art. 4, Sec. 2, cl. 3.

26. Campbell, *The Slave Catchers*, 7–9.

27. Ibid., 6.

28. Carol Wilson, *Freedom at Risk: The Kidnapping of Free Blacks in America, 1780–1865* (Lexington: University of Kentucky Press, 1994), 18.

29. Foner, *Free Soil*, 279.

30. Phillips, *American Negro Slavery*, 445.

31. Ibid., 381.

32. Wilson, *Freedom at Risk*, 40–41; Campbell, *The Slave Catchers*, 11.

33. David Brion Davis, *Challenging the Boundaries of Slavery* (Cambridge: Harvard University Press, 2003), 38.

34. The Northwest Ordinance of 1787 prohibited slavery in the territories northwest of the Ohio River (Fogel, *Without Consent or Contract*, 288).

35. Campbell, *The Slave Catchers*, 26–28.

36. Ibid., 38–40, 46.

37. James McGowan, *Station Master on the Underground Railroad: The Life and Letters of Thomas Garrett* (Moylan, Pa.: Whimsie Press, 1977), 63. McGowan writes that the sum was reduced to $1,500—still a considerable amount.

38. Earl Conrad, *Harriet Tubman* (Washington, D.C.: Associated Publishers, 1943), 43–45.

39. Sarah H. Bradford, *Scenes in the Life of Harriet Tubman* (Auburn, N.Y.: W.J. Moses, 1869; repr. North Stratford, N.H.: Ayer, 1971), 54.

40. Ibid., 27.

41. Campbell, *The Slave Catchers*, 46.

42. Ibid., 114–20.

43. Ibid., 112.

44. Ibid., 87.

45. Linda K. Kerber, *Women of the Republic: Intellect and Ideology in Revolutionary America* (Chapel Hill: University of North Carolina Press, 1980), 36.

46. Ira Berlin, *Slaves without Masters: The Free Negro in the Antebellum South* (New York: Pantheon, 1974), 138–44.

47. Ibid., 139.

48. Ibid., 142.

49. Drew Gilpin Faust, *Mothers of Invention: Women of the Slaveholding South in the American Civil War* (New York: Vintage, 1997), 27.

50. Charles Wesley, "Lincoln's Plan for Colonizing Negroes," *Journal of Negro History* 4 (1919): 8.

51. Harry S. Blackiston, "Lincoln's Emancipation Plan," *Journal of Negro History* 7 (1922): 274.

52. "James Madison's Attitude toward the Negro," *Journal of Negro History* 6 (1921): 85.

53. Foner, *Free Soil*, 267–80.

54. Ibid., 271.

55. Ibid., 272.

56. Ibid., 273.

57. Ibid., 270.

58. Wesley, "Lincoln's Plan for Colonizing Negroes," 10.

59. Ibid., 15.

60. Abraham Lincoln, *Letters and Addresses of Abraham Lincoln* (New York: Howard Wilford Bell, 1904), 257.

61. Foner, *Free Soil*, 273.

62. Janet Coryell, *Neither Heroine nor Fool: Anna Ella Carroll of Maryland* (Kent, Ohio: Kent State University Press, 1990), 66–68.

63. Sidney Greenbie and Marjorie B. Greenbie, *Anna Ella Carroll and Abraham Lincoln*, (Manchester, Maine: Falmouth Publishing Co: 1952), 326, 327, 333.

64. Coryell, *Neither Heroine nor Fool*, 69; Greenbie and Greenbie, *Anna Ella Carroll and Abraham Lincoln*, 355, 356.

65. Lincoln, *Letters and Addresses*, 244.

66. Ibid., 246.

67. Foner, *Free Soil*, 228.

68. Ibid., 278.

69. Coryell, *Neither Heroine nor Fool*, 69.

70. Foner, *Free Soil*, 278–79.

71. Davis, *Challenging the Boundaries*, 58.

72. Charles S. Sydnor, "The Southerner and the Law," *Journal of Southern History* 6 (February 1940), 5.

73. Lincoln, *Letters and Addresses*, 189.

74. Ibid., 266.

75. Ibid., 269.

Chapter 6: The Mantle of Domesticity

1. Brenda Stevenson, *Life in Black and White: Family and Community in the Slave South* (New York: Oxford University Press, 1996), 5.

2. Darlene Clark Hine, *Hine Sight: Black Women and the Re-Construction of American History* (Brooklyn, N.Y.: Carlson Pub., 1994), 49–58, 53.

3. Stephanie McCurry, *Masters of Small Worlds: Yeoman Households, Gender Relations, and the Political Culture of the Antebellum South Carolina Low Country* (New York: Oxford University Press, 1995) 84, 89, 107, 121.

4. Ibid., 80.

5. Mary Beth Norton, *Founding Mothers & Fathers: Gendered Power and the Forming of American Society* (New York: A.A. Knopf, 1996), 14.

6. Hal Roth, *The Monster's Handsome Face: Patty Cannon in Fiction and Fact* (Vienna, Md.: Nanticoke Books, 1998), 69.

7. Sarah H. Bradford, *Scenes in the Life of Harriet Tubman* (Auburn, N.Y.: W.J. Moses, 1869; repr. North Stratford, N.H.: Ayer, 1971), 25.

8. Sarah E. Blackwell, *A Military Genius: A Life of Anna Ella Carroll of Maryland* (Washington, D.C.: Judd & Detweiler, 1891), 48.

9. Shirley Yee, *Black Women Abolitionists: A Study in Activism, 1828–1860* (Knoxville: University of Tennessee Press, 1992), 114–15. Fanny Wright was an advocate of radical social changes beyond ending slavery. Said Cornish, "Ladies are lovely, truly lovely in their place, but alas! When they abandon it!" (114). C. Kay Larson suggests that Carroll's political activities, including the power of her pen, would not have been totally unique for a woman by 1850, but the degree of her political power would be (*Great Necessities: The Life, Times, and Writings of Anna Ella Carroll, 1815–1894* [Philadelphia: Xlibris, 2004], 76). Anne Boylan in private correspondence pointed to the many ways in which women "spoke in public," including women who preached, women who ran their own associations, and women who spoke in public lyceums.

10. Eric Hobsbawm, *Bandits*, rev. ed. (New York: The New Press, 2000), 77–90, 78.

11. Stevenson, *Life in Black and White*, 6.

12. Roth, *The Monster's Handsome Face*, 73.

13. Ibid., 40.

14. Ibid., 76.

15. Ibid.

16. Ibid.

17. *Narrative and Confessions of Lucretia P. Cannon* (printed for the publishers, 1841), 3, 16.

18. Ibid., 3.

19. Ibid.

20. Ibid.

21. Anne Firor Scott, *Making the Invisible Woman Visible* (Urbana: University of Illinois Press, 1984), 92.

22. Marjorie B. Greenbie, *My Dear Lady: The Story of Anna Ella Carroll, the "Great Unrecognized Member of Lincoln's Cabinet"* (New York: Arno Press/ New York Times, 1974), 45–47.

23. Sydney Greenbie and Marjorie B. Greenbie, *Anna Ella Carroll and Abraham Lincoln* (Manchester, Maine: Falmouth Publishing, 1952), 67–69.

24. Greenbie, *My Dear Lady*, 45–47.

25. Ibid., 78.

26. Janet Coryell, *Neither Heroine nor Fool: Anna Ella Carroll of Maryland* (Kent, Ohio: Kent State University Press, 1990), 46.

27. Ibid.; L. E. Barber to Carroll, May 14, 1861, Carroll Papers, Carroll, Cradock, Jensen family papers, Maryland Historical Society.

28. Coryell, *Neither Heroine nor Fool*, 46; Barber to Carroll, May 14, 1861.

29. Evans letter to Anna Ella Carroll, Baltimore: Maryland Historical Society Library, Manuscripts Department, Carroll, Cradock, Jensen family papers, 1738–1968, MS 1867.

30. Ibid.

31. Ibid.

32. Greenbie and Greenbie, *Anna Ella Carroll and Abraham Lincoln,* 164, 165, 219, 230; Coryell, *Neither Heroine nor Fool,* 70–71, 85–88.

33. Charles McCool Snyder, "Anna Ella Carroll, Political Strategist and Gadfly of President Fillmore," *Maryland Historical Magazine* 38: 61; Coryell, *Neither Heroine nor Fool,* 91.

34. Jacqueline Jones, *Labor of Love, Labor of Sorrow: Black Women, Work, and the Family from Slavery to the Present* (New York: Basic Books, 1985), 11.

35. Bradford, *Scenes in the Life of Harriet Tubman,* 27, 7; Ednah Cheney, "Moses," *Freedmen's Record* 1 (1865): 37.

36. Jean McMahon Humez, *Harriet Tubman: The Life and Life Stories* (Madison: University of Wisconsin Press, 2003), 249.

37. Tubman quoted in ibid., 218–19.

38. Holley and Chadwick, *A Life for Liberty,* 139.

39. Anne Firor Scott, *The Southern Lady: From Pedestal to Politics, 1830–1930* (Charlottesville: University Press of Virginia, [1970] 1995), 4.

40. Dorothy Sterling, *We Are Your Sisters: Black Women in the Nineteenth Century* (New York: W.W. Norton, 1984), 33.

41. Scott, *The Southern Lady,* 37.

42. Mary Chestnut, *A Diary from Dixie* (Cambridge: Harvard University Press, 1980), 25.

43. Stevenson, *Life in Black and White,* 238.

44. Ibid., 252

45. Earl Conrad, *Harriet Tubman* (Washington, D.C.: Associated Publishers, 1943), 74–75; Kate Clifford Larson, *Bound for the Promised Land: Harriet Tubman, Portrait of an American Hero* (New York: Ballantine, 2004), 197–202; Humez, *Harriet Tubman,* 47–48, 269–70.

46. Humez, *Harriet Tubman,* 269; Conrad, *Harriet Tubman,* 74.

47. Conrad, *Harriet Tubman,* 74.

48. Larson, *Bound for the Promised Land,* 197–202.

49. Humez, *Harriet Tubman,* 269; Conrad, *Harriet Tubman,* 75.

50. Conrad, *Harriet Tubman,* 74.

51. Humez, *Harriet Tubman,* 270; Conrad, *Harriet Tubman,* 75.

52. Humez, *Harriet Tubman,* 269; Conrad, *Harriet Tubman,* 75.

53. Sherry H. Penny and James D. Livingston, *A Very Dangerous Woman: Martha Wright and Women's Rights* (Amherst: University of Massachusetts Press, 2004), 175.

54. Stevenson, *Life in Black and White,* 252.

55. Holley and Chadwick, *A Life for Liberty,* 175.

56. Ibid.

57. Snyder, "Anna Ella Carroll," 63.

58. James McGowan, *Station Master on the Underground Railroad: The Life and Letters of Thomas Garrett* (Moylan, Pa.: Whimsie Press, 1977), 130.

Chapter 7: Beginnings at the End

1. Arnold Rampersad, *The Life of Langston Hughes* (New York: Oxford University Press, 1986), 73.

2. Hulbert Footner, *Rivers of the Eastern Shore; Seventeen Maryland Rivers* (Cambridge, Md.: Tidewater Publishing, 1944), 7; "Delmarva Redivivus," in Harold Jopp, *Rediscovery of the Eastern Shore: Delmarva Travelogues of the 1870's* (Wye Mills, Md.: Chesapeake College Press, 1986), 4.

3. Alice Dunbar Nelson, "Delaware," *The Messenger* 6, no. 24 (March 1924).

4. Janet Coryell, *Neither Heroine nor Fool: Anna Ella Carroll of Maryland* (Kent, Ohio: Kent State University Press, 1990), 1.

5. Sarah H. Bradford, *Scenes in the Life of Harriet Tubman* (Auburn, N.Y.: W.J. Moses, 1869; repr. North Stratford, N.H.: Ayer, 1971), 50.

6. Ibid., 49; Coryell, *Neither Heroine nor Fool*, 16; Hal Roth, *The Monster's Handsome Face: Patty Cannon in Fiction and Fact* (Vienna, Md: Nanticoke Books, 1998), 226.

7. "I have long been decided in opinion," John Adams wrote his friend Thomas Jefferson, "that a free government and the Roman Catholick [*sic*] religion can never exist together in any nation or Country." John Adams, Abigail Adams, Thomas Jefferson, and Lester Jesse Cappon. *The Adams-Jefferson Letters: The Complete Correspondence between Thomas Jefferson and Abigail and John Adams* (Chapel Hill: University of North Carolina Press, 1959), 571.

8. Frederick Douglass, *My Bondage, My Freedom* (New York: Arno/New York Times, [1855] 1969), 75.

9. Ibid.

10. Ibid., 166.

11. Nell Irvin Painter, *Sojourner Truth: A Life, A Symbol* (New York: Norton, 1996), 30.

12. Peter L. Berger and Thomas Luckmann, *The Social Construction of Reality: A Treatise in the Sociology of Knowledge* (Garden City, N.Y.: Anchor Books, 1967), 92–104; Jopp, *Rediscovery of the Eastern Shore*, 4.

13. Sallie Holley and John White Chadwick, *A Life for Liberty; Anti-Slavery and Other Letters of Sallie Holley* (New York: G.P. Putnam's Sons, 1899), 172.

14. Mary Beth Norton, *Founding Mothers & Fathers: Gendered Power and the Forming of American Society* (New York: A.A. Knopf, 1996), 14.

15. Ibid.

16. In Massachusetts, the Puritans called for the abolition of priests and bishops and smashed statues and stained glass windows as idolatry and sources of distraction from God.

17. In 1689, the Puritans were again overthrown, this time by an association of Protestants ("for defense of the Protestant religion"), who claimed the colony for King William and Queen Mary. A royal governor was appointed in 1690 and a new government formed. Catholics were prohibited from practicing religion or running schools, denied the right to vote or to hold public office.

18. C. Kay Larson, *Great Necessities: The Life, Times, and Writings of Anna Ella Carroll, 1815–1894* (Philadelphia: Xlibris, 2004), 7.

19. Coryell, *Neither Heroine nor Fool*, 15.

20. Eric Foner, *Free Soil, Free Labor, Free Men: The Ideology of the Republican Party before the Civil War* (New York: Oxford University Press, 1970), 9; Drew

Gilpin Faust, *Mothers of Invention: Women of the Slaveholding South in the American Civil War* (New York: Vintage, 1997), 179.

21. George Fox, an Englishman who founded the Religious Society of Friends in 1667, wrote in his journal: "When all my hopes in men were gone, so that I had nothing outwardly to help me, nor could I tell what to do, then, O then, I heard a voice which said, 'There is one, even Christ Jesus, that can speak to thy condition.'" Fox visited the American colonies between 1671 and 1673. On the Eastern Shore he met with both colonists and groups of Native Americans, hoping to convert them to his new faith. Historian Hulbert Footner discovered that "with no house of worship of any sort within the confines of the county" (i.e., the Eastern Shore), most first-settler families joined the Society of Friends. Colonies of Friends were also established in Pennsylvania and New Jersey. Hulbert Footner, *Rivers of the Eastern Shore* (Cambridge, Md.: Tidewater Publishers, 1944), 296.

22. *Faith and Practice* (Philadelphia: Philadelphia Yearly Meeting, adopted 1955, rev. 1972), 30.

23. Footner, *Rivers of the Eastern Shore*, 235.

24. John Woolman, *The Journal of John Woolman* (Boston: Houghton Mifflin, 1909), 61; Kate Clifford Larson, *Bound for the Promised Land: Harriet Tubman, Portrait of an American Hero* (New York: Ballantine, 2004), 81–82.

25. Kay McElvey, "Early Black Dorchester, 1776–1870: A History of the Struggle of African Americans in Dorchester County, Maryland, to Be Free to Make Their Own Choices" (Ph.D. dissertation, University of Maryland, 1991), 112–14. But such positions were not reserved only for Friends. Joseph Nichols of Delaware preached strongly against slavery in the 1760s. Nichols, a farmer, led a group of mostly white followers, advocating that "the practice of slavery or holding of Negroes in slavery and bondage during life is an unchristian custom." He refused to hire slaves from slave owners. Nicolite John Horney of Caroline County "refused to eat with slave holders or to use any goods or commodities either raised or procured through slave labor" (114).

26. Ibid., 114.

27. Joe William Trotter, *The African American Experience* (Boston: Houghton Mifflin, 2001), 126.

28. McElvey, "Early Black Dorchester," 120. Coke later wrote, "In this tour, which has been remarkable above any other tour on the continent for persecution, there arose a great dispute whether I should preach in the Church of England or not."

29. Trotter, *The African American Experience*, 127.

30. McElvey, "Early Black Dorchester," 200–201. By the early 1800s, Methodism was the largest domination in the area but in decline. Some attributed it to the strictness of the slaveholding policies. When Francis Asbury, one of the strongest anti-slavery voices and most influential members, died in 1816, the concern died with him. Historians noted a "profound silence on the subject of slavery" by Methodists after that time (225).

31. Ibid., 115.

32. Trotter, *The African American Experience*, 143.

33. McElvey, "Early Black Dorchester," 116.

34. Ibid., 325.

35. Catherine Clinton, *Harriet Tubman: The Road to Freedom* (Boston: Little, Brown, 2004), 20–21.

36. McElvey, "Early Black Dorchester," 114, 225.

37. Ibid.

38. James A. McGowan, *Station Master on the Underground Railroad: The Life and Letters of Thomas Garrett* (Moylan, Pa.: Whimsie Press, 1977), 135.

39. Kate Larson, *Bound for the Promised Land*, 7.

40. Jean McMahon Humez, *Harriet Tubman: The Life and Life Stories* (Madison, Wis: University of Wisconsin Press, 2003), 209.

41. Ibid., 180.

42. Ibid., 181. Sallie Holley wrote to friends that she met a poor colored man who lived in Pennsylvania a few years and "joined the church one year ago but has not yet partaken of the sacrament. His minister secretly asked him why he had not. 'Oh,' said the poor fellow, 'I once had a brother, and he was sold to buy communion plate, and, somehow, I can't partake.'" Holley and Chadwick, *A Life for Liberty*, 104.

43. Ibid., 259.

44. McGowan, *Station Master on the Underground Railroad*, 135.

45. Bradford, *Scenes in the Life*, 113.

46. Franklin Sanborn, "Harriet Tubman," *Boston Commonwealth* (July 17, 1863).

47. Humez, *Harriet Tubman*, 263–64.

48. Bradford, *Scenes in the Life*, 108–9.

49. Ednah Dow Littlehale Cheney, *Reminiscences of Ednah Dow Cheney (Born Littlehale)* (Boston: Lee and Sheppard, 1902), 82.

50. C. Kay Larson, *Great Necessities*, 114–20; Sidney Greenbie and Marjorie B. Greenbie, *Anna Ella Carroll and Abraham Lincoln* (Manchester, Maine: Falmouth Publishing Co. 1952), 49, 69, 134.

51. Coryell, *Neither Heroine nor Fool*, 14–15.

52. Robert Breckenridge, "The Question of Negro Slavery and the New Constitution of Kentucky," *Biblical Repertory and Princeton Review* 21 (1849), 582–607.

53. Ibid., 593.

54. Ibid.

55. Ibid.

56. Ibid. There can be no question," Breckenridge wrote, "that in this country the blacks are the weaker race, and therefore if emancipated and kept distinct, they must sink and gradually perish."

57. Ibid.

58. Anna Ella Carroll, *The Great American Battle; or, the Contest between Christianity and Political Romanism* (New York: Miller, Orton, and Mulligan, 1856).

59. Coryell, *Neither Heroine nor Fool*, 15.

60. Dr. R. J. Breckenridge, "Emancipation," Kentucky State Convention on Emancipation (Frankfurt, 1849), 530.

61. Max Weber, *The Protestant Ethic and the Spirit of Capitalism* (New York: Scribner, 1958), 80.

62. Ted Giles, *Patty Cannon, Woman of Mystery* (Eastern, Md.: Easton Publishing, 1965), 60.

63. Ibid.

64. Mary Beth Norton, *In the Devil's Snare: The Salem Witchcraft Crisis of 1692* (New York: Alfred A. Knopf, 2002), 6.

65. Dickson J. Preston, *Young Frederick Douglass: The Maryland Years* (Baltimore: The Johns Hopkins University Press, 1980), 203.

66. John Putnam Demos, *Entertaining Satan: Witchcraft and the Culture of Early New England.* (New York: Oxford University Press, 1983), 384.

67. Hal Roth, *Now This Is the Truth . . . and Other Lies: Tales from the Eastern Shore . . . and More* (Vienna, Md.: Nanticoke Books, 2005), 106–19.

68. Norton, *Founding Mothers and Fathers*, 388.

69. Edmund Morgan, review of *Entertaining Satan: Witchcraft and the Culture of Early New England*, by John Putnam Demos, *New York Review of Books*, 29, no. 17 (November 4, 1982); Lindal Buchanan, "A Study of Maternal Rhetoric: Anne Hutchinson, Monsters, and the Antinomian Controversy," *Rhetoric Review* 25: 252.

70. Walter Johnson, *Soul by Soul: Life Inside the Antebellum Slave Market* (Cambridge, Mass.: Harvard University Press, 1999), 218.

71. John Greenleaf Whittier, in Woolman, *The Journal of John Woolman*, i.

72. Ibid., i.

73. Preston, *Young Frederick Douglass*, 162.

74. Ibid., 160.

Index

CAROLE C. MARKS is a professor of sociology at the University of Delaware. She is the author of *Farewell, We're Good and Gone: The Great Black Migration* and *A History of African Americans in Delaware and Maryland's Eastern Shore* and coauthor of *The Power of Pride: Stylemakers and Rulebreakers of the Harlem Renaissance.*

The University of Illinois Press
is a founding member of the
Association of American University Presses.

Composed in 9.5/12.5 Trump Mediaeval
with Myriad Pro display
by Jim Proefrock
at the University of Illinois Press
Designed by Dennis Roberts
Manufactured by Thomson-Shore, Inc.

University of Illinois Press
1325 South Oak Street
Champaign, IL 61820-6903
www.press.uillinois.edu

Shelton State Libraries
Shelton State Community College